"*Dare to Believe!* is an amazing telling of amazing stories about amazing people. I've met believers who live in the Middle East under incredible ob-

stacles and opposition. Amazing because they don't pray for protection—they pray for boldness. You'll be challenged and inspired by the stories of these brave followers of Jesus."

—WAYNE PEDERSON
Global ambassador, Far East Broadcasting

"In *Dare to Believe!* you become Terence Ascott's companion on an epic adventure of faith and obedience. You join him on harrowing pursuits driven by the revelations of what media and technology make possible. You

bear witness to God's master plan and how the hope of the gospel is on its way to the ends of the earth. The story of SAT-7 left me awestruck, praising God, and full of anticipation as the day of the Lord approaches."

—TAMI HEIM
President and CEO, Christian Leadership Alliance

"When it comes to giving the gospel, we must always go where the kingdom of Christ is under assault. Nowhere is the opposition fiercer than in the Middle East . . . yet Christ's church is springing up all over! It's why I thank

God for the remarkable work of SAT-7 and its tireless efforts to make Christ known in this ancient region of the world. In his new book, *Dare to Believe!*, Terry Ascott has captured the danger, intrigue, yet passion and ingenuity behind the unique development of SAT-7. If you are looking for inspiration, as well as a genuine witness of the life-transforming power of the good news, this is a must-read!"

—JONI EARECKSON TADA
Founder and CEO, Joni and Friends

"The Christian faith began in the Middle East, but it is there today where followers of the Risen Christ face constant persecution. In *Dare to Believe!*, Terence Ascott tells the thrilling story of SAT-7's ministry, showing that the faith of Jesus Christ can never be crushed."

—LORD CAREY OF CLIFTON
103rd Archbishop of Canterbury

"As I read *Dare to Believe!*, I found myself moved by the faith and vision required to begin the first ever satellite network in the Middle East aimed at communicating the good news. Terry and Jackie's story was thrilling! King-

dom progress always requires steps of faith, especially in places where such faith can come at a very high cost. We need more believers willing to do whatever it takes to share the story of Jesus in compelling ways. May God use this story to inspire many more people toward bold action!"

—KEVIN PALAU
President, Luis Palau Association

"Who would have thought that one man—daring to believe—could have such an impact for Christ on millions of lives in the Middle East and North Africa? Terence Ascott is that man. In an account that seems to parallel the book of Acts, Dr. Ascott draws upon his own fifty years of faith and actions that only the Lord could design. This fascinating and engaging account of that belief is an astounding revelation of God at work. I was deeply moved

as I read the heart-rending stories of many who paid for their faith in the One presented to them by SAT-7 . . . Jesus. *Dare to Believe* is a must read!"

—RON HARRIS
Chairman, National Religious Broadcasters, and president, MEDIAlliance International

"This is a riveting book filled with miracles! It's amazing that Terence is even alive to write this book. He was thrown out of Egypt, held at gunpoint by the PLO in Lebanon, threatened numerous times, but he stood the course, and the miracle of SAT-7 is now saturating the Middle East, North Africa, and Central Asia with the message of Jesus. *Dare to Believe* is a roller coaster of ups and downs, but God moved the mountains of opposition and today is using SAT-7 to break up the hard soil and bring millions to faith in Christ. SAT-7 is the gospel powerhouse that all of us who serve in the Middle East

thank God for. I highly recommend *Dare to Believe*, and as you read this thrilling book, you will *dare to believe* and trust God for more in your life!"

—TOM DOYLE
Author of *Dreams and Visions* and *Women Who Risk*

"In *Dare to Believe!*, Terry Ascott worries that a Western audience might not be able to cope with reading the harrowing accounts of Christians of the Middle East who, in the face of genocide, atrocity crimes, and persecution, face an existential struggle to survive. But not only do we have a duty to learn their stories and hear their cry, we have a duty to act. Since I first encountered Dr. Ascott, in the 1980s, he has unfailingly and generously devoted himself to the cause of the region's benighted and abandoned

Christians. Through SAT-7's amazing work he has reached over the heads of those who would deny the right to believe, to provide encouragement and solidarity. This book is a timely encouragement to us all to do more."

—LORD ALTON OF LIVERPOOL

"This inspiring volume is really three stories under one cover. It's the auto-biography of a Christian leader with fifty years' experience of working in the Middle East and North Africa. It's the history of SAT-7, a gift of God for the satellite age and a glowing example of entrepreneurial faith, which had the vision to embrace new technologies as an effective servant of the gospel. But above all, it is the compelling story of the suffering church standing firm while the world collapses into anarchy and chaos. It is action-packed with powerful testimonies of dramatic conversions to Christ and a hunger for Christian fellowship and Bible teaching. There are vivid stories of persecu-

tion, intimidation, blood-soaked martyrdoms, and miraculous escapes. Please read it and recognize there is a price to be paid for daring to believe!"

—DAVID COFFEY
Past president of the Baptist World Alliance and former general secretary of the Baptist Union of Great Britain

"This is a story of Christian faith, courage, and perseverance which needs to be heard. It is at times heartbreaking and at times heartwarming. It is a story

filled with pain, love, and undying hope. Western Christians must surely be challenged by its authenticity: if you have ever wondered what the gospel of Christ means in a harsh world, this story is for you."

—STEPHEN GREEN
Baron Green of Hurstpierpoint, member of the UK House of Lords

Dare to Believe!

Dare to Believe!

Stories of Faith from the Middle East

TERENCE ASCOTT

Foreword by George Verwer

RESOURCE *Publications* · Eugene, Oregon

DARE TO BELIEVE!
Stories of Faith from the Middle East

Resource Publications
An Imprint of Wipf and Stock Publishers
199 W. 8th Ave., Suite 3
Eugene, OR 97401

www.wipfandstock.com

PAPERBACK ISBN: 978-1-6667-0039-8
HARDCOVER ISBN: 978-1-6667-0040-4
EBOOK ISBN: 978-1-6667-0041-1

06/07/21

Edited by Ginger Kolbaba

Some of the names and places in this book have been changed to help protect people still living in vulnerable situations. Otherwise, all stories and events are recorded factually.

This book is dedicated to our Christian brothers and sisters in the Middle East and North Africa, some of whom I have been honored to know, and many of whom have made the ultimate sacrifice for their faith.

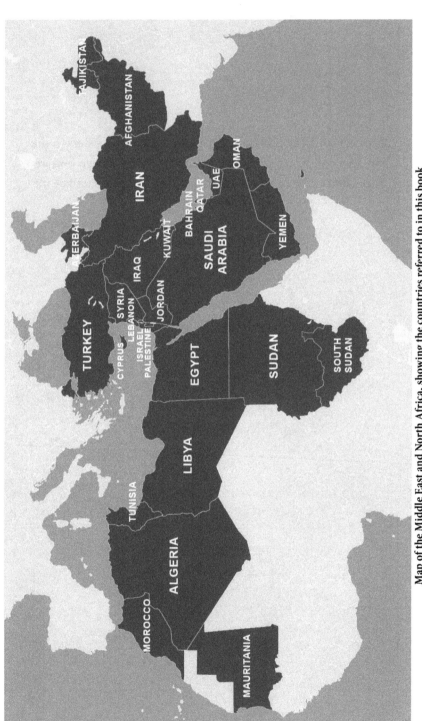

Map of the Middle East and North Africa, showing the countries referred to in this book

Contents

Foreword

What an honor and privilege to write a foreword to this important, and significant book.

I remember Terry and Jackie Ascott when they were active in the early days of Operation Mobilization (OM). Their commitment to taking the gospel into difficult places, despite knowing—and sometimes encountering—the very real risks, is an amazing testament to the kind of people they are. Following their lives and ministry has been a huge encouragement to me and to so many others—especially watching their leadership throughout the amazing birth and growth of SAT-7.

While I have rejoiced in all of SAT-7's work, I found special joy when SAT-7 got involved in Turkey, a country that has been on my heart for well beyond sixty years.

I especially want to add my thanks to those who have prayed for and supported this great ministry. *Dare to Believe!* will be super-relevant to you, as it has been for me. You'll quickly turn the pages as you read the stories of how Terry captured the vision to start a wide-ranging ministry across the Middle East and North Africa and how he and the SAT-7 team overcame numerous practical and spiritual challenges to become a hugely influential satellite television network, reaching literally millions of people in their homes with the gospel. You will find yourself drawn in as you read about the impact SAT-7 has made on so many of those lives. Their stories are immensely powerful and inspiring. And they will create within you a deep desire to want to know more.

Even with all of that, though, the main reason *Dare to Believe!* is so important is that Terry has really made its focus about *our Great God*—and what *He* has done and continues to do among very special people.

Dare to Believe! will grow your compassion toward the people of the Middle East and North Africa. It will help you understand some of the historic background to the region and see the amazing faith of our brothers and sisters under persecution. And you will find your own faith strengthened.

SAT-7's ministry continues to move forward as it faces formidable and unusual days, meeting the challenges of new technology and audience engagement. But as they've shown in the past, they are up to the task—with your prayer and support, and with God's blessings.

Just as I did, as you read Terry's book, I hope you will see the heart of God and be encouraged by the amazing way He uses all kinds of people.

But then don't just read this book and put it on your shelf. Dwell on it. Let it motivate *you* to do something bold for the cause of Christ. And then pass it on! Give copies to others to educate and inspire them as well to . . . *dare to believe* in what God can do when we say yes to Him.

George Verwer
Founder of Operation Mobilization

Introduction

The Shocking Reality

As I looked back at the finished text of this book, I was shocked at the number of stories of death and martyrdom that I included. I wondered if it would be too depressing for Western readers.

But it reflects the reality for our Christian brothers and sisters in the Middle East and North Africa, and it is also the history of much of the global church. In fact, some sections of this book look as though they were additional chapters in the book of Acts.

And while some of the region's Christians continue to leave their homelands, seeking a better and safer life for themselves and their children in the West, many remain committed to stay and be a witness for our Lord, many who see persecution as a badge of honor or a crown that they put on their heads each day.

I remember the day in 1981 when the Sadat government rounded up more than a hundred church and Christian organizational leaders in Egypt, exiling the then Coptic Orthodox patriarch, Pope Shenouda, to a desert monastery, and imprisoning Orthodox bishops, Catholic priests, and Protestant pastors in a common detention center. Together they shared weeks of difficulties and rich theological exchanges, which proved to be a turning point for church unity in the country.

The director of our work in Egypt, Tawfick George, came into our publishing office in Cairo the morning after the mass arrests looking depressed. I assumed he was disturbed by the detentions and worried about potential consequences for our staff and ministry. It turned out he was disappointed that his own activities had not marked him to be one of those the government chose to arrest. He felt as though his life and witness for Christ was somehow inadequate.

These are the Christians of the Middle East. Diverse and disparate. Comprising secret house fellowships to traditional churches that can trace their roots back to the New Testament book of Acts, they remain invisible to most of the world, struggling almost alone in their lives, work, and witness for Christ.

During my nearly fifty years in the Middle East, I have witnessed massive change, perhaps starting with the 1979 Iranian Revolution and going on to the rise of the so-called Islamic State in Iraq and Syria. I have seen everything from disinterest in the gospel to outright hostility toward or the passionate embracing of it. And I have learned and embraced new technologies that have been disrupters in the region, opening doors for the church to come out from behind its walls and be light and salt in the Middle East and North Africa.

This is my story and the stories of some of the wonderful people I have met along the way.

Chapter 1

An Unlikely Beginning

On the early morning of April 17, 1989, I said a sorrowful good-bye to my wife, Jackie, and quietly slipped out of our fifth-floor apartment, trying not to wake our children, who were to assume that I was just leaving on another business trip. I arrived at Cairo airport departures just before 6:00 a.m., as promised. The air seemed still and stifling, and I felt numb; I was going through the motions of completing an obligation because I had no other choice.

A few friends and colleagues had gathered in the car park outside the airport terminal to say their goodbyes.

I looked at our national director, Tawfik, and gave a sad half-smile and a nod. He had pledged to Egyptian State Security on the day of my arrest that I would show up at the airport that morning. His guarantee a few days before allowed me time to go back to my home and office to try and close out my responsibilities, my life. Having lived in Egypt for fourteen years, making it my home, and being responsible for one hundred staff across three different Christian media ministries, not to mention caring for my wife and our three school-aged children, made all this a challenging task to complete in just a matter of hours.

Still struggling to comprehend the reality of what was happening, I reported to the officer from State Security. He took me to the police office in the airport, where he officially handed me over for deportation, in line with Ministerial Decree number 1152, signed by the then-Egyptian Minister of Interior, Zakie Badr.

None of the police officers in the airport knew why I was being deported. Neither did I. The deportation order simply said, "In the interests of national security." But this ambiguity made the officers view me with caution. In their eyes, I was obviously a danger to the state, but how much of a danger?

Two poorly-dressed, lower-ranking policemen escorted me to the Egypt Air check-in counter where I nervously parted with two large, heavy bags, which I had hastily packed with all I considered precious from my years in Egypt. However, they deliberately contained nothing that could embarrass my colleagues in the likely event that my bags were searched—either in front of me or after they left my sight.

The officers then escorted me to a dingy, windowless security office and told me to wait. Only after all the other passengers had boarded the flight to Cyprus was I marched out to the plane by my new friends in black, one keeping hold of my passport until he had personally accompanied me to my seat on the aircraft. Once I was seated, he handed over the document with a flourish, letting everyone on the flight know that I was either a VIP being personally escorted by the police . . . or a criminal. Since I was seated in the economy section, most likely assumed the latter.

On the one-hour flight across the Mediterranean to the island of Cyprus, I had my first real opportunity to stop and reflect on the events leading to this moment, and again to mull over the possible causes of this apparently personal disaster. Yes, the writing was on the wall when my work visa was not renewed a few weeks earlier. I had asked the British Embassy to inquire on my behalf as to why. Their initial, off-the-cuff and unhelpful response was to say, "Since you have been in Egypt for more than a decade, it is probable the authorities feel that an Egyptian should now take over your job."

But something kept nagging at me. *Could it have been that phone call?* I wondered.

A few weeks before, Neil, the Middle East director of Amnesty International, had arrived in Cairo on an official visit. After checking into his hotel, he called me at my office to discuss the possibility of his delegation meeting with some of the local Christians who had recently been imprisoned for their faith. I was horrified by the call and later asked Neil why he had called me at my office to discuss such sensitive and confidential matters—especially when he knew his calls from the hotel were being monitored. I reminded him that all the information I had sent him over the previous three years had been sourced discreetly and communicated from public pay phones or carried out of the country by hand.

Though he had apologized, I feared the damage had been done. I valued my involvement with Amnesty, but I was disappointed. Neil should have known better.

Getting Personally Involved

My work in providing Amnesty, former United States Congressman Frank R. Wolf, and advocacy and media agencies in the West with information on the unjustified detention of Christians in Egypt all began after a close friend, Farid, was arrested, together with his wife, Nabila, and her two sisters, Amira and Eman. They were all believers in Christ who had formerly been Muslims.

Farid and Nabila had six-year-old twins, Michael and Mary, who were classmates of my daughter, Mona. Nabila's life revolved around her twins, who were always immaculately dressed and, unlike my children, did their homework on time. On the day that Farid and Nabila were arrested, the twins were left with no one at home to meet them at the school bus. However, as soon as the news got out, a couple from their church moved into Farid and Nabila's apartment to care for them.

Farid and Nabila's arrest and their subsequent treatment left me shocked. I was aware that some converts could have rough edges that could make them religiously or socially insensitive, and act in ways that could provoke the authorities. But these people comprised a normal, loving, and gentle family who played their part in the church and community, where Farid was a doctor.

They had been arrested under Egypt's Emergency Laws, allowing them to be detained for sixty days without charges or a court appearance. After the first sixty days were up, they were taken to court: Farid from his crowded detention cell in Tora Prison, just south of Cairo, and the three sisters from the women's prison in El Kanarter, north of the city.

In court, their attorney cautioned them that they could be charged with "despising a heavenly religion" and "seeking to disturb national unity." However, these charges were not formally presented and, instead, the court asked each of the detainees to recite *The Shahada,* the Islamic creed—one of the five pillars of Islam, declaring belief in the Oneness of God and the acceptance of Muhammad as God's prophet. One by one, they said they were unable to make this confession. Nabila explained to the court that, while she desperately missed and worried about her twins and wanted to go home, she could not deny Jesus, who had saved her and changed her life.

At the end of the court proceedings, though they were not formally charged and were ordered to be released, their freedom lasted only for a minute or two. Within moments of stepping outside of the courtroom, they were rearrested under the Emergency Laws and held for another sixty days. This cycle continued for most of the year.

The next sixty-day detention fell over Mother's Day in Egypt. While all the children in my daughter's class made colorful cards for their mothers, the twins sat at their desks and sobbed. Their teacher, a kind, Coptic Orthodox lady who knew the children's situation, did her best to comfort them.

But the arrest of converts did not stop with this family. Another man and his daughter and then four North Africans who were attending a discipleship school in Alexandria were detained. At this time, the news about the detainees broke in the West and grew in intensity, becoming an embarrassment for the regime. President Hosni Mubarak, while on a state visit to France, was embarrassingly asked about the detainees on French national television, while photos were shown of demonstrators on the streets of Paris.

On July 18, 1986, a petition, which twenty-nine members of the United States Congress signed, was presented to the Egyptian ambassador in Washington DC, threatening to bring the issue before Congress, with a view to suspending foreign aid to Egypt. Within the week, all ten were released.

Other cases developed and I continued to help keep the world aware of these too.

Now as I stared out the plane window, leaving behind the life and work I'd invested so many years in, I was convinced my association with these cases and Amnesty International's careless visit to Cairo had led to my deportation "in the interests of national security."

Is There a Pattern Here?

As I landed in Cyprus, I felt a God-given sense of peace come over me. Yes, I did hope that I might be able to return to Egypt soon, as different church leaders had optimistically pronounced, but this was not the reason for my inner peace. I reflected on the story of Joseph, out of the Old Testament book of Genesis, and how he had been sold into slavery by his brothers. Later, during the great famine, the brothers came to Egypt to beg for grain and eventually discovered that Joseph was now in a position of great power in the country. They were terrified. But Joseph explained to them how God had allowed their actions so that many lives would be saved, showing how what they had intended as harm, God had used for good. This, I believed, would be my testimony, with the notable difference that I was leaving, not entering, Egypt!

I had seen God use so many experiences in my life that way, so now, as I walked through the airport in Cyprus, it seemed God was moving me once again and I had that deep peace.

Part of the peace I felt stemmed from realizing that my deportation may have been because I had stubbornly missed God's leading to relocate to a place where I could more effectively develop a vision that had been growing within me for several years.

I had to admit that I experienced difficult and draining days during my time in Egypt, days when I would have loved to have been deported. I could not, in all conscience, however, have chosen to leave a place and a ministry to which I had been called. I had seen others leave prematurely from a calling and the results were almost always problematic, for the individual and the families concerned. Perhaps these observations and resulting opinions had become an obsession? Perhaps the desire to faithfully persevere regardless made me insensitive to God's quiet voice? Perhaps I had only ever made a move to where I should be because of God's dramatic interventions in my life?

Where to Go Seemed Obvious!

A few days before my deportation, when I was called into a downtown Cairo security office and detained, I was told I needed to buy and show the authorities a one-way air ticket to leave the country (yes, I did have to pay for my own deportation). I did not need to think long concerning where I should go. For several years we, as a media organization, had said we needed a functioning office in Cyprus, where we did most of our banking, where we sent all our mail for hand carrying into Egypt, and where we printed our magazine for distribution across the region. We also had an established legal presence—if only represented at that point by a plaque on a lawyer's office wall in Cyprus's coastal city of Limassol.

I had also been long aware that Cyprus would provide a better and more secure communications hub to pursue starting a Christian satellite television service. But I certainly did not hear or did not want to hear the call to go.

My now being in Cyprus put me in a place where I was able to step into a ready-made corporate situation and immediately and more efficiently pick up on the organization's communications with people and operations outside of the region. As soon as the staff of

Interserve, a Christian ministry whose international office was located in the island's capital, Nicosia, heard I was in their country, they quickly welcomed me and even presented me with free desk space. Though several of their staff also kindly offered me accommodation, I wanted to be alone for a while, to think things through, and perhaps mourn the loss of my life in Egypt. So I secured two months of free hotel accommodation at the centrally located Cleopatra Hotel in Nicosia, by bartering the cost of my room with advertisements in the monthly Arabic newsstand magazine I had started while in Egypt.

Because Jackie and I agreed it was best for her and the children to stay put to finish the school year, and to give time for the appeal against my deportation to be processed, I would be alone in Cyprus for several months. Staying in a hotel seemed the best option, especially since I had scheduled trips to the United States and the Far East coming up. In any case, I was not yet psychologically ready to give up on being able to return to Cairo and to start looking for a more permanent form of accommodation. Instead, I treated the time as a longer version of one of the many ministry trips I made each year.

My May visit to the United States included taking part in the Folio conference in New York City, a valuable trade meeting for magazine publishers. In July, I attended the Second International Congress on World Evangelization, Lausanne II, in the Philippines.

It was here that the Christian mission strategist Luis Bush first highlighted the need for a major refocus of evangelistic efforts into the "Resistant Belt," covering the middle of the eastern hemisphere. Further research in the mid-1990s led to the 10/40 Window concept, which contrasts the major physical and spiritual needs and few resources devoted to that part of the world, between 10 and 40 degrees north in latitude.

In many respects, with its four thousand delegates, it seemed like just another big and impersonal conference. In the regional breakout sessions, I attended the Arab and Egypt work groups. Though it was great to see friends from the region again, the overwhelming sense of loss, my inability to return with them to Egypt, or to be directly involved in the plans we were making for Egypt, brought me to tears in one session.

But not all was grief. One of the big surprises during those early months in Cyprus was how much work I could accomplish in a day! While I missed my family and work colleagues, I was suddenly free of the many interruptions from staff walking in with questions, and from the endless firefighting that was so much part of life in Egypt. Neither did I have any immediate family, church, or social responsibilities. I felt as though God had "cleared my desk" to be ready for the next chapter in my life. I wondered if that was how Joseph felt while on his way to Egypt as a slave, after the shocking betrayal by his brothers.

Coming to Terms with Reality

At the end of July 1989, three months after my deportation, Jackie and our three children flew to Cyprus for a two-week visit. Jackie still felt optimistic about my chances of returning to Egypt, but a call with our lawyer in Cairo on the first night of their visit gave us a less-than-happy picture. We needed at least a short-term plan, so we decided to move the family to Cyprus for one year.

I hated the idea of having to uproot my family, even for a year—especially Jackie. She had followed me to the Middle East for my work. And she had discovered her own ministry. In Lebanon, she studied Arabic and got involved in a children's ministry. When we moved with a new baby to Egypt, she wasn't happy about it, but quickly fell in love with the country and its people. Over the years, she became involved with St. Mary's Coptic Orthodox Church in Maadi, a suburb six miles south of the capital where we lived. St. Mary's church and monastery were located on the banks of the river Nile where, tradition has it, Mary, Joseph and baby Jesus crossed the river on their journey into Egypt to escape the jealous wrath of King Herod.

Jackie had begun teaching Sunday school at St. Mary's, which was, as in most Middle East countries, held on Fridays. Being an artist, she drew visual aids to use with the children, but during the week, goats wandered into the building and ate her artwork! This triggered her search for more permanent forms of art and a growing interest in iconography and frescos. She enrolled in studies at the Coptic Institute and, in 1988, received her master's degree in contemporary Coptic art, while still finishing her doctoral thesis on the same subject.

She defended her PhD dissertation a year later, on February 13, 1989, just a few weeks before I was deported. It was a memorable night, and the main invigilator at the well-attended, four-hour public event was the patriarch, His Holiness Pope Shenouda III. He had read all three volumes of Jackie's five-hundred-page dissertation and unashamedly defended her when examining professors from the Coptic Institute and Coptic Museum posed tough questions. Twenty Coptic bishops, a number of other VIPs, and more than six hundred friends or interested individuals packed the venue, which was decorated with sixty or so of the amazing icons that Jackie had created over the years, under the tutelage of her professor, Dr. Ishaq Fanous.

I was very proud of her, being able to find her own place in our adopted homeland and minister to those God brought her in contact with. And now I was asking her, in essence, to give it up—even if "just" for a year.

We began visiting potential English-language schools, found a first-floor apartment in Strovolos, just south of the Nicosia city center, and signed a contract to rent it, shopped for used furniture, and put down a deposit on a car.

The family returned to Egypt to pack up our apartment in Maadi, flying back to Cyprus just three weeks later, in time for the start of the new school year. While they were gone, I was able to set up my office, adjacent to the Interserve headquarters, from which I had been working until now. Several staff came from my publishing office in Egypt to discuss the needed changes in the organizational structure and key procedures as a consequence of me setting up an "international office" in Cyprus. They also helped me establish basic office services and email, which, in 1989, was still a dial-up service.

We even hired a local young woman, Louisa Charalambous, to work as my secretary. (She grew with the job, becoming an indispensable part of the team and faithfully working with me until my retirement some three decades later.)

The next months were hard for the family—getting used to a new country and new schools, while deeply missing their friends in Egypt. Jackie especially missed her ministry at the church. In contrast, life in Cyprus seemed sterile, easy, and relatively calm. It felt odd not being constantly faced with people in crises. It was indeed a different world.

Jackie and the children returned to Cairo for the Coptic Christmas in early January, and the following Easter and summer. And this would be the pattern of visits for several years to come, helping at least Jackie and the children maintain relationships in Egypt and keep up the children's Arabic language skills.

Many friends and friends of friends tried to help get my case reviewed. Some were told to leave the matter alone because the charges were very serious. Others came back with promises of help and words of hope. But nothing changed. Then in January 1990, the minister of the interior, Zaki Badr, was dismissed after giving an inflammatory speech, in which he reportedly said that he was prepared to kill up to 1 percent of the population to rid the country of the Muslim Brotherhood. During Jackie's summer visit that year, the door opened for her to meet with the new minister of the interior, Abdul-Halim Moussa. He was gracious, seemed well briefed on my case, and, after raising nonspecific concerns about my past "illegal activities," promised to review my case, and assured Jackie that we would all be allowed to return to Egypt.

After many frustrating delays, I eventually received permission for a ten-day visit to Cairo the following March. During this time, I was able, indeed obliged, to visit the ministry of interior for a review of my case. But I was also allowed to visit old friends and colleagues. It was a happy reunion with our staff and board members, and expectations of me potentially returning soon raised spirits.

My two days of meetings at the ministry included several sessions with General Osama Hamdi and two longer interviews with Colonel Magdy Abed El Ghaffar. They raised a lot of concerns about my publishing work, but I felt that they were mostly going through the motions of a review imposed on them by the minister and that their main concern was never going to be raised. My hopes fell further when I realized that, though they had many questions, no one took notes during the two days. In the end, they told me that the review would take another few weeks and then I would hear from them.

I returned to Cyprus and waited as weeks passed, then months, with promises of decisions "in the near future." When I checked on the status of my appeal, they told me that my papers were on the minister's desk awaiting signature, but that other information had come to light. After eighteen months, at the end of 1992, I began contacting people I knew in different foreign government offices to try to expedite things. Everyone committed to pressuring the Egyptian government, but in April of the following year, Abdul-Halim Moussa was abruptly removed as the minister of the interior. My heart sank. He was replaced by the tougher Hassan Mohammed El-Alfi.

With that key relationship no longer in place and the Egyptian Embassy in Nicosia feeding news to Cairo about my plans to launch a Christian satellite service, people began to feel that any chance of me getting my name removed from the blacklist at Cairo airport was hopeless.

Between 1994 and 1996 I was, surprisingly, able to make several short visits to Egypt, using cruise ships from Cyprus. I had discovered that passengers arriving on such visits were given a "quick-trip visa," which involved no screening. We arrived in Port Said in the early morning, and everyone was loaded onto a dozen or so tour buses, which took us from the port docks to Cairo, where we were to visit the Pyramids, the Egyptian Museum, and other sights before returning to the ship in the evening. By splitting from the tour as it entered Cairo, I had five to six hours to meet colleagues and friends.

The most stressful part of these visits was finding and rejoining my tour bus in the crowded Cairo streets at dusk!

On my last visit, upon hearing that I did not wish to visit the Pyramids with the rest of the tourists, the cruise line assigned me a seat in the "spare" bus, which traveled with the convoy in case one of the buses broke down. Ironically, this bus also carried the police protection force for the convoy, with whom I apprehensively shared the three-hour journey each way.

It was not until the end of 1998 that the security services in Egypt revealed the real reason for my deportation, sharing this information with one of the church leaders who had been trying to help me. As I suspected, it went back to my involvement with advocacy issues starting with the cases of Dr. Farid and Nabila in 1986.

The Big Wedding

In 1998 and 1999, I appealed to Hassan El-Alfi for permission to respectively attend my son Gavin's graduation from the American University in Cairo and again to attend his engagement party to Dina, a lovely young woman he'd known since childhood. I received no response.

When Gavin and Dina announced their wedding for September 1999, I was determined not to miss that event. I appealed to Baroness Caroline Cox and Lord David Alton at the British House of Lords, as well as Rev. Dr. Safwat El-Baiady (head of the Protestant community in Egypt), to intervene on my behalf. It worked, and I received permission—three days before the wedding and twenty-four hours before I was hoping to travel. The minister of interior himself issued the permission, despite a malicious four-page feature in the July 16 edition of the popular Egyptian magazine *Rose El Youssef*, attacking foreign Christians in the country. I had been personally named in the article as having been a deportee ten years earlier because of my activities in the country and for supposedly working with the American CIA!

When I landed in Cairo, a plain-clothes security officer, holding up a card with my name on it, met me in the terminal. He took my passport into the central office, forcing me to wait. After five minutes he returned with my visa and entry stamp completed and showed me through the VIP exit, bypassing the long lines at the passport control booths. No one asked me any questions, and I soon got my luggage and was outside to meet my sons and some former colleagues and friends.

It felt great to drive away from the airport and see Cairo by night for the first time in many years. I stayed in Maadi with my family, who had all arrived in Egypt the day before. The next two days were filled with wedding preparations, family time, and taking my eighty-year-old mother, brother Ryder, his fiancée, and other visiting family members around Cairo's tourist attractions.

The wedding took place at St. Mary's, where Gavin and Dina had first met as children, and where Gavin now served as a deacon and scout leader. The reception was held at the Marriott Hotel in Zamalek, an island in the Nile and a beautiful residential and business district of the capital.

I had been to many weddings in Egypt, but this one topped them all. The wedding started with photographs on the grand staircase of the hotel, a former palace of King Farouk. Then the procession began. Filmed in great detail and accompanied by a band of musicians with drums, bagpipes, and flutes, this started with the formal "giving away" of the bride by her recently widowed father, Nagy Ayad. Then Gavin and Dina led the guests, with the ever-attentive video crew and musicians, on a drawn out forty-minute journey to the hotel's banquet hall.

At 11:30 p.m. the formal entertainment began with a local comedian, followed by another band, then dry-ice smoke, a laser lightshow, and the grand cake cutting. They didn't start serving the dinner until after midnight, when two hundred hungry guests descended on the buffet in droves!

After dinner, we were rewarded with more entertainment, this time in the form of a twenty-four-piece Arab orchestra with yet more performers, including a modestly dressed belly dancer. By 4:00 a.m., all but the most enthusiastic of party animals had quit, including my mother and most of the rest of my family.

I spent the rest of my ten days in Cairo visiting current and former colleagues, church leaders, and, of course, the ministry of the interior. A police general politely received me, and after an hour of questioning about my current work, told me that he would file a positive report, paving the way for possible future visits, but only by arrangement. There was no talk of me ever being able to return to work and live in Egypt. And by now it was increasingly clear that God had established other plans for me. Just as He had done throughout my life.

Chapter 2

Where Faith Leads

My walk of faith began when I was in my early teens. A school friend invited me to attend a boys' summer camp in the west of England. During the ten days of activities and fun, I heard for the first time the story of how Christ had come to die for our sins and that belief in Him would bring eternal life and a whole new meaning to living. The message resonated with me and made perfect sense, and I embraced this new faith unconditionally.

Without any conscious decision to work harder, my life changed for the better. My grades at school improved and each year I continued to advance to an academically higher class for my year.

My relationships were also affected by my new faith. Some of my friends seemed incredulous at the change, skeptically waiting for the impact of my "religious experience" to wear off. I had my first serious girlfriend when I was sixteen and, while she respected my religious beliefs, she found my conservative attitude toward sex odd and eventually moved on.

My father thought I had become mesmerized and laughed at the absurdity of my belief in the supernatural. But soon our conversations became more heated.

As upset as he became about my beliefs, my faith did stick, and I grew in my understanding of it—mostly through attending a weekly

Bible class run by Crusaders, today known as Urban Saints, the same organization that had sponsored the summer camp.

About that time, a local pastor visited our home in Orpington, South East London. My father opened the door and quickly dispatched the young David Boon, saying that he did not believe in the church and its mumbo-jumbo teachings! I overheard the conversation from my bedroom and ran after the pastor for a quiet conversation in the street.

After hearing about his new Baptist church, located near the school I attended as an infant, I told him I would attend the Sunday after my exams. Until then, my only fellowship with other believers was through Christian societies on the fringe of the church, and "church" was an institution, that I had only heard negative things about, especially from my articulate, atheist father.

An Accident to Remember

When the first Sunday came, as I was preparing to make my first-ever visit to a church, some friends arrived with a new grass-track motorbike and invited me to go with them to test it out. The offer was too great, and I accepted.

When my turn came to race the bike around the dirt track, and when I was almost out of my friends' sight, I slid off the track and into a drainage ditch. The bike stopped there but I was thrown into the long grass. I tried to get up but could not move my legs. They felt completely numb. I heard distant cries of "Is the bike okay?" and began to panic that my legs refused to budge.

While I waited for my unsympathetic friends to arrive at the scene, I lay on my back looking up at the failing afternoon sun and made a pledge. "God, if I can walk on the following Sunday, I will be in church, just as I promised."

One of my friends called for an ambulance. At the hospital, the doctors determined that nothing was broken, though my back was severely sprained. And after a few days there, I was released in time for Sunday so that I could hobble into church on a pair of crutches. A painful experience, but one that God ultimately used for good.

A Shocking Revelation

I began to take two of my three younger brothers, Marcus and Brett, to Sunday school at the Baptist church. The following Christmas, the church had a special nativity service. Since my brothers were performing in it, my mother, Peggie, attended. She was so moved by the service, she met with the new pastor, John Doble, and accepted Christ.

I was delighted to hear this news—my father much less so—but surprised when I heard her confession.

"I've spoken with the pastor and he has encouraged me to share some things about my life—our lives, actually," she told my brother Ryder and me. Her demeanor was nervous and fidgety.

"Okay," we said and listened expectantly.

"Your father and I . . ." She swallowed hard and looked down. "We aren't married."

I blinked, not comprehending her words.

She quickly went on to explain that she had been reared in a Christian home and married a man named Cyril in a hurry at the start of the Second World War, just before he went off to fight in France. He was gone four years, returning a different person—changed by the years of horror, and suffering from a serious sexually transmitted disease. They agreed to divorce.

It was during the war that my mother met my father, George. He had helped her and her family, not least of all in procuring black-market drugs for my ill grandmother. My father was in a loveless marriage and wanted a divorce, but "Mrs. A," as we vaguely knew her, refused.

My parents fell in love and decided, despite the stigma of it in the 1940s, to move in together. Once she was expecting her first child, my mother changed her name by deed poll to Margaret Elizabeth Ascott, to give the impression to all that she and my father were married.

She miscarried the child and felt that this was God's judgment on her illicit relationship with my father, though she had never shared this conviction with anyone.

The nature of her relationship with my father was a dark secret that she'd kept from my siblings and me. She admitted that when I became a Christian, this only added to her fears—that I would judge her harshly when and if I discovered her real marital status, and the fact that my brothers and I were illegitimate.

"I shared this information with Reverend Doble, and he suggested that I immediately come clean with at least the two of you, since you're the oldest," she said, referring to the fact that I was her eldest child and Ryder was only eighteen months younger.

Now she stared at us, knowing the power we held over her, her face wearing a worried, almost fearful, expression.

Though I was surprised, even shocked, at the news, I could offer no condemnation. I was too thrilled that she had found peace with God and herself—and with us.

She was relieved when both Ryder and I told her that she had no reason to fear. "That secret holds no power any longer," I said.

As my mother began attending church, my father's ridicule became even more harsh. He derided her beliefs and reminded her of the relationship she was in, and of the fact that much of his income was from shady deals—and how all this made her a hypocrite. And though he attended her baptism, he insisted on smoking his pipe in the church and making loud, embarrassingly sarcastic comments as the service proceeded.

By the mid-1960s, when I was twenty years old, my parents' relationship reached the breaking point, and my mother made plans to move out, despite the pain and guilt she knew she faced at leaving behind the two youngest children, each still in need of her care and love.

I sought to help her find a place to live, but my income as a young engineer was modest. And, at the same time, I needed surgery on my nose, which I'd broken in a fight the year before I came to faith. Almost simultaneously, everything else in my life seemed to fall apart.

I was engaged to a fine Christian girl from Scotland, but we decided abruptly to end the relationship as we both felt it was not helping either of us. We had different values and priorities and were frequently in conflict. I also failed to secure the new job I needed to fund the rest of my way through college, and the house I had hoped to secure for my mother was suddenly no longer available, which meant she reluctantly postponed leaving.

Despite everything seeming upside down, I still felt a deep sense of peace and joy, knowing that God was in control and reorganizing my life for my own good and for His purposes.

I soon found a new job in a bridge design office, one that afforded me a regular salary while working for half the year and studying civil engineering for the other half. This industrial sponsorship enabled me to escape my father's frequent criticism that I too was living off the "ill-gotten gains" of his frequently shady business deals.

Learning about Missions

The mid-1960s was also a time when I met with people from Operation Mobilization (OM). They had set up their UK headquarters just a few miles from the college where I was then studying, and I invited them to present their work to the small Christian meeting we held on campus each week. I began working though the books on discipleship and evangelism they left with me and, from 1966, began spending my summer holidays volunteering with them, distributing Christian literature in Europe. Initially I traveled to France, though later I made frequent trips into Eastern Europe and behind the Iron Curtain, at a time when the church there was heavily under siege. I found each of these overseas trips faith-building as I saw God provide in the most basic ways and sensed His leading and protection. These trips made me want to be involved even more in sharing my Christian faith.

The end of the 1960s saw a worldwide escalation of social conflicts, typically characterized by popular demonstrations against the military and the bureaucracy. In the United States, as well as in London, Paris, Berlin, and Rome, these protests were mostly in opposition to the Vietnam War. But the most spectacular manifestation of these protests were the May 1968 protests in France, in which students joined up to ten million striking workers. For a few days the movement seemed capable of even overthrowing the government.

Venturing into Publishing

I was convinced that Christians needed to respond to all that was going on and began looking for Christian materials suitable for young people on the front line of these protests. I came across a pamphlet entitled *The Permanent Revolution*. But it was only available as duplicated, typewritten pages. I spoke to its young authors, Denis Alexander and Peter Hopkins, to find out why they had not printed it in a more attractive format, for a wider distribution on college and university campuses. They explained that Christian publishing houses considered it too radical. So I visited a Christian-owned press and discussed how the document could be properly typeset and printed in a more attractive way. I printed ten thousand copies, which was all I could afford, and distributed them at my college, and at demonstrations in London's iconic Trafalgar Square. Soon I received requests for bulk copies from all over the country and ordered another twenty thousand copies from the press, then one hundred thousand, and within a couple of years, I had printed and shipped nearly two million copies to Christian associations in universities across the UK, and received dozens of requests from others seeking permission to reprint the tract in the United States and in other languages for Europe.

This was my first experience with designing, producing, and handling the large-scale distribution of Christian literature. And even though it was a steep learning curve, I found it rewarding. I was witnessing firsthand the power of Christian literature. Seeing the take up on this single pamphlet and the amazing responses that came to me at our local church, whose address they allowed me to put on the reply-coupons, I was sold! I put together other publications and distributed them as well.

In January 1972, before starting my last academic term at Enfield College of Technology, now Middlesex University, I felt God impressing upon me to take off a year after graduating to work full-time with OM.

I left the UK in July, before my exam results were published, to join the OM team based in Munich, Germany, driving literature into Eastern European countries using special vehicles with cavity walls and floors. But soon I had another decision to make. When I received my exam results, I learned I had graduated with the university's first ever first-class honors degree in civil engineering and had also been awarded the Institute of Civil Engineers' 1972 prize for outstanding undergraduate work. With this news came an offer from the University of Wales in Cardiff to join a doctoral program in the autumn. While all this sounded attractive, I had committed the next year to full-time service to God, wherever that might take me. Which meant I had to turn it down. I was not even in the UK for my graduation ceremony, but my mum proudly attended to collect my diplomas!

Earlier that year, I had begun courting Jacqueline "Jackie" Ann Doble, the daughter of the pastor who baptized my mother. Though we had met several years before, and she had volunteered to help me with my part-time publishing efforts, it was only after she had been away to college in West London, studying languages, that I saw her in a new light—as a grown woman. She had also spent summers serving with OM and was also now thinking of taking a year to work with the organization. In the late spring, we became engaged, and in late September, after the annual OM planning and orientation conference in Belgium for new one-year workers, we returned to the UK to marry.

Needless to say, neither the news that I was going "to waste a year of my life in service to the church" nor news of my marriage to the pastor's daughter went down well with my father, who did not attend our October 14 wedding, and later disinherited me.

Eastern Europe

After a short honeymoon in Majorca, Spain, we left for Vienna, Austria, where we would be based for the coming four months. We lived in a close-knit international community of believers committed to supporting the church in the East and even more committed to keeping our work secret. Not even friends and family were to know what we were doing, other than "ministering among immigrant workers in the city," which we did on Sundays, when we were actually in Vienna.

All addresses in the East were to be memorized or coded, no cameras were allowed on trips, no maps were to be marked-up, the titles of the literature we were carrying were coded, and we all had code names. For a reason I no longer remember, my code name was Nero, which some of the Christians we met in the East found to be a strange choice by my parents—considering Nero, an ancient Roman emperor, was well-known for persecuting Christians!

When we were not actually "tripping," which is what we called traveling into the different Eastern European countries, we were working in the vehicle workshop—where it was freezing cold in the Austrian winter months. Some of the vehicles were exceptionally sophisticated for the 1970s. Most of my tripping was in "the Arab," a converted Ford Transit, which had a massive V8 engine and extra suspension springs to carry the one ton of literature we needed to conceal in its walls and floor, and which was disguised as a camper van. Opening the floor required the use of magnetic switches applied to the dashboard, and from the floor, one could access the wall panel releases.

Since it used to take several hours to unload all the cavities, we always needed to find a quiet place to get all the literature from the floor and walls and ready for a quick drop off. Once, after having retrieved all the literature from their hiding places, we were on our way to the appointed drop-point in the west of Czechoslovakia when the road suddenly ended and we drove into sand, which formed part of the foundations for a section of road being rebuilt. The powerful V8 engine could have gotten us out of the sand had it not been for the rather standard Ford clutch, which quickly burned out. We had to call a tractor to get us back on the paved road.

Keeping prying eyes from seeing all the Bibles and books piled high inside the vehicle was nerve-racking! But we eventually made the drop and then limped back to the Czech-Austria border.

On another visit to Czechoslovakia, we successfully unloaded all the Arab's cavities and were parked on a Prague street adjacent to the one on which our contact lived in a second-floor apartment. He needed all the literature discreetly delivered at night, in plain suitcases. So one of the team stayed in the transit packing the cases while my codriver, Ray, and I nonchalantly sauntered up and down the street with alternatingly very heavy and very light cases. At the end of my third delivery, while walking back to our vehicle, I was surprised and confused to see it was gone. I was left standing in the street wearing an ill-fitting raincoat, which I had quickly borrowed after a light rain had started, but with no identification or money and two empty suitcases! As I later discovered, Ray had spotted someone observing our movements and decided to pull the plug on the delivery, leaving in a hurry.

We had protocols for this kind of situation, but my mind had gone blank as to what they were. I dumped one of the suitcases in a doorway and headed down the street toward the iconic Wenceslas Square, thinking this would be a possible landmark at which Ray may think to look for me. As I walked toward the statue of Saint Wenceslas, two armed soldiers in Soviet-style uniforms walked toward me, as though to intercept me, so I casually veered off and headed to the railway station. It had only been a matter of months since the twenty-year-old Czech student, Jan Palach, had set fire to himself in front of the statue. His self-immolation was in protest at the 1968 invasion of Czechoslovakia by Warsaw Pact armies, ending the so-called Prague Spring. The state was in no mood for any new incidents in the square, and I must have looked like potential trouble.

The main train station was the next possible rendezvous point on my mental list of options. Eventually, as I made my way through the hundreds of Soviet troops milling around the station, I spotted the Arab parked near the adjacent bus terminal and reconnected with my colleagues.

Sometimes leaving an Eastern European country was more dangerous than going into one. If they discovered the hidden compartments, they could accuse us of having just smuggled in armaments or people. So occasionally, we would "accidentally" leave a single copy of a New Testament in one of the cavities, as evidence of what we were really doing.

Each country differed from its neighbor. Some, like East Germany, were very difficult to get into and the border checks thorough. It was on the East German border that the Arab was eventually confiscated. In other countries, customs officials were obsessed about the movement of drugs. So when Romanian border guards drilled a hole in a suspicious panel on one of our other vehicles and pulled out paper from a Bible they had drilled into, they dismissed it as insulation, just because it did not smell suspicious.

Other countries, though, like Yugoslavia, were wide open. We used to drive a vanload of Bibles and books into the country, with only a few sleeping bags and a pair of skis covering the load. In fact, we even set up a depot in Yugoslavia for storing books so that "tourists" who had just passed through Hungary and dropped their cargo there could refill their vehicle in Belgrade before returning home through Hungary, dropping off a second shipment on the way.

Each country also had its special needs and opportunities. In Hungary, Christians could publish Christian books and Bibles, but only in small quantities. However, we could take out samples of such books and reprint them in much larger quantities in the West and then smuggle these back into Hungary. Unless we had too many of the books in one place at one time, no one would know they were not part of the locally produced quota. It was in Hungary, after dropping literature early in the morning at a farmhouse deep in the countryside, that I first heard a wood saw being played with a violin bow. The pastor, the shipment's recipient, insisted on giving us breakfast and then played several internationally known hymns on his saw. It was beautiful and somewhat surreal in the circumstances.

In Poland, the believers had established an underground printing press, so their need was for printing press parts, which we could take in through Czechoslovakia.

When committing to spend a year with OM, my plan was to continue working into Eastern Europe. But at that point, I didn't realize it does not take long for couriers to become well known enough at borders and for me to become a liability. I knew it was time to move on. So did OM. They asked me to spend the second half of my year helping with a publishing start-up in Beirut, Lebanon. I needed to consult an atlas even to know where Lebanon was! But, by faith, both Jackie and I committed to going there in the spring of 1973 for the second half of our year with OM.

Bombs and Bullets in Beirut

Driving overland to Lebanon, through Eastern Europe, Turkey, and Syria gave us a little time to adjust to the Arab World. It was so different from Eastern Europe. Life was much more chaotic and unpredictable, people friendlier, everything more negotiable. And it was warmer!

But the accommodation situation was not quite what we had expected. When we arrived in Beirut late on a Sunday evening in March, we were shown to our new home. It was a single room at the back of the OM publishing office on the fourth floor of a building in West Beirut. And we were to share the single small kitchen and bathroom with the ten or eleven single men from four different countries that made up the OM Lebanon boys' team! Our room had a single bed in it and nothing else, but it had been proudly repainted by a couple of guys from the team, just in time for our arrival. We could still not touch some of the wet paint. The first thing to do the next day was to buy a closet, so we could at least hang up our clothes.

One of my responsibilities in Lebanon revolved around being a camera-carrying media worker. My first and rather humorous run-in with the authorities arose not long after I'd arrived in the country. I was taking photos of street protests from the roof of our office in

Rue Bliss, across the road from the American University in Beirut (AUB). A lieutenant from Lebanon's rapid-deployment force, Squad 16, spotted me on the roof with a camera and came to investigate.

I had only been in Lebanon a few weeks and was still dependent on others to translate. My assistant, Joseph, stepped in. Several times Joseph told me to give my camera to the lieutenant, but I said—in both English and Arabic—no!

In the end, the angry officer left, and Joseph turned to me. "You liar!"

I was baffled. "When did I lie?"

"He asked you if you were the man on the roof taking photos."

"But that is not what you said to me," I insisted. "You asked me to give him my camera!"

We both laughed at the mix up, happy that I had not lost my camera.

The next month, in the early morning of April 10, 1973, Israeli commandos led by Ehud Barak, who later became Israel's prime minister, secretly arrived on speedboats at a beach south of our offices in Beirut. Mossad agents awaited them with cars rented the previous day, and then drove them to their targets—three prominent Palestinian Liberation Organization (PLO) leaders in different parts of the city, who were then assassinated in their homes.

Several days after, I was on my way to the Chinese consulate in the southeast part of the city to get some photos needed for a new book. Gary, a tall American agricultural student at AUB, accompanied me. We left early to avoid the morning rush hour. But not far from the consulate, I took a wrong turn onto a desolate road, which had not seen a road sweeper in several years. After passing a sign in Arabic, which neither of us could read, I realized we were well off-track. As I was turning the car around in the narrow street, a PLO jeep pulled in front of us, blocking our movement. Three armed men jumped out and forced us out of the car. Perhaps we would have gone unnoticed in this part of town were it not for the fact that Gary was so tall and had blond hair and bright blue eyes.

They took us to a nearby PLO command center where they then separated us. A tired-looking man in military fatigues questioned me. He was obviously suffering from a bad head cold, and continuously pulled tissues from a grubby box on his cluttered desk.

"Why are you not carrying any ID?" he asked me. "And why do you have a bag of camera equipment on the back seat of your car? Are you here to take photos ahead of another Israeli raid?"

As I tried to explain what had happened, I spotted something through a window. People outside were removing the door panels from my car in search of suspicious items. They even dismantled my wristwatch in front of me.

I liked that watch, I thought, wishing I'd never made that wrong turn.

After about half an hour of more questions—Why was I living in Beirut? And exactly who did I work for?—an unshaven man in worn civilian clothing entered the room. He looked carefully at my face, then suddenly pulled out a knife and came running toward me, shouting in Arabic that I was the man he had seen taking pictures in the neighborhood of one of the murdered PLO leaders ten days earlier. The two guards standing behind me rushed to intercept and drag out the knife-wielding and screaming false witness! In the end I surmised that the whole thing was just a ploy to test my reactions. I must admit—I was momentarily horrified!

After three hours of them circling back to the same questions over and over, one of the guards led me to a detention cell, where I was reunited with a very shaken Gary. He had also been questioned for several hours and unhelpfully admitted to me in a whisper that he'd lied to his interrogators about never having visited Israel. He also told me an equally unhelpful story about an American who had mistakenly gone into one of the PLO camps in the city the previous year and had never been heard of again. We must have remained alone for another two or three hours before they took us to meet someone from their information department.

This man was clearly well-educated and spoke excellent English, but did not explain why we were there or whether our fate had been determined. Instead he began to tell us about the struggle of the Palestinians, beginning in the early twentieth century, quoting European philosophers and writers, and including direct quotes from the works of Shelley and Keats. It was a strange experience. We were obviously emotionally vulnerable, and his story of the suffering Palestinian people moved us, even to the point of tears. At the end of his presentation, he unexpectedly announced that we were free to go, but were welcome to return next week, by which time he would have some new literature for us in English about the Palestinian cause.

We got back into our car, with the door panels (mostly) reinstalled. I also received back my bag of camera equipment (without the film), and we were given a military escort to the ill-defined camp perimeter.

We felt relief, as perhaps I never experienced before or since—as if we were lost and then had been given back our lives. The whole experience lasted just over six hours, and when I walked back into the office, people were packing to leave for the day, unaware that we had been "missing" at all.

I guess I must be a slow learner because, since those early days, I have experienced many other detentions or warnings for having a camera near strategic installations—government buildings, bridges, dams, train stations, telecommunication centers, and the like.

At the end of our year with OM, because Jackie and I better understood the needs and opportunities in the Arab World, we committed to stay another year, and then another . . . never suspecting that we would never again live and work in the UK.

Even though we became more streetwise, we still suffered a number of close calls, especially during the beginning of the civil war in 1975. A car bomb took out all the windows of the building we then lived in. It blew glass all over our bedroom. Fortuitously, to escape the heat that night, we were sleeping in the open air on the back balcony. Another time, someone planted explosives in front of the shop on the ground floor of our building, again blowing in all the windows.

In the late summer of 1975, we moved out of the city and to the Druze village of B'Chemoun, in the hills to the south of Beirut, overlooking the international airport. As the war gained momentum, check points began appearing, with local communities organizing their own controls on the approach roads to their respective villages. One night when returning from Beirut to B'Chemoun, armed men outside the village stopped me. As they were checking my vehicle, other men came out of the dark and began firing at the car behind me, which was scrambling to turn around. The gunfire was so loud that I could not hear anything else and could not move out of the conflict zone, because the local militia were using my car as cover against any expected return fire from the escaping vehicle! That was my only taste of real panic, the kind where my mind ran wild and tried to fill in details that may or may not have been true. I assumed that, because people were using my car as a shield, there must be return fire, and I was caught in the middle of it. When I got home, however, I was astonished not to find any bullet holes in the vehicle.

I've always loved reading the heroes list in Hebrews 11. One thing I've noted is that a life of faith does not guarantee us protection from an early or painful death or other woes. And as disciples of Jesus, how can we expect the world to treat us any better than it did our Lord, who died an agonizing and premature death on a Roman cross? But in this life of faith, we do know that nothing will befall us unless our heavenly Father allows it.

As Jesus said in the Gospel of Matthew, "Are not two sparrows sold for a penny? Yet not one of them will fall to the ground outside your Father's care. . . . So do not be afraid; you are worth more than many sparrows" (10:29, 31). Understanding this truth gave me the assurance of immortality until my God-appointed time to leave this world has come.

Middle East Media

As my work continued with OM, we began expanding our publishing role. In the autumn of 1974, we created Middle East Media (MEM) as a separate division of OM, which specialized in the production of Arabic Christian literature, mostly for distribution through secular bookshops. But the organizational strategy was increasingly out of step with OM's main work, so we agreed with OM's leadership to spin off this unit as a separate organization, effective September 1975. But, as this date approached, we found ourselves some four months into the start of Lebanon's civil war, making the start-up of this new entity challenging.

I was responsible for the ministry's publishing work, as well as much of the photography and graphic design. Bill Musk, who later was to become the Anglican bishop of North Africa, joined the team in 1973 and, a year later, conducted a survey for us to find out the most popular formats of printed matter read in the Arab World. The results were not encouraging for a book publisher: excluding school and university textbooks, the typical Arab spent an average of just two *seconds* a year reading a book! What they were reading avidly were newspapers and magazines, many of which were highly subsidized by political or religious interests.

So we decided to publish a Christian newsstand magazine—unfortunately, at that time we struggled to find the right people to manage the editorial and artistic content.

"What if we went to Egypt to find who we need?" I asked the team in the summer of 1975. It seemed the perfect idea, given the fresh openings in the country after President Sadat declared his new "Open-Door" policy. We knew that many gifted Christians lived in Egypt, including writers and artists—in fact, half of all the Christians in the Middle East live in Egypt. We knew we needed to get better involved there. But we put it on a back burner for the moment, determined to look into it at a later date.

However, things still weren't working for us in Lebanon. By the end of 1975, the main post office was backlogged with tens of thousands of undelivered letters, our staff often could not travel to work because of insecurity on the roads, we had many days without electricity, and the printing press we mostly used for our ministry got shelled. And then, on a personal level, I was concerned for Jackie, who was expecting our first child at any minute, and we did not know if the road to the hospital would be open or not when the time came.

Our son, Gavin, arrived on the night of December 11—one of the heaviest nights of fighting between the rival militia groups holding the Holiday Inn Beirut and the Murr Tower. Both of these tall buildings were only a few hundred yards from the American University Hospital and clearly visible from the maternity floor. Ours was the only child born in the hospital that night, though many visitors crowded onto the otherwise deserted floor to watch the rocket-propelled grenades and other fire trade-off between these two frontline positions.

"You know how we've been wanting to check out Egypt?" one of my coworkers said to me.

I nodded. "Yes. Now seems like a very good time to go."

Leaving Lebanon

A few days later, in the cold early morning, a dozen of us packed into four vehicles and left for Syria, where we hoped to get a ferry from the port city of Latakia to Alexandria on Egypt's north coast. We assumed we'd be there only a few months, until the civil war finished. We did not even take any of our summer clothes, we were so confident that this was all going to be over in a matter of weeks. But it was a year before I could even return to clear out and hand back the keys to our rented apartment in the village of B'Chemoun. We would never live in Lebanon again.

We arrived in Damascus at dusk. People were out on the streets, casually strolling along the sidewalks. *Are they mad? They're not even carrying weapons?* But then it dawned on me, and others in the car, that our shock at the relaxed atmosphere was our shock at normality. What we had become so used to, after months of conflict in Lebanon, was abnormal.

We could find only two available hotel rooms in Damascus, such was the flood of Lebanese into the country. So the men slept in the cars and the women and children, including my eight-day-old son, slept in the hotel.

In the morning, we learned the December 20 ferry to Egypt had no space left on it, so we booked spaces for our vehicles and a few of the group on the next boat, leaving on January 6. We then drove to Amman, Jordan, where we had friends with whom we hoped to stay over the Christmas and New Year period. We arrived in Amman during the late afternoon to again find a city crowded with Lebanese citizens who had fled the fighting. All the hotels were full, as well as our friends' guest rooms—though they did offer whatever accommodation they could. For Jackie, the baby, and me, the best that could be found was an empty car garage, cut into the steep hillside of Jabel Amman. It was basically a twentieth-century "stable," and we began to feel like Joseph and Mary with baby Jesus on that first Christmas! And now we were even "fleeing to Egypt" as they had.

Our hosts provided us with a one-bar electric heater for the garage, which we plugged in and did not turn off until the day we left. We all slept in our car, a Volkswagen minibus, showered at our host's home, and ate meals with the brothers and sisters from the local church.

Eventually, January came, and we set out for the Syrian port of Latakia, finally sailing in the late afternoon for Alexandria.

We landed the next day and, after negotiating the port's customs and immigration, arrived in Cairo at dusk. As we drove into this bustling megacity with its noise and chaotic traffic, Jackie burst into tears.

"What's wrong?" I asked her.

"I didn't know Egypt was like this! I imagined this country as villages, with a slow pace of life. This is frightening!"

I did my best to calm her, realizing that she was an exhausted new mother who'd had to live as a refugee for the four weeks since giving birth to our son.

As we settled in, she soon fell in love with the country, adapting her Lebanese Arabic to the very different Egyptian Arabic dialect and making new friends.

He and She

Early on in our stay, we met with some gifted Egyptian Christians who, though skeptical about the idea of a magazine with Christian content being allowed to go on sale on public newsstands, were excited to be involved. But the logistical challenges were enormous. Even to buy a dozen rolls of camera film from Kodak, we needed a letter from our company to explain why we needed so much film. Darkroom supplies weren't easily accessible, and we either had to buy the basic chemicals from the market and mix up our own developer and fixer or hand carry them into the country. Even getting a post office box for correspondence with our future readers took months of red tape.

After several frustrating delays, however, on the first of October 1976, the first edition of *Huwa wa Hiya* (*He and She*) magazine finally hit the newsstands in a dozen Arab countries. Only Saudi Arabia proved to be a difficult market. The Saudis used to tear out pages they did not like from the magazine and then invoice us for their work in doing so. After a few months they banned the magazine altogether.

Huwa wa Hiya grew in circulation, and the content expanded over the next decade. We were able to promote it on Egyptian television, on outdoor billboards, and through competitions and novel content, such as covers made of die-cut stickers that people could use, in much the same way that people use emojis in social media today. We were also able to sell advertising space in the magazine to commercial businesses and take part in national book fairs in several countries. Many of these new initiatives opened the door for other Christian publishers and local Bible societies to follow.

As we began MEM, and to develop ministry projects that required thousands of dollars, I saw miracles happen over and over. It began with the need to fund publishing books and then to subsidize the production of our monthly newsstand magazine in Arabic, competing with other religiously and politically subsidized magazines. The magazine was a serious step-up on the need for funding. A magazine was unlike a book, the printing of which could be postponed until funding was received. A magazine needed to go out every month! The printers needed to be paid each month; the air-freight bills needed to be paid each month; and so on.

In faith we had taken our first edition of *Huwa wa Hiya* to the press in Cyprus in the summer of 1976. It was to go out on newsstands in October. We had the funds in the MEM account only to pay for the first edition, nothing more. At the end of September, I traveled to Nicosia to pay for the first edition of the magazine, oversee its dispatch to a dozen Arab countries, and deliver the working materials for the second, November, edition—for which we had no funds!

At the end of October, I returned to the press with the films and artwork for the third, December, edition, and to pick up the bill for the second edition that was about to be shipped out. The invoice totaled $6,122. I went to the bank to check our account balance. I had heard that, after praying and fasting for this new initiative, a group of Bible school students in Örebro, Sweden, had taken up a collection to pay for an edition.

But how much can Bible school students contribute? I wondered. To my amazement, when I got to the bank, I found an incoming transfer of Swedish krona, which exchanged to $6,120.

This kind of experience occurred again and again, sometimes at the very last minute, but adequate funding for the magazine continued.

Keep on Keeping On!

What is a life of faith? Chapter 11 of the New Testament book of Hebrews talks about the many Old Testament heroes of faith, people who lived by faith in God and pleased God through their belief and trust in Him. Interestingly, all of them were, like us, frail human beings with their own failings. To mention only a few: Noah was a drunk; Moses had a short temper; David was an adulterer who sought to cover his sin by murder; and Rahab was a prostitute.

In other words, perfection is not a prerequisite for living a life of faith! But without faith it is impossible to please God.

Another aspect of the life of faith is perseverance. We can find many verses in the Bible about persevering. In Luke 11, Jesus teaches His disciples, and us, to pray and to keep on praying. In verse 9, He tells us to ask and to seek. But the English loses the present imperative of the Greek, where *ask* means to "keep on asking" and it will be given to us; and *seek* really means to "keep on seeking" and we will find.

But why do we need to persevere? If God is our good Father, who knows what we want before we even ask, why do we need to keep on asking?

The answer is very often, because it strengthens us. I once watched a chick trying to get out of its shell. It kept pecking at the shell for which it had grown too big but could not break free. It kept on with its little beak, breaking bits of the shell and fighting to get free, and eventually it did. I had been tempted to reach down and help the chick, by peeling away some of the shell, but the farmer explained to me that this would hurt the chick's chances of survival. It was only through the struggle to get out of its shell that it could develop enough strength to begin the next phase of its existence.

Or as Paul puts it in Romans 5:3: "We also glory in our sufferings, because we know that suffering produces perseverance; perseverance, character; and character hope."

There were many times Jackie and I could have put up our hands and called it quits, saying it was too difficult, too scary, too dangerous, too . . . And yet we recalled James's words: "Blessed is the one who perseveres under trial because, having stood the test, that person will receive the crown of life that the Lord has promised to those who love Him" (James 1:12).

Though we were no longer in Lebanon—refugees, as it were—we were set and ready to go where God was leading, to follow with perseverance the life of faith He had planned for us. And this time, He had led us to Egypt.

Chapter 3

The Fear of Christian Television!

Daring to believe that God is faithful doesn't guarantee that our paths will be easy. Throughout the years many times I clung to the second half of 1 Corinthians 10:13: "God is faithful; he will not let you be tempted beyond what you can bear. But when you are tempted [or tested], he will also provide a way out so that you can endure it."

Not long after we moved to Egypt, in 1978, our entire family contracted hepatitis A, apparently through eating at one of Egypt's first KFC outlets! I was the first to develop a high fever, and the tell-tale yellow eyes and straw-colored urine. Then Jackie's parents in the UK came down with it, having visited us a short time before. Then our now-two young boys came down with it, and finally, Jackie who was eight months pregnant with our third child.

I was still bedridden and carted off to stay with friends from church as the two boys went with Jackie to London to receive the best possible medical care. With the boys staying with Jackie's now-quarantined parents, she was hospitalized within hours of her arrival, and our daughter, Mona, was born premature in the hospital's isolation ward that night.

It took six weeks before Jackie could return to Egypt with the now-three young children. How she managed with them on the flight, I have no idea! I was still not fully recovered and could not even go to the airport to meet them.

It was a few weeks later that we began to have concerns about Mona. She was not responding to any visual or auditory stimuli. We took her to a number of specialists in Cairo, and they confirmed that she was not able to see or focus on anything. Her pupils were not responding to changes in light, and that she apparently could not hear at all.

What did all this mean for her? For us? What special care would she need? Would this be available in Egypt?

I was committed to do everything I could to ensure she got the best possible care, but what if that meant returning to the UK and leaving a ministry that God had called me to, and which was rapidly expanding in an exciting way?

I had always believed that God could heal, but not that God *always* heals, even if we have faith. I had seen too many good and faith-filled saints not recover from serious illnesses. And sometimes God has a special blessing to bestow on us during illness, whether this be our own or that of a loved one.

But in this matter, I felt that I had, for the first time in my life of faith, reached the end of myself, my endurance. I claimed the promise in 1 Corinthians 10:13, that God would provide a way of escape—knowing, and willingly accepting, that God may one day bring me back to such a test again for my own spiritual growth. That weekend, together with friends at church, we prayed specifically for Mona's healing.

Two nights later, I was sitting in the car holding Mona while Jackie did some grocery shopping. As Jackie clicked open the door of the vehicle to get back in, the noise startled Mona and she jumped in my arms. I looked down in amazement. This was the first time she had responded to any sound! Over the coming days we revisited the specialists, who confirmed that she was now able to both hear and see—a change that they could not explain. Mona would need surgery later to correct a minor visual squint, but other than that, her physical development was perfectly normal. God had not tested me beyond what I was able to bear at that time and had performed a miracle.

He had provided for my family. And now I was about to need a miracle in my professional life.

This Is a Terrible Idea!

By the time we reached the early 1980s, my team and I had gotten a handle on the publishing part of the work, but we continued to struggle with the circulation numbers. Despite publishing hundreds of thousands of magazines and books packed with the message of the gospel, a huge swath of the population in the Middle East was excluded from accessing these because of their functional illiteracy, something that affected about half the adult population.

How do we increase our reach? I wondered many times and prayed for God to open doors for us to make the gospel available to many more in the region.

One evening in 1982, while walking home from my publishing office south of Cairo, I approached the six-story building in which my family and I lived and saw the strangest sight. Construction had begun on a similar high-rise apartment building on the lot next to our home, and the workers had brought piles of building supplies— sand, cement, timber, and tons of steel-reinforcement bars. They had hired a guard to protect these materials. He lived at the side of the road in front of the site with his wife and three kids. They had nothing but a stretched tarpaulin to keep off the sun and the rare winter rainfall, a few cooking pots, a gas-burner . . . and a television.

As I walked past them, the sight of this family huddled together around this little black-and-white television stopped me in my tracks. *How do they have such an appliance living here, on the edge of destitution, by the roadside?* I spotted a power-cord running right across the building site to a ground-floor neighbor's home. I stood and blatantly stared, though no one from the family noticed me— their eyes were all glued to the little screen!

Eventually I walked on, but that sight stuck with me. *How could such an assumedly illiterate family ever be exposed to the Christian faith . . . unless . . . it was through a medium such as television.* I groaned inwardly.

I really should not have been surprised at this encounter. For a year or two before, local newspapers had been full of stories about how television was changing centuries of culture in Egypt. *Fellaheen* (Egyptian farmers) who used to go to their fields before first light each day were now turning up after 7:00 a.m., bleary eyed and unfit for a day's work—because they had been up late watching the latest soap opera on national television. Suddenly, poor rural families aspired to have appliances and services they saw advertised on television or being enjoyed by city people portrayed in the daily soap operas. Other articles talked about the family planning aspect of the new television services—now rural Egyptian families had something else to do in the evenings other than procreate.

I decided to tuck that roadside scene in the back of my mind— far, far in the back. We needed to reach a broader audience, but television? No. I wasn't prepared to get into that.

My first love was literature. This had been an important tool of choice ever since I became a follower of Christ in my mid-teens. I had published literally millions of tracts for use during the years of student unrest in Europe. I had spent several summers and eventually the first four months of our married life smuggling Christian literature into Eastern Europe. And in Lebanon I had been involved in book publishing and now, in Egypt, I was publishing a monthly magazine that landed on newsstands across fourteen countries in the region. Yes, I believed in and was committed to the use of Christian literature.

But that scene kept forcing its way to the forefront of my mind and offering an option for us. *What if we could make Christian programs and somehow get these onto popular television channels in the Arab World? Or even, one day, start a Christian channel?*

I shook my head in disgust. *Even if it could be done, that's a terrible idea!* I thought. *Literature engages the imagination! I can go back to it as many times as I choose and reflect on content, highlighting points of interest.* On the other hand, television is mostly a transient "lean-back experience," watched for its entertainment value, to relax or distract oneself. Also, television distorts our perspective on global news by being heavily driven by available footage, reducing the coverage of significant events in hard-to-reach places. And when it came to Christian television, well, do not get me started! I had always had a low regard for much of what we call "Christian television."

Apart from some of the disturbing tales of fallen televangelists in the past, and the manipulative on-air appeals of some networks for funds, one has to ask the fundamental question, "Is television a morally neutral enough medium to use in purveying Christian truth?" And the answer I came up with was no, it was *not* a morally neutral conduit for truth.

When I casually mentioned to Jackie what I'd seen with that family and the television, her face lit up. "Maybe that's your next ministry."

"No," I explained. "Listen. The first problem is that you need to have a 'face' for television—that rules many of us out from being watchable contributors. Second, you sit in front of an artificial set, wearing makeup to disguise your facial blemishes and reduce glare from the carefully positioned artificial lighting. Everything is so phony, and, with today's graphic techniques, people cannot begin to separate true images from false. And then you also need to possess a certain level of self-confidence, which we can also call ego, even to put yourself in front of a camera. The stronger the ego, the more confident and competent you look."

She was listening but shaking her head.

"Oh, it gets worse!" I continued. "Television, unlike print media and radio, makes the implicit text of the Bible explicit. Perhaps deliberately, the New Testament does not tell us what Jesus looked like . . . but TV dramas about Jesus do."

"Terry—"

"And—*and*," I interrupted to hit home my point, "there is the questionable economic model of Christian television. Most Christian TV stations or networks make their money from two sources: selling their airtime to others and on-air appeals for money. While this may work in some parts of the world, it won't work in the Middle East. You know why. Because it is only western, mostly North American television ministries who have the funds to buy such airtime—and, good as some of these programs may be, the last thing Middle East Christians need is for us to reinforce the common misconception in the region that Christianity is an import from the English-speaking world."

I wanted to go on and remind her that Christianity was born in the Middle East! But I knew she already knew that. There has been an unbroken, faithful witness to Jesus in the region ever since Pentecost, with tens of thousands dying as martyrs for their faith—at first under pagan Rome, later under Islam, and then even during the Crusades, when ignorant Europeans slaughtered Arab Christians along with their Muslim neighbors.

And as for the idea of raising money from audiences in the region, one that has the smallest percentage of Christians (3.5 percent) in the world and all kinds of economic or currency restrictions—how would that work? And how would on-air fundraising, often associated with audience manipulation, make us look in the eyes of the non-Christians we were also seeking to serve?

No, I thought again, feeling more determined than ever. And I felt as if God was backing up my decision, since I didn't really feel that He was leading us to do something with this medium.

Redeeming the Visual Media

As the weeks passed, though all these disturbing aspects of television, and specifically Christian television, worried me, the image of the building guard and his family watching television became a nagging reminder that the only way to reach out to millions in this part of God's world was through the visual media.

Sometime later, I attended a Lausanne Movement's Young Leaders conference in Singapore. Interestingly, the topic of television arose, so I shared my concerns.

"You don't remember how, a few decades ago, Christians rejected the theater as an evil that Christians should not be involved with, and how others believed that an organ was the only musical instrument that should be allowed in church?" one young leader from Uganda asked. "Don't you know that God can use many ways to communicate with humankind and, that in the book of Numbers, we even read of how God spoke to Balaam through the mouth of his donkey!"

I had to admit this man's challenge made me think. I had other such conversations in Singapore and left with a new clarity and resolve. Despite all its intrinsic weaknesses, I realized, we should not put aside television and its unique power to reach and influence children, the illiterate, women in closed homes, and those beyond the reach of other forms of Christian witness. For the sake of the kingdom of God, we *had* to find a way to mitigate for its weaknesses and maximize the positive and powerful aspects of this increasingly ubiquitous media—and nowhere more so than in the Arab World, where functional literacy was below 50 percent and where it is primarily an oral culture. Despite the great respect all in the area have for the Holy Books and for sacred writings, important things are nearly always communicated orally.

Bit by bit, I began seeing that the visual media had to be used and, as the prospect of un-censorable satellite television services began to seem more probable, this became an obvious opportunity for us. It would be a chance to address all the misunderstandings that had been propagated against the church for centuries, and it was an amazing opportunity to present to everybody, openly and in a form they were familiar with, the basic message of the gospel.

Ultimately, when it came right down to it, the driving force behind my eventual openness was my deeply held belief that it is a basic human right that everyone in the world should have the opportunity to hear the claims of Christ in their own language and without unnecessary foreign cultural baggage, and thus be able to make an informed decision as to how they will respond to the claims of Jesus.

Okay, let's do it, I finally thought.

But how to start? Especially when there were so many other skeptics—among the church's leadership, the donor community, and even within my own team—people who held similar opinions as I'd had?

Getting Started

About this time, I heard from several others in the leadership of radio and print ministries that they too had noticed the growing influence of television, so we agreed to meet and discuss our thoughts and ideas. In March 1983, we convened a "Christian Television Consultation" in the southern Egyptian town of Itsa, where the evangelical church had a conference center. I attended as MEM's representative. People came from Lebanon, Jordan, and Egypt, though just a few had previously been involved in any professional television production. To help facilitate and contribute to the discussions, we also invited several international guests, people who had either a media or film background or had been involved in establishing new ministry partnerships of some kind.

Over the course of our time together, we heard from people who shared their own experiences about the impact of television and, more importantly, how the church could get involved. When the meetings ended, we committed to building on the discussions.

I felt energized, especially since I already had a clear mandate from the MEM international board to conduct a series of studies that would look at the state of video distribution, cinema and broadcast television in the Arab World, the church's use of video and television in the region, and how Christians outside the region were using video. I was to present these studies, with recommendations for action, to our next MEM board meeting at the end of that year.

At the time, the only Christian television being broadcast in the region was from a terrestrial television station in the then-Israeli-occupied South of Lebanon, Middle East Television (METV), an initiative of the US Christian Broadcasting Network (CBN). While it feigned to be a station for Lebanon, many were aware that two-thirds of the signal strength was directed south, toward the Israeli public. This is perhaps why most of its programming was in English and only subtitled, not dubbed, into Arabic.

In 1984 I visited the station, hoping to learn more about it and the lessons they had learned. But it was a difficult trip, as the south of Lebanon was still under Israeli military control. It was a surreal situation. The television station was in a fortified compound in the Lebanese Christian town of Marjayoun, right next to the headquarters of General Saad Haddad's Israeli-backed South Lebanon Army (SLA).

Whenever the general was upset with the actions of the local, mostly Shia Muslim population, he would march next door to the METV compound, take over the studio, and rant at and threaten the Shia population, an event that was usually followed by the shelling of specific troublesome villages mentioned in his tirade. There was nothing METV executives could do to stop these unannounced political broadcasts, as they and their transmission mast were there by the grace of the Israeli government and their puppet military force, the SLA. I left with a strong conviction that whatever we did, we needed to avoid external political interference if we were to be able to broadcast an uncompromised, authentic Christian message.

Then, a year later in June 1985, NASA launched Arabsat 1B, a satellite that could share live television programs between Arab states as well as broadcast television channels directly to homes (DTH) in the region. The launch of this satellite was highly publicized because one of the seven-man crew on the space shuttle Discovery was a Saudi prince, Sultan bin Salman Al Saud, who was on board as a payload specialist. Al Saud became the first Arab, the first Muslim, and the first member of a royal family to fly into space.

In reality, and because of tensions between various Arab countries at the time, Arabsat 1B was never deployed for television broadcasts, and only used for telephony. But the idea of being able to broadcast television channels directly into homes across the region, without the traditional censorship controls imposed on all Arabic broadcasts, did not escape me. I had lived with censorship controls for most of my time in the Middle East. *Huwa wa Hiya,* our newsstand magazine, was subject to censorship every month as it entered each Arab country where it was sold. If it were possible that a day would eventually come when we could broadcast uncensored Christian television programs into the region, however fantastic that seemed at the time, then we needed to prepare for such an opportunity.

Collaboration

This was an era of unprecedented collaboration between both Christian agencies and different churches in the Arab World. In the mid-1980s I helped to establish the Arabic Literature Convention (ALC) as a forum for Christian publishers to meet, share ideas, and launch new collaborative initiatives. Then in February 1990, I had the privilege of helping bring together other media ministry leaders to establish the Arabic Broadcasting Convention (ABC) as a forum to bring greater synergy to the work of organizations involved in Christian radio and television.

But as media ministries were expanding, we were all aware that many in the West were woefully ignorant of the situation in the Middle East—including the plight of its Christian populations and the potential of Christian media. If we were to see the needed support for our new initiatives, we had to change this. To pursue some of that change, I took on the role of executive producer for *The Real Story*, a six-part video series and study guide to help western Christians better understand the Arab World. As executive producer, part of my job was to get as many ministries involved in the project as possible, not just to share in the production costs but to maximize the distribution of the series to churches, universities, and home-study groups.

Later I also became very involved in establishing a human-rights forum, which was later registered as Middle East Concern (MEC).

All these different cooperative forums helped those of us in ministry to coordinate our efforts and brought a level of synergy to much of what was being done in or for the region. They also opened the door for me, as MEM's international director, to initiate the

Cooperative Strategy Group (CSG) study, with its goal to map the state of Christian presence and mission in the Arab World; analyze the megatrends shaping the future of the region; and seek agreement on a set of mission-related priorities for the 1990s. Apart from the strategic importance of the study itself, I hoped that this might justify the concept of a Christian satellite television channel to a wider audience of church leaders and western supporters.

With funding from the Maclellan Foundation, a full-time facilitator on loan from Interdev, and the participation of more than ninety mission agencies and another sixty Middle Eastern church leaders, we started in April 1992 by developing and using a comprehensive survey and a series of consultations.

I spent most of my summer holiday in 1993 editing the final 220-page report, which flagged up half a dozen priorities for Christian ministry, including: the need for more prayer for the region; more effectively discipling new believers; a focus on children's ministry; greater collaboration between local churches and foreign ministries; and a greater use of electronic media—with a strong endorsement for the creation of a Middle Eastern Christian satellite television service.

The CSG report gave a mandate for interested churches and agencies to begin collaborating on such a project, and MEM became the lead agency in the next phase of it—mostly because people realized that, as its international director, I had both the passion and the time to focus on this bold new initiative, because of having been kicked out of Egypt and now being based in Cyprus.

I turned my eyes toward the next phase of the project: taking the vision and developing it. But I quickly realized creating a satellite television service had several dimensions to it, the first being to visit and talk with the leadership of as many different churches in the region as I could, including the Protestants, the Orthodox, and the Catholics. We had to listen to their fears, their hopes, and their aspirations for such a project.

But What Do We Call It?

First, however, we needed a name! Until now, the project had been referred to with the tongue-in-cheek title of "Operation Bigfoot," because of the big coverage or "footprint" of the satellite we were hoping to use. But since most people in this region didn't quickly understand the humor in the double meaning of the title, or feel it was culturally appropriate (given that feet and shoes are considered unclean in the region and the idea of a footprint over the Middle East was insulting), we quickly had to find a more suitable name.

"It needs to be something that won't be an immediate religious turn-off for potential viewers outside the small Christian community," I said to our team. "And yet it needs to be something that has at least some symbolic Christian identity"—a sort of twentieth-century version of the sign of the fish, which early Christians in Rome used to identify themselves discreetly.

"But we also need something short enough to work as an on-screen logo and that would work in several languages," one of the team members said.

"Well, there is always 'SAT,'" I said, referring to shorthand for Satellite Channel.

"Yes, but there are already European channels with the names SAT1, SAT2, and SAT3," another team member offered.

We sat quietly, pondering our next brainstorm. Then it hit me.

In the original languages of the Bible, mostly Hebrew and Greek, there are no separate symbols for numbers, so the writers also used letters of the alphabet to indicate numbers, with the numeric value of a word being the sum total of all its letters.

Seven is the most prolific of the mathematical series that binds Scripture together. The very first verse of the Bible, "In the beginning God created the heavens and the earth," contains more than thirty different combinations of seven.

But then there are more than five hundred specific references to "seven" in the Bible. Just a few examples: "By the seventh day God finished the work [of creation]"; "Take with you [on to the ark] seven pairs of every kind of clean animal"; "After seven days the flood waters

came on the earth"; "[In Egypt] the seven years of plenty were followed by seven years of famine"; and "Lord, how many times shall I
forgive my brother or sister who sins against me? Up to seven times?"
Jesus answered, "I tell you not seven times but seventy-seven times!"

Seven is often referred to as "God's seal" or the number of spiritual perfection—a lot to live up to!

"What about SAT-7?" I said. "The number seven is a holy or
'complete' number, one that Middle Eastern Christians would quickly identify with."

The team smiled and nodded. We'd found our name.

Getting Everyone on Board

We knew our goal was to reach all the people of the Middle East and
North Africa. But we had to start with one language. We chose Arabic, hoping to get to Persian and Turkish broadcasts at a later time.

Armed with our name, I headed out to visit as many leaders as I
could. One I visited was His Holiness Pope Shenouda III, the patriarch
of the Coptic Orthodox Church in Egypt, the largest Christian community in the Middle East. Founded in Alexandria by the evangelist
St. Mark, this church has survived under often brutal waves of persecution. In fact, the massacre of Christians in Egypt by the emperor
Diocletian in the early fourth century was so severe that the church's
Coptic calendar dates itself from Diocletian coming to power in AD
284. The Coptic church has also given us the teachings of the Desert
Fathers, the original Monastic Orders, helped to screen and select the
contents of our current Bible and was even responsible for taking the
gospel to many other parts of the world, including Europe.

When I met with him in 1994 to discuss SAT-7, Pope Shenouda
had been the patriarch in Egypt for more than two decades. He was
a wise and compassionate leader who knew the Bible better than any
evangelical I knew. But he was aging and, in his revered ecclesiastical
position, had been somewhat shielded from the changing world of
technology and communications. He graciously listened with interest to the plans I presented for an Arabic-language satellite television

service for the churches without comment or commitment, other than asking us to engage with His Grace Bishop Marcos, in the Bishopric of Shoubra El-Kheima. Bishop Marcos was known to be someone who stayed up to date with technology.

As I would later learn, though the Pope and his staff appreciated the consultative approach, and my enthusiasm, they felt the project was unrealistic and unfeasible. (Interestingly, the Pope's secretary at that time was a monk, who later became the Coptic Orthodox archbishop of London, Archbishop Angaelos. In 2019 he became the chair of the SAT-7 international council!)

Similarly, most church leaders I was able to visit in Egypt, Jordan, Lebanon, and other countries did "humor me" and "hypothetically" shared their hopes for and concerns about such a proposed Christian television service. However, most tended to focus on their fears—most notably, questions about funding and the potential inappropriateness of foreign-sponsored programming; the possible backlash on the church or individuals who showed their faces (this was not radio); concerns about how different churches could work together on such a channel; where we would find the on-air talent and technical staff for such a project; and how we would avoid being jammed by Arab governments.

Father Antoine Gemayel, who headed up the Catholic Information Office in Lebanon, was one of the more encouraging people I met at that time. He introduced me to his boss, Bishop Roland Abou Jaoudeh, who eventually became a SAT-7 advocate and much appreciated member of our international board.

Eventually, the then general secretary of the Middle East Council of Churches (MECC), Dr. Gabi Habib, appointed a working group to collaborate with us—in the design of an organizational structure, which would ensure that policy and strategy decisions remained in the hands of trusted leaders in the region, and to formulate an all-important programming policy for the proposed channel. We put together guiding documents and agreed to them in the spring of 1995, ahead of the founding meetings for the new channel in November of that year.

Collaboration and approval were slowly coming together.

Obstacles to Face

As I moved through this first dimension of the feasibility studies, I was already beginning to tackle the second dimension. That included forming distinct working groups from the potential partners in the project. Each group focused on one of the following challenges: technical and licensing issues; funding options; production and broadcast logistics; potential program suppliers or production partners; human resource development; and audience relations.

These potential partners were mostly Western Protestant agencies, many of whom were initially skeptical about the idea of working with one another, and even more skeptical about partnering with non-Protestant churches. Slowly, through their commitment, despite their skepticism, God began to soften their stance and change their attitudes. One Swedish Pentecostal agency director admitted that not only was he surprised by being able to work in this SAT-7 ministry alongside Swedish Lutherans, but he felt blessed by having met and learned from some of the local Arab bishops on the board—people who had manifest spiritual wisdom and had shown love and openness toward him and the work.

Yes, of course, in Egypt and in other places, I also met Orthodox clergy and laypeople whom I considered petty and narrow-minded and caught up in traditions, as well as people who were biblically illiterate. But I also found these same kinds of people in Protestant churches around the world, and it dawned on me that church labels do not mean an awful lot. I realized that God is, and always has been, working in all traditions, even if not in all the individual churches of a given tradition or denomination all the time. My quest thus became to seek out and work with those in whom God was working, in different countries and churches, putting aside the misconceptions that I and others had gained from perhaps meeting poor representatives of those traditions.

In May 1994, while I was on a visit to the United States, Jackie discovered a lump in her left breast. I cut short my trip but was unable to get back in time for the lumpectomy she had performed two days later. The lump turned out to be malignant, and a few weeks later, she began a course of six chemotherapy sessions, which continued until September. In all our married life and years in the Middle East, we had never had medical insurance, but just the year before, a dear friend, Cedric, had convinced us to take out some, even taking it upon himself to raise the cost of the annual subscriptions from among members of our home church in Orpington, Kent. As a result, we were able to get the best possible treatment for Jackie, then and in the days that followed.

In October, a tall Swede named Erling Wennemyr joined our team as SAT-7's first full-time employee. In his late fifties, Erling had a business and finance background, as well as mission experience in Asia, and had been loaned to work with us by the Swedish agency InterAct, then known as the Örebromissionen. Many of my days in Nicosia began with him coming into my office, pushing aside the other, mostly MEM paperwork on my desk, and saying, "Today you need to focus on these issues!"

Erling did indeed keep us all focused upon SAT-7 and shared passionately the vision of different churches and western partners working together in the spirit of John 13:34–35, "A new command I give you: Love one another. As I have loved you, so you must love one another. By this everyone will know that you are my disciples, if you love one another." This passion endeared him to many of the Middle East church leaders we were meeting at that time.

A Time for Self-Improvement

In many ways we all felt we were going beyond our comfort zones. None of us involved in the research or the feasibility studies had much personal experience with television or satellite broadcasting, and with the unknown comes a sense of fear or inadequacy. But we wanted to break this barrier by self-education, better informing people of the need and opportunity, and creating a road map that would somehow make such a bold strategy tangible, doable—to bring it within reach.

In this regard, I needed to begin with myself. MEM had started a television production and dubbing ministry in Egypt, but most of this work had expanded after I had been deported. So I read books on television production and watched instructional videos on satellite technology, all of which were beneficial. But it was a later trip to a television station in the United States that proved to be the most helpful.

In the spring of 1995, David Alton MP (now Lord Alton of Liverpool) graciously hosted a presentation of the proposed satellite channel at the Palace of Westminster—home to the British Parliament. This was well received, especially by the few Middle Eastern clergy who also attended, and it helped to raise the profile of the project, opening doors for similar such meetings in the years to come.

Also during that spring, I made a visit to the United States. A major Christian foundation that had helped fund some of the earlier research, which led to the SAT-7 initiative, had received our business plan for the channel. They wanted us to attend a two-day workshop with their advisory group, Ron Blue and Company in Atlanta, Georgia, bringing with us some key leaders from the Middle East to review the plan in detail. This was a promising opportunity, so half a dozen of us flew in for the workshop, including Ramez Atallah from the Bible Society of Egypt and Amira Khaldis from World Vision Egypt.

Things seemed to be going well, until toward the end of the two days, when news began to break about the collapse of what turned out to be a massive Ponzi scheme run by John G. Bennett Jr., a Christian businessman from the Philadelphia area. His Foundation for New Era Philanthropy had raised more than $500 million from more than a thousand mostly Christian donors and institutions, including the foundation we were meeting with. Investors had been told that if they contributed a minimum of $25,000 for three months, New Era would double it. Bennett explained that he had identified secret donors who would match charitable contributions raised by his friends. The whole thing turned out to be nothing more than a scam. There were no secret donors, and new funds were being used to pay out existing investors in the program. More than $130 million had been embezzled before the pyramid scheme collapsed.

This news obviously was a major distraction for some of the Americans in the meeting, which then closed abruptly. Whether it was the haste with which the meeting ended or the properly considered opinion of the experts around the table, the bottom line on SAT-7 was that our business plan did not work for them. They did not see how we could run an operation of this size based only on donations from non-beneficiaries of the service. So if we were not going to change our plan and fundraise from our audiences, they did not see the venture as sustainable and would not fund it. We were all shocked—at both the conclusion and the abrupt way in which the discussions ended.

Regardless, back in Cyprus, we knew God wanted us to move forward, so we agreed to hold the founding meetings for the new channel in the third week of that November.

The meeting with the Americans had so thrown me off, that I was unsure how many of the churches and agencies we had invited would sign up to help fund and support the proposed new channel. But that was not the only uncertainty hanging over me personally.

During the feasibility studies, I was hoping to find a channel director who would head up "the great adventure," as Erling frequently referred to SAT-7. Because I did not have a strong television background and because it had become increasingly clear that this was not a project that could come under the umbrella of MEM, I approached several people who had been constructively involved in some of the studies and partnership forums to see if they would be willing to serve as SAT-7's founding CEO. Their responses surprised me. One asked, "You are really going to do this? Oh, this is scary." For them, their work on the feasibility studies had been a kind of exciting and interesting exercise but, in the final analysis, none of them thought it could be done. No one whom I felt was even vaguely qualified for the job wanted to risk actually trying to undertake such a seemingly impossible responsibility.

I was then faced with a difficult choice: to stay in my current role as international director of MEM or leave and head up the proposed new partnership of SAT-7. To leave MEM was going to create in me a sense of guilt, especially as I had been involved in the ministry since its creation in Lebanon in 1975, had a deep commitment to its staff and programs, and because I suspected that some of the existing MEM supporters might transfer their funding to the new channel, especially if I were to be its founding CEO.

On the other hand, with my inability to freely visit Cairo, I was becoming out of touch with day-to-day developments in Egypt, and this progressively eroded my ability to lead such a work. I had already, three years before, gone through the painful decision to hand over the leadership of the magazine ministry to a new, locally based director. Furthermore, the isolation from the work in Cairo was sapping my ability and even my enthusiasm to adequately represent the ministry to others. Eventually, the difficult choice was made for me when the MEM international board recognized that this was God's will for me and were unselfishly supportive of the plan. So they decided that fall to release me to work full-time with SAT-7, effective January 1996.

The Founding Meeting

November 17, the day of the SAT-7 partnership council's founding meeting, finally arrived. About sixty people from forty different churches and Christian agencies turned up.

At this meeting in Larnaca, Cyprus, we initially outlined the historical background to the initiative, including our consultations with both church and agency leaders, the feasibility studies, the resulting draft organizational structure and program policies, and our proposed approach to audience relations. We again reminded everyone of the vision and mission for SAT-7, the latter being, "To provide the churches and Christians of the Middle East and North Africa an opportunity to witness to Jesus Christ through inspirational, informative, and educational television services." And by Middle East, we meant not only the Arab countries but deliberately also included Iran and Turkey.

We then presented an overview of secular television and satellite television in the region, along with our preliminary business plan and choice of satellite provider for the initial broadcasts.

Many questions came from the floor. How would we produce the initial programs when we did not have a studio, any equipment, or on-screen talent? How would we be able to produce programs that would be theologically acceptable to such a wide range of partners and churches? What percentage of our programs would be originally made in Arabic? When would we start with the Persian and Turkish programming? How would we finance the initial 1995–96 budgets? And the questions went on.

We also held a session on the value of being a partner in the project before proceedings closed for the day. While I felt exhausted by all the discussions, I was pleased at the way people engaged with the issues we had ourselves struggled with for the previous two years, and pleased that we had good answers to all the concerns raised.

The next day, we went over the need for all partners to respect the publicity guidelines, which we had carefully drafted with input from the churches, the interested party most likely to suffer any back-lash to the start of a Christian satellite television service.

Then we asked for the attendees to step up and commit to being part of SAT-7. Sixteen did, including thirteen agencies and churches, as well as three individuals. The founding partners included Middle East Media (MEM), the United Bible Societies, the Finnish Evangelical Lutheran Mission, Interserve, Life Agape (Cru), the International Ministries of the American Baptist Churches, Trans World Radio, the Örebromissionen (later renamed InterAct), and Télé-Lumiére. Another twenty-five agencies or individuals signed up as "Friends of SAT-7," requiring a token annual subscription as opposed to the minimum $10,000 annual fees that full partners would pay.

Following this encouraging beginning, the partnership council went on to formally approve the initial constitution, statements of faith, and council officers, affirm the initial SAT-7 international board, the program policy, the business plan, and me as SAT-7's first CEO.

The first chair of the partnership council was Rev. Lucien Accad. Lucien was the general secretary of the Bible Society in Lebanon but was nearly always involved in interagency and new church initiatives, bringing his words of encouragement and wisdom. Over the years, he had become a wonderful friend and mentor to me, and someone who always promoted collaboration of the sort that SAT-7 now typified.

When asked, "Why, with so many other commitments, are you accepting this responsibility with SAT-7?" Lucien replied, "Because my main responsibility is to make the Bible accessible to those in the Arab World. And I cannot imagine a Christian television channel that will not include the Bible in a prominent way!"

The founding international board included: Rev. Dr. Habib Badr, a member of the MECC executive board, a senior pastor in Beirut, and later SAT-7's longest-serving board chair; Sana Nassar, a woman from the Maronite community in Lebanon who was elected as the first board chair; Hanna Shahin from Trans World Radio, representing the SAT-7 partnership council; Jean-Pierre Barry, the founder of Euro Media, Paris; Nicolas "Nicola" Abou-Samah, the owner of a television production facility in Lebanon, where we put together all the early programs; David Adams, a lecturer at the Oxford Center for Mission Studies; Makram Mehany, from Egypt; and me as a non-voting ex-officio member.

We closed out our time by setting the next board meeting for early in the new year, when we would begin the long process of fine-tuning the policies that would fully address my long-held fears about Christian television and allow us to use its great potential as a conduit for Christian truth.

I couldn't believe this was actually happening, and that I was leading this endeavor—not least of all because of a desolate family on the roadside watching a tiny television.

Chapter 4

How Do We Start a TV Station?

In early January 1996, the first SAT-7 office opened in a rented suite on the third floor of an old building on Themistocles Dervis Street, Nicosia, Cyprus. As in the case of most start-ups, we wondered what just eight of us were going to do with all the space! But of course, that was not an issue for long.

Erling, our first business director, had everything up and running within the first few days—phones, fax, computers, a copier, and a satellite dish and receiver. We had also registered with the Cyprus authorities for duty-free permits for the office and staff to import equipment, registered with the Tax and Social Security departments, and had all our basic office systems in place—including our charts of accounts and banking arrangements, with cash assets of $65,000.

In a report to our board on January 1, I concluded: "We face many seemingly impossible challenges. At the same time, we have the support and good will of many partners and friends who share the belief that SAT-7 is important and has to happen. With God's help, we are moving toward the realization of our vision!"

The new office was officially opened and dedicated in the presence of local clergy on January 15.

Our new programming director, Mousa Hossain, was a Jordanian American in his mid-forties and had moved with his American wife and children to Cyprus in early 1996. His first job was to assemble a team to put together a pilot two-hour broadcast for our board's review. We would produce it in Lebanon where there was more political freedom; we could more easily find talented Christians willing to go on-screen; and we could rent studio space, editing, and technical services at Filmali, the television production facility owned by our board member Nicola Abou-Samah.

Mousa would also oversee acquiring any suitable materials from the West—cartoons for children and Christian movies or documentaries—the kind of high-quality programming that would be of interest to Arab viewers and might not be possible for us to produce ourselves, especially given our modest budgets. To help with this, we recruited Rabie, a young believer from Beirut. His job was to research suitable programs that could be translated and dubbed. Now we were set to move forward.

Finding On-Air Talent

Early that year I again traveled to Lebanon, this time with Erling and Mousa, to explore technical facilities and hopefully identify and audition potential on-screen "talent." My friend Derek Knell, the area director of FEBA radio, suggested we visit the Baptist recording studio that they were renting a part of in Mansourieh. The place included a television studio that had never been used and was also available for rent.

To prepare for the visit, a young FEBA employee, Rita El-Mounayer, was to host us and give us a tour of the facilities. We were supposed to arrive around 1:00 p.m. but, as so often happens in Lebanon traffic, we were running late that day. By the time we arrived at 3:00, everyone was in the process of finishing their workday and getting ready to leave. Rita was the only staff member left, waiting just for us.

We introduced ourselves in English. Mousa, although Jordanian by birth, had lived in the United States since childhood and therefore had a strong American accent. But Rita was annoyed that we were late and did not really listen to what we said, missing the point that Moussa had an Arab name. She wanted to leave as soon as she could to go to the movies with a friend who had also just arrived at the studios.

She started the tour, introducing what they did in each part of the building and showing us the poorly maintained semi-basement television studio with its mostly out-of-date equipment and several inches of water on the floor, the result of recent heavy rain.

As we walked around, Mousa turned to Rita and, with his thick American accent, said, "Are you interested in television?"

"What do you mean?" she said.

"We would like you to try for a screen test and to get to know you better. Maybe you will be good on television."

"No, thank you!" she announced immediately. She turned to her friend and said in Arabic, "So this 'uncle' wants to recruit me into television! He wants to make me a star!"

They both laughed.

Mousa asked her a second time.

Rita again looked at her friend. "Seriously," she said in Arabic, "they turn up so late and then they are asking me all these questions! We want to go to the movies. What is wrong with this uncle?" She continued showing us around, all the while complaining to her friend in Arabic and making fun of Mousa's offer.

Moussa persisted as we all went back to the offices for coffee. "So you seriously don't want to give it a try and go on television?"

"No! I am happy with my job." She again turned to her friend and joked in Arabic: "I am indeed the superstar! He really wants me to be on television."

"So you write and produce programs and then host these on FEBA radio?" Mousa said to her as we all sat down.

"Yes."

"Can I have a sample of your writing?"

"Sure." Rita stood to get the files and then stopped dead. "I'm sorry but my scripts are in Arabic," she said nervously, turning around. "Do you read Arabic? Do you understand Arabic?"

He looked her in the eyes as a big smile crossed his face. "Of course I know Arabic. I'm Jordanian!"

Rita turned bright red and disappeared into the office kitchen, with her friend following.

"Do you think he understood that we were making fun of him?" her friend said softly, though we could still hear them.

"Yes, of course he did!" She sighed. "Even if I wanted to be a TV star one day, I know he will make sure that I don't become one."

Mousa found it all very amusing, and when she returned, he made her the offer for a screen test once more.

By way of apology, she agreed.

On the day of the screen tests, Rita turned up in her radio studio clothes, while the other people auditioning came in their best outfits, with full makeup and elaborate hairdos. Everybody was rushing around and seemed stressed about being in front of the camera and worried about saying the right things.

We asked each candidate to do two things for the screen test: read a brief script in formal Arabic from the teleprompter and then look at the other camera and say something impromptu.

When Rita's turn came, she seemed uneasy. "I didn't prepare as the others did," she said apologetically, seeming insecure.

"That's okay," we told her encouragingly. Her natural character, the heart and wisdom in the scripts she had shown us at the studio— these all counted for much more.

She read out the script. Her classical Arabic was very good and working in radio had honed that skill. Then she looked at the second camera. "Hello, everybody! Today you have the opportunity to win $100,000 if you call this number!" She was clearly having fun and continued, enjoying the chance to act the part of a secular television announcer.

After she finished, Mousa asked her to meet us all in the office. "Everyone, I'd like you to meet Rita. She is our on-screen presenter for SAT-7's new children's program!"

Her face showed surprise. But when he looked at her, she nodded.

The next week Rita recorded a whole pilot program, which they sent to me in Cyprus to evaluate. The program, which we called

AsSanabel (*Ears of Wheat*), included a drama, songs, Bible readings, an art competition, and even birthday greetings to specific viewers.

In those days, to avoid long delays with government censorship and customs, we had to hand carry all such tapes in and out of Lebanon. Tino was our main coordinator in Lebanon, and he brought me the pilot program.

I was impressed with Rita's raw talent. *She's going to work out well for us*, I realized.

Rita met Tino at the airport upon his return to Beirut to find out what we thought.

"They really like you," he told her. "You're the person they want to do the children's programs."

She grimaced slightly. "I don't know about this. I like my job at FEBA. I'm not sure I can juggle both responsibilities."

"No worries. It's only twenty minutes a week. Write the scripts in your spare time, and we will record the programs on a Saturday or in the evening. Please, we need your help."

She took her responsibility seriously and got to work writing scripts and preparing. But three weeks before the launch of the first two hours of programs on the new SAT-7 ARABIC channel at the end of May, Rita asked to speak with us.

"I have been struggling," she began. "Being in front of the camera, with people seeing my face! And writing for children all over the region . . . I don't know a lot about children. At FEBA radio, my boss checked my scripts, but here I'm writing and hosting the programs alone. Also, I know Lebanese children, and having been one myself, I know something of their challenges, and I speak in their dialect. But how am I supposed to talk to children in Morocco or Egypt or Dubai?"

We listened quietly as she shared her concerns.

"Last night, I felt this sense of responsibility weigh so heavily on me that I couldn't get to sleep. So around midnight, I went to my living room and started praying. In a way, I was arguing with the Lord, asking Him, 'Why are you challenging me beyond what I can do? I don't know if I will succeed. If I fail and it's a terrible program, then it is worse than if it happened on radio, as people will recognize me! And what if I don't say or do things that are relevant to the children watching? Please, Lord, I don't know these children. I don't know how to serve them!'

"I felt God give me a vision: the call of serving the children of the Middle East and North Africa through SAT-7. As I was praying, I saw children in the streets, children barefoot, children eating ice cream and it dripping on their clothes. I saw children in their school uniforms going off to school, and I saw lots of children having fun. And I felt love for them all! It was like that love you feel when it is so strong you cannot take it anymore, too much love to bear because you love so much that it hurts. God gave me this huge love, and, in my heart, I heard Him tell me, *Rita, I don't need your skills and I don't need you to look good in front of the camera. All I need is for you to be a channel taking My love to these children. Human love often ends or changes, but My love is unfailing. It is always there.*"

Her eyes glistened with tears and excitement. "So I'm ready!"

A month after the first broadcasts began, Rita was sitting in the FEBA office when she looked up to see Tino coming toward her carrying a large box. "What is that?" she asked.

"These are the letters you have received for the program," he said.

Rita looked into the box in amazement and started opening envelopes and reading letters. They were from children in Syria, Palestine, Egypt, Lebanon, Tunisia.

Soon after, one of our production partners, a Swedish ministry, offered to sponsor Rita's program on SAT-7 and make her one of their "missionaries." As part of the arrangement, she had to go to Sweden three or four times a year to record the children's programs in their studios in Linköping. She initially did this on a part-time basis, for six months, but in the summer of 1997, they asked her to work with them full-time, as their employee in Lebanon, on loan to SAT-7.

Based on this verbal offer, Rita resigned from FEBA, but not long afterward, something went wrong, and the Swedish partner decided they could not open an office in Lebanon or employ Rita there after all. Instead, they wanted her to live in Sweden and work for them there. She told them, "I live in the Middle East. I'm sorry; I can't do that."

Suddenly Rita found herself without a job. She telephoned me for advice and explained the situation.

"Don't worry, we will take you," I told her without hesitation. "We want you in SAT-7 full time. I'm coming to Lebanon next week. We can discuss it then."

The next week Rita met me in the studio in Beirut. I sat across from her with my briefcase open and confirmed that we were offering her a job.

"Thank you, but I do need some written assurance from you that you definitely would like me to be in SAT-7," she said. After what had happened with the Swedish mission, she was being understandably cautious.

"Yes, of course, I'll give you a written commitment," I reassured her. I took a Swiss army knife out and casually said, "I'll write it in my blood."

Rita did not know my sense of humor. She jumped up. "No! No! No!"

I broke out in laughter, and soon she realized the joke and joined in. It was my clumsy way of conveying how serious we were about wanting her in SAT-7.

In March 1998, Erling signed the official employment contract and handed it to her. "This is a very precious contract for SAT-7," he told her.

Rita signed it. At that time, no one would have guessed that twenty-three years later, she would succeed me as SAT-7's CEO.

Getting the Broadcasts Up and Running

The SAT-7 board met several times during the spring of 1996 to look at pilot programs, to discuss the practical application of our detailed program policies, and to try to shape the content of future broadcasts.

We negotiated satellite time on one of the Eutelsat satellites, getting on a time-share channel with TV Albania and a few others. While these satellites were not designed to cover the Arab World, their wide European coverage footprints spilled over into North Africa and the central Middle East—where they provided the first uncensored television services for Arab countries.

We reserved the midday slot on Fridays for our two-hour broadcasts, presuming this would most likely be the best time to find people at home, as Friday was the main day off in most countries across the Arab World. We signed an agreement with an Anglo-French company to uplink our programs to the satellite from London, starting May 31, 1996. Then the company asked for our Independent Television Commission (ITC) issued content license. We had not known about the need for this and we had only a couple weeks to secure it, which was not feasible. Fortunately, we discovered we could call the initial broadcasts "experimental broadcasts," which did not require us to have a license.

We had six phone and fax lines installed, and rented post office boxes in Nicosia, Beirut, and Amman, enabling us to offer contact addresses in both Latin-script and Arabic. We had also just set up the sat7.org domain, mostly to manage our email accounts, but with a view to providing resources to our audience through it in the future. Only about twenty thousand websites existed in the world when SAT-7 was formally launched (compared to the 1.8 billion sites in 2020). And very few people in the Middle East had an email address at that time.

We also visited the embassies in Cyprus of key Arab countries to give each ambassador a heads-up on the start of broadcasts, explaining to them who we were and who we were not. The most sensitive visit was to the Egyptian embassy, who were aware of my earlier deportation from Egypt. The ambassador was gracious and said that they would let the channel speak for itself, and that they would watch it for a year before rushing to any conclusions.

We scheduled a May 31 meeting of our international board, so we could watch the first broadcast together.

I am not sure if it was a head cold or stress, but by the day of the meeting, I had completely lost my voice. Erling had to read my written report, and I had to resort to writing notes in order to respond to questions or when trying to make a point. But by the time I had done so, the board conversation had usually moved to another issue.

The board adjourned between 1:30 and 3:30 p.m., so everyone could watch the first broadcast.

We had not really expected any immediate responses to it—thinking it would take time for people to find a two-hour-a-week Arabic broadcast on a European satellite that otherwise broadcast in Albanian and Romanian, but we did get calls and faxes! Within minutes of the broadcast's start, a call came into our Nicosia number. It was from a man in the Arabian Peninsula who was astonished at the program presenter he had just seen. "What is this channel? I just saw a woman wearing a cross around her neck and speaking Arabic!" Here was someone who did not even know Arabic-speaking Christians existed!

When we started, we wondered if anyone would be willing to take the risk or go to the expense of making an international phone call to get in touch with us. Up to this point, none of the international radio ministries had offered a phone number to their audiences and instead relied on mail. In the coming days we were astonished at the number of people who were willing and wanted to make international calls to speak to us.

A Steep Learning Curve

The partners—especially those interested in program production or audience relations—met immediately following the May 31 board meeting. We had workshops on each topic, trying to distribute responsibilities across the group. This was when our Swedish partner, TV-Inter, offered to get more involved in the children's programming and our Paris-based partner, Life Agape, with the audience follow-up.

In the coming months, a lot of new doors opened for us. We were amazed to watch how SAT-7 actually being on-air changed people's attitudes. People who, before, gave us words of encouragement but did little to try to help us, now wanted to be engaged, coming forward with offers of practical help. I had experienced the same thing twenty years earlier when we launched *Huwa wa Hiya* magazine. Once the magazine hit the newsstands, people saw that the vision was no longer an optimist's dream of what could be but a God-given reality, and they wanted to be a part of it.

Now, people were flocking to us—clergy who were ready to write or present teaching programs, Christian musicians, would-be producers, counselors who wanted to offer their services to counsel our viewers, camera operators, technicians, and many more. But we were still in the early stages of growth and our infrastructure could not keep up. Typical of this challenge was when we hired a cameraman in Beirut before we even owned our first camera!

During these first few years we were on a steep learning curve. We had few precedents or models we could look to. We had to create new policies and procedures for almost everything we did. We were learning in so many areas simultaneously: production and program acquisitions; co-production with partners; master control room; playout and satellite uplink services; navigating censorship and customs procedures, as well as the legal and financial structures for new offices. We had to develop personnel policies that would not stifle creativity and creative people, had to be flexible for staff needing to work evenings and weekends, and were equitable across different offices and between loaned mission staff and locally employed nationals. We needed training and procedures for staff answering phones in different countries. And the list went on. At times, it seemed overwhelming having to invent and refine everything as we went along!

It seemed that we could gain a better understanding of the industry from spending time in functioning television stations and on-the-ground visits to parts of the region we were seeking to serve. So in early 1997, at the kind invitation of Jerry and Shirley Rose, and with the financial support of the Jerusalem Trust, I embedded myself as an annoyingly inquisitive guest at Channel 38's Chicago studios. Each day, I spent time in a different department, interrogating managers and staff about what they did and why they did it that way, and making copious notes.

It was a very cold and snowy week, and so my visit with Channel 38's chief engineer to the station's transmitters on the top of the Sears Tower (now Willis Tower and once the tallest building in the world) in the Windy City was kept as brief as I could make it! Overall, I experienced an extremely valuable visit and left with a big picture of the different elements and processes that make up a television and broadcast operation.

That week Craig, a representative for an anonymous foundation in Michigan, approached me, saying they wanted to learn more about what we were hoping to do. Craig and I had a late dinner meeting and then he left, with me not knowing if anything would come from the encounter. As it turned out, this foundation went on to play a major role during the first four years of SAT-7, helping fund the launch phase of the ministry.

I returned to Cyprus and began implementing the lessons I'd learned from the visit to Channel 38, but was also able to supplement them in the next few months by attending the Cabsat '97 and MID-TV regional television industry trade fairs in Dubai; participating in meetings of the National Religious Broadcasters in Los Angeles, the Fellowship of European Broadcasters in Utrecht, the Christian European Visual Media Association in Amsterdam; and attending a BBC course in Norton Wood entitled, "Making Television Work."

Key Visits to North Africa and the Gulf

The other learning strategy I had was to listen to people on the ground in the Arab World—to better understand what was working, what was not, and what we were missing altogether. This involved getting out to North Africa, Arabia, and places where we did not yet have local staff or board members.

Most impressionable and informative were my trips that year to Morocco, Tunisia, and Saudi Arabia.

In Morocco I attended a meeting of people whose job was to follow-up on contacts made by Christian radio. I was shocked how few people made it through all the courses and screening procedures before they actually got a face-to-face visit from anyone—it was less than a dozen people a year. And what shocked me most was the way our methodologies were shaping the demographics of the emerging church in North Africa.

First, international Christian radio was a medium that attracted a younger, mostly male, audience. Second, the way to get more information about the Christian faith was to write to some address in Europe for a Bible Correspondence Course (BCC), which, in itself carried a degree of risk—that the government or a family member might intercept the correspondence, creating potentially serious problems for the person. And, of course, one had to be functionally literate even to begin down this track. For these and other reasons, almost all the people able to jump through all the hoops and eventually be brought into a house fellowship of some kind were single, sixteen-to-twenty-two-year-old, literate males. These people then needed to meet in the homes of foreigners because there were so few indigenous families where all the members were believers.

It was clear that Christian television was going to break through these limitations. First of all, satellite TV, unlike international radio broadcasts, was not something a person could listen to alone in their bedroom at night. No, people owned one television and one satellite dish per household, and it was firmly planted in the family's living area. So people who watched SAT-7 mostly did so with the mutual consent of the family or not at all. This led to whole families coming to Christ, creating new nuclear home groups. Satellite television was being watched by the illiterate, by the women and children in the household—by everyone.

Before I left Morocco, I met a Christian schoolteacher working near Casablanca. He excitedly told me that the children in his class had told him about a Christian satellite TV channel called SAT-7. He had heard about this new initiative coming out of the Middle East but had not realized just how available it was in North Africa.

"Almost every home seems to have a satellite dish," he exclaimed. "And families sit and watch by the hour whatever comes on screen! I was in one home at midday on a Friday and I could hardly believe my eyes. I saw Jesus portrayed as the Bread of Life, with John 6:35 on the screen in Arabic. There were songs for the children and adults, and a Christian movie. And it was totally unreal to hear the 'Hallelujah Chorus' there in that village and see flashed on the screen, 'King of kings and Lord of lords!' And they enjoyed it! One lady came up to me and said, 'I always watch it. It's better than what usually comes on the other channels at this time.' What potential, and what a challenge for our prayer!"

While his comments encouraged me, I had more to learn from my visit to Morocco. Some of the new believers I met thanked me for the worship songs we broadcast. They would gather around their televisions at noon each Friday and treat the weekly broadcasts as the basis of their own worship service, standing for the songs and prayers and listening hungrily to the teaching segments. What shocked me was what they said about the worship songs: that these were their only hymns and that they videotaped them to enjoy throughout the week and share with their friends. In other words, we were giving the North African church their hymnology.

There were lots of recorded Arabic Christian songs but very few had been professionally videotaped. And what we broadcast were the only music videos we could acquire or make ourselves. We gave no thought to providing a balanced theological hymnology or to understanding that these music clips might be the only worship songs a church would have. I realized that we needed to be more deliberate with our worship music. But that realization didn't stop with music. We needed to consider how balanced and how complete we were in our on-screen teaching. This led to developing teaching curriculums and special program series that sought to "teach the whole counsel of God."

Tunisia

My visit to Tunisia in June that year also proved a valuable learning experience. I spent time with satellite dish wholesalers and retailers in the capital to better understand the kind of programs and channels that motivated people to invest in a dish, and which satellites had the most popular channels for Tunisians.

Of course, this was a country where French was widely used, and so satellites with French-language channels were popular. In general, people were looking for sports (especially soccer), music, Arabic-language movies, and uncensored news. In this regard, the new Saudi-owned Arabsat satellite was of little interest, while the Eutelsats at 13 and 16 degrees east (where the SAT-7 channel was) were by far the most popular, with increasing numbers of people buying the more expensive motorized dishes so they could move their antenna between the two satellites.

Interestingly, the Tunisian government had been one of the few Arab countries to initially ban dishes. However, at the end of 1996, in the face of public resentment over the ban and the widespread smuggling of dishes, smaller-sized dishes were allowed so long as owners registered them. There were now about 150 importers officially bringing in dishes and tuners.

This was consistent with the government's efforts to secularize Tunisian society and suppress what they saw as growing Islamic fundamentalism in the country.

I also visited some private television production companies in Tunis. One had just produced a one-hour documentary on the Christians of Tunisia before the rise of Islam. They were very open-minded and had actually helped produce some biblical films for a South African company the previous year. We discussed the possibility of coproducing a series on the early Church Fathers, which could be shot on location in nearby historic Carthage, or in Hydra, out near the Algerian border where massive Roman ruins, with churches, stood. In the end, nothing came out of this particular relationship, but it did confirm for me the interest we could elicit among North Africans to learn about their pre-Islamic, Christian past—a topic not taught in the vast majority of schools. Years later, the popularity of a locally produced movie about the life of St. Augustine bore this out.

I was also able to meet with a number of church leaders and Christian workers while in the country, including the bishop, Monsignor Fouad Twal, at the massive Catholic cathedral on Tunis' Avenue Bourguiba. The bishop was originally from Jordan and very positive about SAT-7, which had been discussed the previous week at the Conference of North African Bishops in Algeria. They felt that this new television service was sensitive to their situation and would be effective in bringing a better understanding of the Christian faith to those in North Africa. He also welcomed the idea that SAT-7 would begin to publicize their church services in Tunisia, including the services held in Arabic. He was always looking for ways to gently push the envelope when it came to the rights for Christians to witness in the country, and this fit right in with that agenda. And so began a series of SAT-7 on-air announcements, promoting church services in North Africa and, soon after that, the Arabian Peninsula.

Arabia

My visit to Saudi, a few months later, took a bit more work than going to North Africa. It began with needing to apply for a visa, which in turn needed an invitation from a Saudi national or company. "Pastor Andrew," a Korean believer in Saudi, secured it for me. He had friends in the construction business who could legitimately invite a civil engineer, like me, for such a visit. But getting the letter was just the beginning. I then needed copies of my work and residence permits in Cyprus and a police report, certifying my crime-free past. Fortunately, my deportation from Egypt did not appear in any police records in Cyprus. All these documents then needed to be couriered to the Saudi embassy in Athens, together with my passport, grounding me for two weeks while the application was processed.

Eventually, after three weeks and half a dozen phone calls, the visa came through.

The Cyprus Airways flight to Saudi was uneventful, until we stopped in Jeddah to pick up more passengers for the final leg of the flight into Riyadh. We were supposed to be on the ground for just forty-five minutes, but this turned into three hours as the plane was loaded to capacity with pilgrims returning from the Hajj in nearby Mecca and Medina. Men with closely shaved heads, mostly dressed in traditional national costumes or white robes, some with their well-covered wives in tow, struggled to find their seats and enough overhead bin space. Everyone had excessive amounts of hand luggage as well as at least twenty liters each of holy water from the well of Zamzam.

The well is located near the holy Kaaba in Mecca and, according to Islamic tradition, is a miraculously generated source of water from God, which spontaneously sprang from the sands thousands of years ago when Abraham's son Ishmael and his mother, Hagar, were left in the desert, thirsty and crying. Millions of pilgrims drink from the well each year while performing the Hajj pilgrimage.

Despite the chaos and shoving on the plane, a spirit of camaraderie settled among the new passengers, much like that found among friends returning from a church picnic. However, the water bottles in the overhead bins soon proved to be a problem as some were leaking and Zamzam water began dripping on passengers through the light sockets and air vents.

The plane was further delayed by a Pakistani lady from Bolton, England, who refused to be separated from her husband. She had been assigned a seat in the forward part of the aircraft with the women, while her husband had one at the back. She sat next to him, in someone else's seat, and refused to move, even when the captain came and appealed to her.

"If we do not leave soon," he explained, "the flight will need to be cancelled as the crew are approaching the maximum number of hours they can work."

She was unmoved.

Under normal circumstances, one could have easily moved a few passengers around. But due to the strict segregation of the sexes among these pilgrims, the negotiated seat exchanges took an hour!

As we eventually took off, I felt a sense of relief, hoping that Andrew, who was meeting me in Riyadh, was informed of the delay. But just when I thought things were back to normal, and even before the seatbelt signs were switched off, white-robed men everywhere got out of their seats and knelt for prayer in the aisle, facing toward the back of the plane and the holy city of Mecca, from which we were departing. The mostly Greek Orthodox Cyprus Airways crew, who were concerned about the safety of the passengers, as well as how they were going to move their food trolleys, just stood in despair.

In Riyadh, a polite but very thorough immigration service welcomed me. It was a matter of routine for them to open and search all bags, although my person was not searched. I had with me overhead projector transparencies and single hard copies of some SAT-7 information materials for reproduction in the country after my arrival. These were all in between the pages of an in-flight magazine and went unnoticed. I also had a single VHS videotape, however—samples of our programming. This was buried deep between different pockets in my shoulder bag. They found it and took it with my passport to a special video-viewing gallery at the end of the customs hall. Since no one seemed to care, I followed my tape and passport to the censorship room and stood in the doorway to see what was happening. The official went through the entire tape, fast forwarding through sections of little interest but stopping each time a Christian symbol or church appeared, sometimes rewinding to listen carefully to what was being said. They went through the English and then the Arabic versions of the program. By this time, I thought I would never see the tape again and would be fortunate even to get into the country! However, the tape and my passport were returned, with no comment, and I was advised I could leave.

Andrew met me at arrivals, and we drove to his home in the city's suburbs. It was typical of much of the housing in Saudi—a two-story villa surrounded by a high-perimeter concrete wall. Its flat roof also had a six-foot-high perimeter wall. This level of privacy, which Saudis seemed to feel the need for, did give a level of security for Christian activities, and provided all citizens with a way of hiding their rooftop satellite dishes! These were mostly huge C-band dishes, up to ten feet across, which were illegal in the 1990s, but already widespread in the kingdom.

In fact, official figures released during my visit put the number of homes with at least one dish at 65 percent, with an additional ninety thousand homes per month installing dishes. In percentage terms, this meant these illegal sales had one of the fastest growth rates for any domestic appliance in the world. The percentage of homes with a satellite system would grow to 99 percent before dishes were legalized. In the meantime, Saudis I met complained that the *mutawa,* or religious police, continued to shoot at any of these "satanic dishes" they could see from the street.

I attended my first "church meeting" in Saudi in the basement of a cultural center for mostly Asian expatriates. Different areas were marked out for men and women with conspicuous signs on the doors to adjoining rooms: "Sewing Lessons," "Arabic Lessons," and so on. The main meeting room could accommodate about eighty people sitting on the floor. The walls were covered in heavy drapes to help contain the sound of singing and music, of which there was plenty.

Before the service began, some leaders passed around the mandatory Arabic language study folders and spent time teaching a few words of Arabic. During the actual worship service, closed-circuit television monitored the outside of the compound, and next to the staffed monitors was an alarm switch. In the event of a raid by the mutawa, the service would immediately revert to an Arabic study class.

This particular fellowship was perhaps more security conscious than most, partly because it did not meet on a diplomatic compound and because, five years before, their meeting had been broken up by the mutawa, and their pastor beaten and deported. It had taken a long time for the members of the congregation, each of whom had received a severe warning, to regroup and recommence worship services. Some of the members had joined other fellowships, which could be described as more charismatic than the Presbyterian-style of worship they enjoyed at this particular venue. After an hour of prayer and worship, the leaders asked me to share. With translation, this lasted two hours. But even then, at 10:00 p.m., people were still not in any hurry to leave.

The next day I had the chance to see more of Riyadh, the capital and perhaps the kingdom's most religiously conservative city. Its streets were wide with a growing number of modern buildings. The diplomatic quarter of the city was architecturally beautiful and its gardens and expanses of well-watered lawns well-manicured. But, even in this cosmopolitan and diplomatic zone of the city, all street signs were only in Arabic. Riyadh was not only the seat of government and the headquarters of the security services but also the center of power for the mutawa. While their numbers and influence were being curtailed, several thousand full-time mutawa remained on government payrolls.

Each day, the newspapers published the exact times of prayer, and all stores, restaurants, businesses, and public offices were required to close their doors at the start of these prayer times—and remain closed for about thirty minutes. People already inside shops or restaurants were usually allowed to continue their activities but the doors had to be locked and signs displayed, saying, "Closed for Prayer Time." The mutawa checked for compliance. However, few nationals seemed interested in participating in all the prayer times, and the traffic was at its worst during prayers, with many using the occasion to run errands or take care of personal business.

The mutawa also checked to ensure that women were not out by themselves. They were expected to be with a male relative or with other women. In the 1990s, no women were allowed to drive, or even to travel in the front seat of a vehicle, unless the driver was a male relative. And, of course, all women were obliged to wear a black outer garment and normally have their head covered, although this was not usually forced on Western women.

I was surprised to see the prevalence of American-style fast-food outlets, including McDonald's, Wendy's, and Kentucky Fried Chicken. These, like other public eating places, had segregated areas for men and for families. Women did not usually go to such places by themselves or even with just their children. I found it strange to see, in a McDonalds, that the booths were surrounded by high partitions and sliding doors, so that customers could enjoy sufficient privacy for the women to remove their veils and eat.

During the following days, I was invited to share about SAT-7 at a number of other Christian fellowships in the capital, including the US Embassy Fellowship, which met on Fridays. Security made it difficult for any except Americans to attend this fellowship, and the security services made an open show of collecting the number plates of all cars pulling into the embassy compound each Friday.

Some of the brothers I met in Saudi were what they call "tent-makers," people who worked in the Gulf to support themselves (as the apostle Paul did, making tents) but whose real motive for being there was to share their faith with others. I was amazed that some had huge stores of Bibles and other Christian resources. While it had been relatively easy to get these into the country, the real problem was their distribution to end users. This carried considerable risk to those involved in such distribution. The personal ownership of a single Bible, in a person's own language, was not a problem, but possessing even one Bible in Arabic would create questions. Having a box of them was a recipe for deportation.

During ten days in the kingdom, I also traveled to the eastern provinces and again to Jeddah. I met with many wonderful and courageous people. I listened to stories of bold personal witness, of hundreds of nationals attending Christian gatherings and thousands of Asian believers meeting in sports arenas. I also heard stories of need and pain.

One such story was typical of the unusual opportunities for witness in Saudi. The mother in a Saudi royal household was termi-nally ill, so the father asked their Indian servants, who were com-mitted Christians, to pray for the lady of the house. The wife was miraculously healed, and the story spread quickly within the royal family. One of the servants, who was relatively young but had been the main actor in leading the prayer, was called in by the mutawa. They told him of another sick person, saying that on the following day, he must heal him or face execution. The next day, while on his way to the meeting, the leader of this particular mutawa group was killed in a car accident. The mutawa dropped the whole matter, and the Indian brother began to be treated by his employer, and certain members of the royal family, as a special prophet.

Farshad, a "tentmaker" from Iran, also told me a story of a friendship he had developed with a former chief of police in one of the provinces. For some days, he felt God guiding him to offer this man an Arabic Bible but was naturally concerned as to his possible reaction. The sense of compulsion to do this became overwhelming and so, in fear and trembling, he went to the official's home and, after some pleasantries, asked him if he would accept the gift. The official's eyes lit up and he said, "You mean this has all the verses I have been trying to write down from the recordings?" He then turned on his video recorder and showed Farshad the teaching programs he had recorded from the SAT-7 broadcasts.

I left Saudi on the eve of the Islamic new year. I had learned much and felt inspired by what I'd witnessed. It made me feel that, even if we were only broadcasting SAT-7 to the Kingdom of Saudi Arabia, it would be worth all the effort and cost. People were hungry for the Good News, and there was a growing new church that needed support, encouragement, and building in the faith.

A Reminder of Life in the Middle East

Though we were excited about ministering to people in the Middle East, we never forgot the risks we faced in the region. In April 1997, less than a year after SAT-7 had begun broadcasting, I was on a regular visit to Lebanon, and our local coordinator, Tino, had picked me up from the airport. We were on our way to the official opening of the new Bible Society office to the north of the city.

Along the main road from the international airport in Beirut is the Al Rassoul Al Azzam Hospital with its nearby Great Prophet Mosque, which, at that time, had atop its minaret the television transmitter for Hezbollah's Al-Manar TV. It made a great photo, and I asked Tino if he thought they would mind if I took photos of it. He was confident they would not, so we stopped the car on the main road, and I got out to take pictures, to be used in our next newsletter focusing on religious television in the region.

As I climbed back into the car, plain-clothes security guards from the mosque came around the car. One reached in though the open window on the passenger side and pressed the muzzle of a revolver against my kneecap. Another snatched Tino's car keys from the ignition.

"Get out of the car," they told us.

My first reaction was not to get out. I had all my papers and luggage in the car, and, in any case, I would rather confront them in a public place with dozens of witnesses than be taken behind closed doors to be interrogated. Two things changed my mind: they began slapping Tino, and a Lebanese policeman sauntered past, displaying no interest whatsoever in intervening in this unfolding drama!

We got out.

The men took us to a windowless room on the first floor of the mosque where the questioning began. Within seconds, my cell phone rang. They allowed me to answer it, and discreetly explain that I may be late to the office opening event. The security guards wanted to know who I was and why I had taken the photos. They already had my passport and briefcase from the car, so it was not difficult to convince them of my name and leadership role with SAT-7, a channel with which they were familiar. As to why I needed the photos, I explained the uniqueness of there being a television transmitter on a minaret and how this was of novel interest to those in the television industry. I also made the point that, if my intentions were bad, I could have just snapped a photo from the car as we drove past. I had no real need to get out of the car and walk across the road to get a better frame for my photos.

By now, Tino was visibly pale and shaking. He was of Palestinian origin and understandably felt very insecure in this situation.

After an hour of questioning, they let us go. I reached for my camera and offered to remove the film for them, but they said I was welcome to keep it and to use the photos! All our belongings in the open car, still at the side of the airport road, were intact and we hurriedly left for the tail end of the reception at the Bible Society.

A Personal Blindside

In early July 1997, my family and I again moved to a new house, to a ground floor apartment in an older building near the Cyprus Museum, behind the Russian school, and much closer to the center of town and the churches where Jackie was now serving. Preparing for the move was bizarre. Jackie could not stay focused. She would begin to pack a box and then get distracted, leaving me alone to complete most of the preparations for the move. On moving day, as porters were carrying in boxes and furniture, she fell asleep on one of the unmade beds. In the following days, she began coming home very late. Her behavior was inexplicable. When I asked why she had not come home for dinner, she would just say that she was talking to her friends and express surprise at how late it was already.

A few days later she traveled to the UK to spend six weeks with her parents in Devon. I planned to join her for the last two weeks and her father's seventieth birthday celebration on September 4.

On the appointed day at the end of August, our daughter, Mona, and I flew to London. But soon after landing we had a call from Jackie's father. His pained voice told me immediately something was wrong.

"It's Jackie," he said. "She's in the hospital, in a coma."

I stopped midstep. "What?"

"She's been diagnosed with a brain tumor."

I felt my world shake.

He explained that after arriving in Devon, Jackie had complained of headaches and went to the doctor several times, but it was not until she went into a coma and was rushed to the hospital that they discovered the brain tumor.

On the long drive from the airport, Mona and I began piecing together her bizarre behavior, now knowing the reason.

The next day and after more tests, Jackie and I met with the consultant physician. He explained that they had put her on steroids to reduce the swelling, so she was now lucid, but that the tumor was inoperable, and she had only about two weeks to live. We were all in a state of shock.

I called the boys, who were both in Cairo, and explained the situation. "You need to come to England immediately if you want to say goodbye to your mother," I told them in the most difficult conversation I'd ever had with them.

They arrived three days later.

The doctors ran more tests and returned with news. "It may be possible to try surgery," they told us. "But the chances of her surviving, and not suffering any brain damage, are slim."

Jackie wanted to try, so they moved her to Frenchay, a larger hospital in Bristol, where the doctors performed the surgery a week later. It was an amazing success but, because the tumor was malignant, she then needed to stay on in the UK for several weeks of radiation therapy. Jackie was encouraged by the love and prayers of her many friends, and by phone calls from Egypt's Pope Shenouda and Lila Clerides, the wife of the President of Cyprus, with whom she had become good friends.

The boys returned to Cairo, and I drove Mona up to Manchester Metropolitan University, where she was to start a BA in fine arts.

During these difficult months, I continued to travel and oversee the work, with several passes through the UK to check on how Jackie was doing. By October, Jackie was well enough to remotely organize a surprise fiftieth birthday party for me in Nicosia! She was able to return to Cyprus at the end of November and underwent her additionally needed chemotherapy there.

As we looked back on the year, we could clearly see God's hand in getting Jackie to the UK in time to undergo such a complex surgery, as well as in our earlier house move, which put Jackie within an easy walk of her studio and the churches where she serves, especially now that she would not be allowed to drive for some time.

Throughout this experience, Jackie could have felt that God had let her down after all she had given up to follow Him, but instead, seven months after the removal of her brain tumor, and while still undergoing chemotherapy, she used her experience to share God's faithfulness.

She wrote an article about the new world into which she had so unexpectedly been thrust—a world full of sick, suffering, needy, and dying people, not to mention all the doctors and nurses, all the visitors, and the world of MRI scans and lab tests. She shared how she reached a turning point in which she was able to accept her situation when she realized that perhaps Jesus *wanted* her there in this new world, to share His love and care with others. Her article, "Working from a Hospital Bed," was later published in the UK magazine, *Woman Alive*.

From this time onward, she had a different perspective. Instead of looking at the months of being in and out of hospital as simply a period of treatment and waiting to be well enough to return to the "real world," she now understood that this was her real world, a world that was as tangible and significant as the world outside. It was full of real people, like her, people who were her brothers, sisters, and friends.

In accepting this as her world, her calling, her journey, she also accepted it as the Lord's plan for her. Out of His love and compassion, God had chosen this path for her—not only to bring her closer to Him, but to bring her closer to others who were also suffering and in pain, often without any hope or personal faith.

Through these experiences, both personally and professionally, we learned the truth of Paul's words to the Philippians: "Do not be anxious about anything, but in every situation, by prayer and petition, with thanksgiving, present your requests to God. And the peace of God, which transcends all understanding, will guide your hearts and minds in Christ Jesus" (4:6–7).

As a young civil engineer, September 1971.

My marriage in October 1972 to Jacqueline "Jackie" Ann Doble

Studying Arabic in Jordan, August 1974.

Evacuating Beirut with one-week old Gavin, December 1975.

The first copy of *Huwa wa Hiya* magazine hits the newsstands, October 1977.

Our family in Egypt, 1982. L to R: Jon, Jackie, Gavin, me, and Mona.

A family watching television in rural Egypt, circa 1982.

Our family unintentionally desecrating an Egyptian monument in 1987!
L to R: me, Mona, Gavin, Jackie, and Jon.

Jackie graduating with a masters from the Coptic Institute, 1988.

Our family in Cyprus, 1993. L to R: Me, Jon, Gavin, Mona, and Jackie.

Sharing the SAT-7 vision with church leaders in Lebanon, 1994. Me with Bishop (now Archbishop) Paul Sayah and Rev. Dr. Salim Sahyouni.

The founding meeting of SAT-7's international board, November 1995.

Rev. Lucien Accad chairing the first Annual General Meeting of SAT-7's partnership council, November 1996.

Production Manager Ray Lovejoy and Audience Relations Manager Makram Barsoum with the founder of SAT-7 Egypt, Fouad Youssef (seated), circa 1997.

"The Cairo Dream," as it was when purchased in 2000.

Accepting the "International Ministry of the Year" award at the NRB convention in
Dallas, Texas, February 2001.

SAT-7 Lebanon Production Manager Patrick Tayah with Rita, recording in a
Moroccan school, April 2001.

Chapter 5

Moving to 24/7

SAT-7's needs for regular monthly funding was similar to that of the magazine but on a whole new level. We had the usual expenses for salaries and rent, but also monthly bills for satellite time and programming, which had to be covered every month, month after month. Not to be able to pay our satellite costs would result in our being taken off the air!

In the first year, we were only on-air for two hours a week, but our total expenses were averaging $130,000 per month. I would be dishonest if I said that the money always came in to pay all vendors on time, and we did occasionally need to negotiate delayed payments, but the money always did come. God continued to provide.

By April 1999, more than sixty satellite channels were broadcasting in Arabic—more than in any language other than English! SAT-7 had expanded its broadcasts to twelve hours per week, two hours each day for four days a week on the Eutelsat satellite and two hours for two days a week on PanAmSat, a satellite that gave us better viewership in the Gulf region.

Consequently, SAT-7 realized a 40 percent increase in audience responses, typical of which was this message from a lady in Morocco: "Please send me the Bible in Arabic, so I can know more about Jesus in a personal way. Thank you for this beautiful channel!" But this increase in responses again raised the question of how to overcome the barriers to audience response, which included: illiteracy; the costs of calling internationally; the interception of mail by governments or family members; and the need for immediate help for an immediate need.

To address these barriers, we resolved to strengthen our network of local telephone counseling centers in Arab countries, as and when we could find people willing to run these. We also worked to "do follow-up" through on-air teaching programs, addressing for all viewers the questions most commonly asked by those contacting us. Additionally, we wanted to direct people to the growing number of Christian resources available online in Arabic, as well as promote through our broadcasts local Christian events or church services to which people could go to learn more about the Christian faith or get help. And finally, we resolved to encourage the use of email, though in the late 1990s, many business cards still did not have an email address on them and 97 percent of all our thousands of responses came by letter, phone, or fax.

In early 1999, the international staff of SAT-7 was still only twenty-six people, and we had key positions that still needed filling. Our annual budget was now $3.8 million, and fundraising was also a challenge.

In the UK, in 1997, we had established a separate SAT-7 charity, under the chairmanship of John R. T. Douglas OBE (Order of the British Empire). I first met John in the mid-1980s. At that time, he was the chair of a UK-Egyptian joint venture company in Egypt, Lift-slab Misr. John's company had pioneered a new building technique, using prefabricated units to speed up the construction of high-rise buildings. Their pilot phase in Egypt included several fifty-floor buildings by the banks of the Nile, where I had lived south of Cairo.

But there were so many problems! Often the locally made prefabricated units were not quite to specification, making construction difficult; none of the preassembled bathrooms fitted properly; and when they had eventually been installed, there was no water supply to test the plumbing. And, despite the beautiful views of the Nile and Pyramids from the upper floors, no one was sure they wanted to live up that high without a more reliable electric supply to ensure that the elevators would always be available. In any case, John would visit me on his frequent trips to Cairo and pour out his woes to an ex-fellow engineer.

He would sometimes just show up at our door unannounced (the phones rarely worked in those days and letters took forever) with presents for all three of my young children. He always had with him a pilot's bag and he became known to my kids as "Uncle John with the big black bag." He and his wife, Sheila, became good friends to us over the years and were very supportive of the work we were doing.

John was one of the founding partners of SAT-7 in November 1995 and then helped to set up SAT-7 in the UK. In the spring of 1999, together with Baroness Caroline Cox, he hosted an important SAT-7 introductory event at the Royal Society of Arts in London. The response to the invitations was so great that it became impossible to accommodate everyone on the scheduled date, so we offered a repeat of the event the following day in the same venue!

Each year, SAT-7 also hosted an international meeting for its supporters and official partners, under the title of "Network." In 1999 this was held in Cyprus with more than one hundred delegates from forty different churches or agencies. Ramez Atallah, general secretary of the Bible Society in Egypt, led the morning devotions. And our plenary sessions were led by Dr. Graham Mytton, the former director of International Audience Research at the BBC in London; Dr. Samir Saif, a prominent Egyptian television director; and Patrick Roddy, a former executive producer of ABC's *Good Morning America* show.

In many ways, 1999 was a turning point for the ministry. We doubled the number of hours per week that we were broadcasting, paving the way for daily broadcasts to start in 2000. We more than doubled the staff to fifty-five people, with 90 percent of the new hires being Arab media professionals wanting to use their talents to serve God. Audience responses from North Africa and from women were significantly up. Six new in-country telephone counseling centers had opened across the region. And we broadcast our first drama series from Palestine, *The House of Abu Youssef.*

This drama series was important as it was our first attempt to put into practice our vision of holistic Christian programming, which, apart from spreading the Good News, would also "contribute to the good of society and culture" (from SAT-7's vision statement). Among other things, this twenty-two-part soap opera looked at issues of child labor and domestic violence. If anyone doubted the influence of such programs, they needed only to see the responses we received. For example, a medical doctor in Cairo called our office in Nicosia to complain that we had ruined his marriage! Apparently, after watching *The House of Abu Youssef,* his newly enlightened wife went to their local police station to report her husband for continually beating her, correctly citing that this was unlawful!

Other such programs followed, in which we addressed such issues as personal health, hygiene and safety, microenterprise start-ups, and the needs and rights of the disabled and ethnic minorities.

At the end of 1999, SAT-7 covered several millennial events, including a special concert in Beirut and an international gathering in Switzerland. On December 27, 1,500 Christians gathered in Beirut for a celebration concert entitled "Breaking Chains." This included Christian musicians and singers from Egypt, Jordan, Syria, and Lebanon, and videotaped greetings from churches as far away as Kuwait and Morocco. Leaders from different denominations prayed for God's guidance and blessing on His church in the twenty-first century. Immediately following the concert, the SAT-7 crew and I, equipment and tapes in hand, flew to Lausanne, Switzerland, where 6,500 Christians had gathered from all over Europe for EXPLO 2000, a five-day millennial event that was being broadcast to ninety countries.

We showed twenty minutes of edited footage from the Beirut concert to the whole assembly and its remote venues. SAT-7 also recorded the highlights of each day's messages, editing and translating them into Arabic during the early morning hours and then hand carrying the finished tapes to the broadcast center in London for the following day's broadcast. Though it was a lot of work, with many logistical challenges, we didn't want to miss this unprecedented opportunity to show the life and unity of Christ's body at a time when many in the Arab World were asking, "Two thousand years since what?" And the answer we delivered was clear: two thousand years since the Word became flesh and dwelt among us!

Near the end of the Lausanne event, on New Year's Eve, I took the whole team out for a late dinner at a nearby Swiss restaurant to celebrate both their efforts and the new millennium about to dawn. Most of the restaurant staff were already drunk by the time we arrived, and the meal was chaotic, and perhaps the most expensive I have ever hosted!

SAT-7 EGYPT

Even though I had been deported from Egypt and was unable to have a lot of in-person connections there, the SAT-7 work in that country, which had started in December 1997, continued to flourish. With the support of Bishop Moussa and Bishop Marcos, we had been able to set up a modest four-person office and small studio space inside the Coptic Orthodox Bishopric of Shoubra El Kiema in north Cairo. Though the staff later moved to a rented apartment in Heliopolis, having adequate space was a continuous challenge. The leader of our Egyptian team was Fouad Youssef, an engineer with an ambitious vision to acquire or construct a purpose-built facility for the ministry to expand. After all, half of all Arab Christians lived in Egypt and, within this community, there was a unique pool of gifted Christian writers, singers, actors, theologians, and teachers—people who fortunately saw SAT-7 as a wonderful new opportunity for them to share their faith with the fast-growing satellite television audiences in the region.

By 1999, the staff in Cairo had grown to nearly twenty people, both producing programming and responding to the thousands of people now contacting us as a result of the Arabic broadcasts. Fouad saw that the staff and facilities needed to dramatically expand once daily broadcasts began. He presented his plans for "The Cairo Dream," an unfinished three-story villa in the Mokattam area of Cairo, built on a quarter of an acre of land. The building was for sale even though unfinished, which meant we still had time to make changes to the layout, to facilitate a large central television studio; an audio studio for dubbing projects; edit suites; meeting and training rooms; offices for the administrative, audience, and church relations work; set-storage areas; a place to park an outside broadcast (OB) van . . . and all we could ever need! The cost to buy, convert, and finish the building was about $500,000, excluding any new production equipment or studio lighting we would need.

This seemed like a huge investment, but Fouad was committed to finding the funds, which included raising money from Christians in Egypt. By faith we proceeded with the purchase and began carrying out the work as funds became available. We started with expanding the basement area, painstakingly cutting into solid Mokattam rock to create a precious audio studio and a secure equipment storage room.

The hills of Mokattam, a few miles south of Cairo's city center, have a long and rich history of faith. The story of Simon the Tanner is perhaps the most notable. He lived toward the end of the tenth century, when many Coptic Christians in Egypt were engaged in handicrafts. Simon worked in tanning; a craft known there till this day.

According to tradition, Caliph al-Muizz, who reigned over Egypt and much of the region from AD 972–975, used to invite religious leaders to debate matters of faith in his presence. In one such meeting, at which the Coptic Patriarch Abraham and a Jew named Yaqub ibn Killis were present, the patriarch got the upper hand in the debate. To get revenge, Ibn Killis quoted Matthew 17:20, in which Jesus said, "Truly I tell you, if you have faith as small as a mustard seed, you can say to this mountain, 'Move from here to there,' and it will move. Nothing will be impossible for you."

Ibn Killis then demanded that the patriarch prove that his religion was the right one by demonstrating this act of faith. After hearing this challenge, the caliph asked Patriarch Abraham, "What sayest thou concerning this word? Is this what it says in your gospel or not?" The patriarch answered, "Yes, it is." The caliph then demanded that the patriarch himself perform this same miracle or else he and all the Copts would be killed by the sword. Upon hearing this the patriarch asked for three days to complete the miracle.

Patriarch Abraham called together a group of his monks, priests, and elders, asking them all to stay for three days in what, today, is called the Hanging Church, in a state of penance. On the morning of the third day, while the patriarch was praying, he had a vision of Mary, the mother of Jesus. She told him to go to the great market where he would find a one-eyed man carrying on his shoulder a jar full of water. He was to seize him, for it was through him that the miracle was to occur.

The patriarch went to the market as instructed, where he met the man, who turned out to be Simon the Tanner. Simon had plucked out one of his own eyes because of his strict interpretation of Jesus' command in Matthew 5: "If your right eye causes you to stumble, gouge it out and throw it away. It is better for you to lose one part of your body than for your whole body to be thrown into hell. And if your right hand causes you to stumble, cut it off and throw it away. It is better for you to lose one part of your body than for your whole body to go into hell."

Simon told the patriarch to go out with his priests and all his people to the mountain with the caliph and all his soldiers and to cry out three times, "O Lord, have mercy," each time making the sign of the cross over the mountain. The patriarch followed the words of Simon, and the mountain was lifted, so that everyone could see under it. The caliph turned to Patriarch Abraham and declared, "O Patriarch, I have seen a miracle this day and recognize the correctness of your faith."

After the miracle, the patriarch searched for Simon, but he had disappeared, and no one ever found him again.

The thirteen-thousand-square-foot SAT-7 studio building officially opened in mid-January 2002, although one floor of the building was not yet finished, pending the needed funds. Gifts to fully complete the building came from all over the world, including Egyptians in the Gulf and underground churches in Saudi Arabia.

Nine months later, however, as staff were beginning to get the most out of their amazing new facility, a devastating fire at the studio broke out, causing $350,000 in damages and putting the facility totally out of action. We soon learned the cause: On the night of September 4, arsonists poured gasoline under the studio doors at the rear of the building and set it alight. Despite night security staff quickly raising the alarm, it took several hours for fire trucks to arrive, by which time the studio was destroyed and the rest of the building was fire or smoke-damaged.

The SAT-7 staff was devastated. To make matters worse, we were unsure how to begin any rebuilding. And yet we discovered one clear sign of hope: a completely undamaged Bible we found on the floor of the burned studio. A clear miracle!

Robert A. Seiple, whom I had met a few years earlier when he was the president of World Vision USA, had recently served as President Bill Clinton's first ever United States ambassador-at-large for international religious freedom. His kind intervention resulted in us getting exceptional help from the Egyptian government, with both added security on our premises in Cairo and the unprecedented early release of the fire insurance money—something that in Egypt can take many years, especially in the case of an arson attack.

But what was most touching was the concern, prayers, and practical support of local Christians and sister Christian organizations, many of whom came forward with sacrificial gifts to help rebuild The Cairo Dream. Women brought all kinds of personal jewelry that they wanted us to sell in order to help restore the studio. Even widows gave us their no-longer-needed wedding rings.

We completed the restoration within a few months and, in the process, were able to carry out small but helpful modifications to the structure, building on lessons we'd learned from the first nine months of using the building.

We will likely never know what provoked this attack. Some speculated that it was a reaction to the start of new Christian channels broadcasting from outside the region that took a more aggressive approach, attacking Islamic belief and practice. Others felt it might be related to the start-up of Farsi-language programs on the channel. In any case, God provided and blessed in the midst of that dark challenge.

The New Millennium

For the rest of SAT-7, we were also seeing God's provision and guidance. The new millennium had begun with a sense of optimism. At our Network meetings in November 1999, we committed ourselves to move to daily broadcasts, effective April 2000. Though this felt like an ambitious and exciting step, as April got nearer, we still had challenges. Our programming and production teams were mostly self-taught or had learned on the job and were already feeling stretched just keeping up with our current four-days-a-week broadcast schedule, not to mention the five-hours-a-week of weekend broadcasts on PanAmSat! How were they going to put out nearly twice this number of hours of programming each week?

Some voiced their concern that this expansion would lead to a drop in program quality, or that we would just be physically unable, with the current staff, to achieve this output. But it was clear that the single greatest complaint we received from viewers was that we were not on-air every day. We also knew from media surveys that the best way to build audiences was to be predictable, to be available at the same time *every* day. Furthermore, in the new satellite contract, we had already secured a new primetime slot for our daily broadcasts.

As the first of April approached, the team did rise to the occasion and what seemed like an impossible challenge eventually became a weekly routine. We also found that the quality of our programs actually went up. It seems that the more programming we produced, the better and more creative we became at it. With the start of daily broadcasts, SAT-7 at last came of age and became a proper channel!

We also experienced many other encouragements and much growth in this first year of the new century.

In the spring, I traveled to Tunis with Patrick, our programming director, and Rita, who was to record new programs in Tunisian schools. We spent the first day in a private villa, recording the testimonies of new believers in the country. I chatted with one girl in her early twenties, Miriam. She told me about her journey to faith and how her father, an imam at the local mosque, had concerns that she had joined a weird religious sect. But Miriam was able to turn on SAT-7 and show her father a church service from a cathedral in Cairo where thousands of Christians were worshiping in Arabic. The program had helped her father see that there were Arab Christians who were allowed to openly worship in Egypt, and who even had their own television channel. Miriam's faith and her affiliation with the Christian church had been legitimized by the SAT-7 broadcasts, and her father began to better accept Miriam's new belief.

On the following days, we were able to record with children in different schools and shoot music videos at the excavations of old Carthage, once home to the church in North Africa and Christian writers like Tertullian, Cyprian, and Augustine who contributed so much to the development of Western theology.

In that first quarter of 2000, I was also honored to receive the Fellowship of European Broadcasters' Bridgebuilder award. This had special meaning to me, as a former builder of bridges, and I was reminded of why I had left that profession.

It was not so much that the work of building physical bridges was unimportant as the fact that any engineer could do this—he or she did not need to be a Christian. But in the world of building bridges between Christians and those outside the church, Christians were needed. We needed bridges across which we could send messages of God's unconditional love, messages of hope and encouragement to people in despair, or messages about the rights of women, the unborn, and the disabled. These were the bridges I wanted to spend my life building.

Give Us More!

During this time, the satellite broadcast industry was going through a major change with the transition from analogue signals to digital ones. To the average viewer this change made little difference, other than they would get a slightly sharper picture. They did, however, need to buy a different type of receiver to pick up the new digital channels. If there was a big difference, it was this: satellites could now carry six or seven times the number of channels at the same cost. Ultimately this would drastically lower the cost of broadcasting, and spur a growth in new and more specialized channels.

In May 2000, just a few weeks after we made the big step-up to daily broadcasts, we also began broadcasting 24/7 on a new digital channel. Recognizing that most of our viewers and potential viewers were still only able to view analogue channels, we committed to broadcast on both analogue and digital channels until the audiences for analogue broadcasts diminished.

We were now paying only the same for our twenty-four hours per day on digital as we were paying for the two hours per day on the analogue channel. The only problem was that it would be another four years before we could fill the whole of the digital channel's twenty-four-hours-per-day schedule with programming. In the meantime, we had to include many hours of repeated programs, music, and promotions for programs, our telephone counseling centers, and other Christian media. At the same time, it would also take another four years before most Arab viewers upgraded their analogue receivers to the new digital ones and we could discontinue the much more expensive analogue broadcasts.

Again, viewer responses grew rapidly, especially through emails. But despite our bold move to daily broadcasts on analogue and digital satellites, we still received complaints of not having enough new programming! One man in Algeria wrote, "Please broadcast *more* than two hours a day of new shows. Your unique programs are so genuine and honest, we viewers need to benefit more from them!"

Each year we analyzed the nature of the responses. The most common requests we were now getting were for Bibles or Christian books, followed by questions about the identity of Christ and how we can know our sins have been forgiven. Others expressed gratitude for the spiritual encouragement the channel gave viewers, and parents shared how pleased they were with the children's programs. Still others requested help in searching for the truth, the right way, along with questions concerning how viewers could meet other believers or how they could get copies of our programs.

To strengthen the relationship with viewers and help preemptively address some of these issues, we created a viewer magazine. This publication also gave our viewers insight into the shows and the people they were seeing on-screen each week.

Later that year we also began preproduction on "Project 104." Working with local theologians and under the guidance of apologist the Rev. Colin Chapman, we developed a curriculum of theological content that we would work into two series, each consisting of fifty-two episodes. The first, *The Seeker Series*, was aimed at non-Christians, addressing questions and specific common misunderstandings they have about the church, what Christians believe and practice, and Christian ethics and values. The second, *The Discipleship Series*, was aimed at new believers or Christians who had very little understanding of their faith. It delivered basic Christian doctrine about God, Christ, humankind, sin, salvation, the Holy Spirit, the Bible, the church, and interpersonal relationships, such as living as a Christian in a non-Christian world.

Each teaching series included drama, music, animation, and other segments to make them attractive and help reinforce the core messages.

That summer we expanded our premises in Nicosia, moving to another floor in the same building where we had begun five years before. We also rented additional space for our growing staff in Lebanon and the United States. These expansions, and the new building in Egypt, led to jokes about us moving the whole operation to one big SAT-7 office in satellite orbit around the earth—giving us unlimited room for expansion, allowing all staff to be together, and saving us money on satellite uplink costs and international phone and fax!

In September 2000, we appointed Kurt Johansen as the part-time general secretary of our new office in Denmark. He would be responsible for fundraising in the Nordic countries. We had a growing number of valued partner agencies in Scandinavia, and Kurt's part-time involvement soon moved to full-time.

In November, we hosted Network in Lebanon for the first time. We met at the beautiful hilltop Al Bustan Hotel, half an hour's drive into the mountains north of Beirut. Everything was well managed by our SAT-7 Lebanon team, who could draw on their production staff for a professional event.

In February 2001, several of us attended the National Religious Broadcasters (NRB) convention in Dallas. They had chosen SAT-7 as their International Ministry of the Year, and I was privileged to accept the award on behalf of the ministry.

During the meetings in Dallas, a well-known American Christian broadcaster approached us. They knew we were struggling financially and offered us $2 million a year and some of their programming in exchange for two seats on our international board. At face value, this seemed like a good offer, but I had seen the way they had operated in other parts of the world. They would come alongside financially strapped indigenous television ministries, offer help, and then more help . . . and eventually take over full control of the operation, rebranding the channel with their own name. To our US executive director's dismay, I politely declined.

I felt at peace about the decision, even though a report had just been released about the financial state of affairs for overseas ministries. Dr. David Barrett's year 2000 update on "The Status of Christianity" showed that only 0.07 percent of the $120 billion in global funds given to more than twenty thousand Christian agencies and churches worldwide went to ministry in the Middle East and North Africa. This made it the most underfunded region in the world.

In April 2001, I went with several from the Lebanon team to Morocco. For me it was a research trip. For Rita and her cameraman, it was another opportunity to bring the faces of more North African children to the screen.

Over that week, I visited an international telecom exhibition in Casablanca and a dozen satellite-dish retail outlets, conducting an informal survey of present sales and the penetration of new digital receivers in Morocco. Unlike in Tunisia, most of the sales were conducted from small shops or even unregistered open-air markets. There were fifteen or so such outlets in one bazaar, which had no electricity, and so had to demonstrate their equipment to potential buyers using small generators.

Few distributors had reliable or consistent estimates concerning the present penetration of digital receivers in Morocco, though the local representative for Eutelsat put the number at less than 10 percent. However, everyone agreed that 95 percent of all new sales were for digital receivers.

One of our key contacts for this trip was Jack, an American who ran a nongovernmental organization (NGO) and a respected school in Casablanca. He had been open to us recording programs with the children there, but our scheduled visit was cancelled at the last minute because of fears concerning the parents' reactions to seeing their children's faces on SAT-7. Jack did introduce us to two other schools, however, one of which had more than eight hundred children and was run by nuns from Lebanon. They welcomed Rita and invited her team to return a few weeks later, when they were able to record amazing stories and songs with the children.

During our visit we also learned many other things about Moroccan society and the mostly underground church. One surprising fact was the high level of divorce in the country and the open interest people had in getting help with their marriages—something for future programs to focus on. I left feeling the need for us to conduct or acquire more qualitative research into people's felt needs, attitudes, and opinions as we planned programming.

From those in the NGO community, I also learned that the unemployment rate in Morocco was at a new high of 50 percent; that illiteracy was at 70 percent and, of course, much greater in rural areas; that the government was now putting a higher emphasis on children learning English rather than French in school; and that internet usage was on the rise, especially among students who frequented the growing number of internet cafes around the universities. All these facts would help shape the content for future programs, promoting microenterprises, teaching Arabic and English on-air, and so on.

During our visit we needed to buy a new microphone and ended up in a shop in Marrakech where one of the owners recognized Rita and began a debate about SAT-7 trying to evangelize Moroccans. Rita clarified that we were a channel for the Christians of the Middle East, but, in any case, we had the full right to openly share our faith since Moroccans who had a satellite dish had the right to choose what they watched. The man was obviously a regular viewer of SAT-7 and asked why we did not have newer versions of the Jesus Film to show, complaining that we were rerunning the same old films too many times!

We also spent time with Ahmed, our Moroccan SAT-7 international board member. He worked as an instructor at the airport and hosted a church in his home in Casablanca. He shared many anecdotal stories of believers being encouraged through SAT-7 programs and people coming to faith through the broadcasts.

He especially appreciated the way in which SAT-7 was showing the life, work, and witness of Arab Christians, letting people know that Christianity in the Arab World was not restricted to foreign priests and nuns, as was very much the perception in his country.

"Interestingly, SAT-7 has imitators," Ahmed told us, then showed us a new Moroccan television program that appeared to be a sad imitation of Rita's *AsSanabel*, with a Rita-type character and a clown like the one in her show, using similar program segments.

"Imitation is the best form of flattery, they say," I said and laughed.

"Ah, yes, but this one is missing the main ingredient," said Ahmed. "It lacks the Christian hope and joy of the SAT-7 show!"

September 11, 2001

On September 6, 2001, I flew to Cairo to meet with Ron, the president of the foundation whose representative I had met during my time with Channel 38 in Chicago four years earlier. Ron helped us to finish and equip the new studio in Egypt and wanted to actually visit and learn more. It was a positive few days, and we both flew out of Cairo on the morning of Tuesday, September 11. I heard about the first plane crashing into the World Trade Center in New York City when I was in transit at Beirut's International Airport. I searched desperately for a television screen but could find none, even in the business-class lounges. I was dependent on calls with our staff in Beirut to follow what was happening.

As I sat in a departure lounge near the gate waiting for my flight, I caught the eye of a man sitting nearby, sipping a drink.

"You've heard the news?" he said.

"Yes."

"I'm planning to get as drunk as possible before this flight. I'm afraid of flying anyway. But this news from America has pushed me over the edge."

Another man overheard us. "This will make for a new round of retaliation against Arab nations and Arab people."

"We don't know yet for sure who is behind the hijacking," I said.

He raised his eyebrows. "Do you doubt?"

I didn't. I was still trying to absorb the news of the attack as I landed in Larnaca later that day, only to be told about the additional plane going into the World Trade Center and another into the Pentagon.

I thought about Ron. He was flying back to the States. I learned several days later that his flight was going fine until midway across the Atlantic, when passengers were informed that US airspace was closed and that they were being diverted to Toronto. From there, Ron managed to rent a car and eventually drive across the border and back to his home in Grand Rapids, Michigan.

If this was perpetrated by someone in the Middle East, I feared that Westerners would blame all of the Middle East—not understanding that many Middle Eastern Christians and innocent Muslims would also suffer the consequences of any retaliation.

Seminary on the Air

Ever since my earlier visit to Morocco in 1996, I'd had a growing concern that we should be more deliberate and systematic in the Christian teaching we delivered on-air. In some cases, our programming would be the *only* theological input that new Christians or even those born into Christian families would receive. Some people who were leading house churches had never been to a Bible school or seminary and could never go because of visa requirements, financial difficulties, or for some other reason. Their only qualification to lead was the fact that they were the first person in their village or town to have become a believer and had introduced others to the faith.

Were we equipping these leaders and giving our viewers a full and balanced diet of theological teaching or were we delivering a random selection of teaching programs—the ones our program makers and content providers wanted to make?

In an effort to move this approach to the next level, in December 2001, I called together representatives from the major theological institutes in the area for a two-day consultation in Cyprus. We had good presentations, and I left knowing that everyone attending had understood what we wanted to do. At the same time, it was obvious that many felt threatened by the idea of a "seminary on the air." Would this replace the Bible schools? What would happen to a teacher who had recorded all their best lectures on a given subject, and these then became available on-air and online? Would there still be a place for the Bible correspondence courses that were so popular in the region? Others worried that distance learning could never replace the full experience of mentoring that takes place in a seminary. Of course, we did not want to replace any of these things; we just wanted to make some of it available to those who would never have the chance to attend such a place of learning.

We appointed an Egyptian Canadian to help move the project forward. But given the concept's newness, the latent resistance to it by some in the seminaries, and the fact that he was based in Toronto, he had a tough job! In fact, the project would flounder for six or seven years, until we would begin anew in partnership with the Overseas Council.

By the end of 2001, the number of staff working with SAT-7 worldwide had grown to ninety and we had added four new telephone counseling centers, bringing the total to twelve. These were now based in Cairo, Alexandria, Jerusalem, Amman, Beirut, Dubai, Oran, Barcelona, Limassol, London, Stockholm, and Paris, and some forty or so of the volunteer counselors had attended our most recent round of training workshops. This all took place in the aftermath of 9/11, an event that raised many questions in the minds of thinking people. The number of responses to our programs grew dramatically, with more than half of the total now coming from Egypt, Algeria, and the Palestinian Territories.

When we began to promote on-air the new number for the Algerian telephone counseling center, we wondered how long it might be before the government blocked the line, but they didn't!

On the first day we advertised the center, a believer from the south of Algeria called in. He was so excited. "Are you a follower of Jesus? I thought I was the only one in Algeria! Where are you? I must come and meet you."

The following day he made the seven-hour bus journey to visit the brother he had spoken with, leaving again that night, much encouraged, with new friends and with a precious pile of Christian books in Arabic.

Another Algerian man wrote to us: "On your channel, people talk about loving each other, which is so different from any other channel I have ever seen! I was overcome with emotion, to the point of tears, because I never imagined that there could be so much love, peace, and forgiveness between peoples. Thank you!"

Just a few days before Christmas, and in order to gain more space, the SAT-7 international office moved from its offices on a part of the third floor to occupy the whole of the sixth floor in the same building. I spent most of the quiet period between Christmas and New Year in the new office, sorting out my boxes of files and getting settled in for a new start in January.

I needed that time. The following year was challenging, financially. The political and economic uncertainty after 9/11 and the anger at and in the Muslim World, and at Arab people in particular, was impacting support for the ministry. By April 2002, we were struggling to pay for our satellite time and GlobeCast, the UK provider of this service, threatened to cut off our broadcasts. But despite the seriousness of the situation, I had a quiet confidence that God would provide. And, as has happened several times since, last-minute donations enabled us to meet all our obligations and even ramp up our programming for the following eighteen months.

Security Issues

In March 2003 the Iraq war began, something that seemed to displace any sense of peace or rational discourse from the region. Special prayers went out on the channel for the people of that country, whose suffering never seemed to end. The country of Jordan had long hosted the thousands fleeing Saddam Hussein's regime, and now they were being joined by hundreds of thousands more fleeing the war.

In December, security services in Egypt, Cyprus, and the United States advised us that there was a "credible threat" from a radical Sunni Muslim group against our offices in those locations. One night we had a bizarre experience in which the FBI stormed our empty offices in Wayne, Pennsylvania, while a helicopter hovered overhead. They had reason to believe that a bomb had been placed there, even though we had moved from that rented office complex earlier in the year. Fortunately, in Egypt, we enjoyed increased government protection on our building, and our office in Nicosia was secured for several months by armed police, making our neighbors feel quite uncomfortable! Eventually the threat passed and life returned almost to normal, other than visitors being security-screened before they could enter our offices.

During this chaotic time, we were advised to acquire a letter scanner to check for potentially dangerous contents in incoming mail. Unfortunately, it was a poorly thought-through strategy. After two weeks, a member of staff entered my office with a small packet.

"The scanner is showing suspicious contents," he said. "What should I do with it?"

I had no idea. But being the most expendable member of staff, I checked the sender and decided to open it. It contained some data tapes, and no one died.

Though we continued under the shadow of the events of 9/11 for some time, good things were happening. In May 2004, we finally had enough programming to better use all twenty-four hours per day available to us on the new digital channel. We did this by designing a "smart schedule" that allowed a viewer to watch two hours of new programming at the same time each day or to watch new programming nonstop for fourteen hours on any one day, perhaps their day off work or school. The other ten hours per day were still filled with program and channel promos and advertisements for the telephone counseling centers, Christian websites, or radio channels. It now also included regular Farsi-language programs, which we had begun to produce for audiences in Iran . . . but that is a story for later.

The First Audience Survey

In 2004 we commissioned an extensive audience survey, conducted for us by Intermedia in eight different Arab countries. Such studies are not inexpensive or easy to conduct for a Christian channel. It relies on people being willing to admit to the total stranger conducting the survey that they watch a Christian channel. Even if some people were afraid to admit that they watched us, the data we received indicated that our regular viewing audience was now some five to six million people, with half of these watching daily or at least several times a week.

The same survey also indicated that the number of Arabic-speaking people with satellite television had now grown to more than 150 million, with about 90 percent of these owning a new digital receiver. This gave us the confidence to discontinue the relatively expensive analogue broadcasts.

That year we also decided to build our own master control room (MCR) in Nicosia. This would put an end to the laborious daily process of assembling all the programs, promos, and other elements for each two-hour broadcast onto two master tapes in Beirut; taking the tapes to the Lebanese censorship office for clearance; and then sending them by courier to the playout center in London. Having our own MCR would end all this, give us more flexibility to change the schedule at last minute, and save us about $100,000 a year! In addition, we could add a continuous crawl along the bottom of the screen with information on programs, telephone counseling centers, as well as greetings and other feedback from viewers, all in near-real time. We planned for the new MCR to begin operations in early 2006.

Apart from equipping the MCR and installing an uplink dish on the roof of our office building, this new initiative would also necessitate moving thousands of master program tapes from our studio in Beirut to a new air-conditioned tape archive in Nicosia. Over the following year, most of these professional-format tapes had to be hand carried to Cyprus to avoid the cost and time of each tape needing to go through government censorship once again before official export from Lebanon.

In January 2005, we began live web-streaming our broadcasts for the first time, as well as starting a subscriber-based satellite distribution to Arab viewers in Australia.

On May 15 we conducted our first-ever live broadcast, where the signal was sent directly from our studio to the viewer in real time. It was a participation in the Worldwide Day of Prayer and broadcast from our studio in Cairo. The whole thing was a nerve-racking experience. Apart from all the technical things that could have gone wrong, for the first time, we had no option to edit out mistakes or shoot a scene again. But the team did an amazing job and it worked flawlessly.

Live programs allow us to respond in real time to events happening in the region and give people the opportunity to call in and be heard, help shape the direction of a discussion in a program, and so on. To prepare ourselves for regular live broadcasts, which we planned to start in the next year or two, we began to record some of our regular programs "live to tape," as if they were live shows. This was not so much to save time or money on post-production editing as to develop the procedures and disciplines needed for live shows.

By now I was traveling for almost 40 percent of the year, with two or three annual trips to the United States and Canada, several visits to the Scandinavian countries, the Gulf, and Palestine, frequent visits to Lebanon and Turkey, and even trips to Egypt, when I could get Egyptian government approval. It was a rare month that I did not make at least two overseas trips. Thankfully, Jackie remained in remission and generally in good health, although my frequent coming and going must have taken its toll on the family.

Finding the Right People

SAT-7, though doing well with programming, had other growing pains with which to deal. We needed to fund our growing budget, but even more challenging was finding the right people. By the end of 2005, we had 120 staff, excluding those in the support offices. Each year we needed to make many staff changes, with sometimes painful dismissals. It was hard to find people who were both competent and committed to the vision and mission of the organization. Many had baggage from their difficult past lives, while some could not work well with others, or with those of another Christian tradition. And a few had ulterior motives for engaging with us or were even plainly dishonest. This was all disappointing to find in Christian work, especially when our expectations of others in such a ministry were so high. While it was disheartening at the time, God did provide over the coming years a dedicated and talented team of professional staff without whom SAT-7 could not be where it is today.

In July 2005, we appointed Rita El-Mounayer to the position of Arabic programming director. She had grown in her understanding of the work, was sometimes frighteningly honest with people, and was a fast learner. In recognition of her potential, SAT-7 had sponsored her to study for a master's degree in communications practice at The Oxford Centre for Mission Studies (OCMS). Despite needing to be based in Oxford for much of the two-year course, she kept her children's programming team moving forward and even expanded their weekly output of programs. She had graduated just the year before.

One of the first changes Rita made to the schedule, starting in September, was to introduce special programming blocks for different audiences and for different genres of programs. We would have special blocks for women and youth, in addition to the daily children's block. Then there would be a regular broadcast slot for movies and dramas, current affairs, Christian teaching, music, and so on, involving sixteen genres of Arabic programming, plus the now daily two-hour blocks of programming for Iran.

Audience responses doubled in 2005 to more than eighteen thousand phone calls, emails, and letters, plus another twenty thousand responses to a popular program on marriage produced by IBRA Media. The new SAT-7 Arabic website was getting 1.2 million hits per month by the end of the year, mostly because of the new schedule and the many new programs focusing on important subjects relevant to different audiences. The start of Arabic SMS text messaging was also giving many people a new, inexpensive option for contacting us.

Though the first few years of the new century had been chaotic for the Middle East, it had been an exciting time of learning, growth, and change for SAT-7 and resulted in more responses from our audiences than we would ever have imagined.

Chapter 6

From a Channel to a Network

On February 2, 2006, the new Master Control Room (MCR) in Nicosia began operations. Our staff all excitedly crowded into the small room at noon as we took over the program playout from the London-based contractor and uplinked the signal to a feed satellite. The signal was then received at a broadcast center in London, where it was, with other channels, beamed up to the HotBird satellite so our viewers could watch it.

Of course, most of our viewers were unaware of the technology, or the switchover, except for the unfortunate and unplanned fifteen minutes of blank screen as this took place! However, viewers did begin to see improvements to the service, beginning with the messages now crawling across the bottom of their screen, providing near-real time information and audience feedback.

We saw immediately the value of the crawl when one day it included a request for prayers for families in Baghdad, whose loved ones had been injured or killed in a terrible car bombing incident. In response to this news, a man called from Morocco to say how touched he was by the concerns of Christians for the Iraqi people and asked us to send him a New Testament.

Arab audiences now had to cope with new Turkish language programming blocks on Tuesdays and Thursdays, which we were carrying for a sister ministry in Turkey, as well as the existing daily Farsi blocks of programming for Iran. This was disruptive for those who were watching, as each time we switched to broadcasting programs in a different language we would lose the current viewers. But it was the only way we could incubate these fledgling language services.

On May 31, we marked our tenth anniversary of going on air. To celebrate, we planned a special event from the Emile Lahoud Center, just north of Beirut. More than eight hundred local and international clergy, ministry partners, supporters, staff, and viewers crowded into the hall for this two-hour event to mark all God had done during the past decade. This was also the first live event that SAT-7 both produced and broadcast through the new Nicosia control room.

It nearly got off to a disastrous start. Just before the opening curtain rose, a local dance troop were hiding under the low-lying fog created by the dry-ice machines, struggling to breathe. While in the control room, the staff were experiencing delays in connecting the live feed through to London and they asked the director of the event to hold the start. Though it was only a delay of less than a minute, by the end of the time, the director was begging for the show to start before any of the dancers passed out! In the end, however, it turned out to be an evening to remember, with moving contributions from church leaders, SAT-7 partners, our own on-screen presenters, and well-known local Christian singers and musicians.

We were still riding the high of the celebration when just six weeks later, things went sideways in Lebanon. On July 12, the so-called "July War" began, precipitated by Hezbollah fighters attacking armored Humvees that were patrolling the Israeli side of the disputed border fence between Lebanon and Israel. Three Israeli soldiers died and two more were abducted. Following a failed rescue attempt, things escalated and the Israelis began airstrikes and artillery fire against military and civilian targets in Lebanon, including Beirut's International Airport, key roads, bridges, and a power station. Israel also launched a ground invasion of Southern Lebanon.

For many Lebanese, the bombing brought back depressing memories of the civil war.

The conflict continued until a United Nations-brokered cease-fire went into effect on the morning of August 14, 2006. One thousand three hundred lebanese and 165 Israelis died in the conflict and about one million Lebanese were displaced.

With the closure of the airport, we were unable to fly out our program tapes to Cyprus. However, within a few days, we were able to contract for regular link-satellite time, enabling us to send our finished programs and promos to Nicosia overnight, when satellite time was less expensive.

This satellite link also enabled us to start our first-ever weekly live shows, initially focusing on messages and stories of hope amid the pain and hopelessness of the situation in Lebanon. Our program *Nafitha* (*Window*) showed how Christian schools were opening their premises to hundreds of displaced, mostly Muslim families from the south of the country, and how Christian NGOs were providing food and emergency medical aid. These programs stood in stark contrast to the rage and political anger being broadcast by other channels.

But with people being fearful to move around the country and even more fearful to let their children do so, we had to curtail producing children's programs during the normally busy school holiday period.

Despite the power shortages, SAT-7 operations in Lebanon were able to continue, thanks to having our own generator, though fuel for this became increasingly difficult to find, forcing us to carefully ration power.

With some 40 percent of all our programming being done in Lebanon, the war highlighted our vulnerability to the closure of the airport. This led us to buy our own satellite truck, enabling us to more effectively go live from the studio at any time, or live from anywhere in the country. But it would be many more months before we could import it and make it operational.

And in Egypt, where we were not licensed to uplink live programs to a satellite, we began experimenting with a Teradek device, which enabled us to use a number of mobile phone chips in parallel to go live from almost anywhere in the country using the mobile telephone network.

In 2006 we were able to increase the number of new programs we produced by almost 60 percent, with only a 5 percent increase in costs. We achieved this by implementing both economies of scale and more efficient production techniques, which Rita had introduced after becoming programming director.

The schedule now included a number of social-impact programs. These included a game show with disabled and able-bodied children, which sought to challenge the many misunderstandings about people with disabilities, and their potential and rights in a "shame culture" that tends to hide away its disabled. And soon after, we added a literacy program for the millions in the region still unable to read and write. But it was the amazing responses we were getting to our children's programs that became our focus.

SAT-7 KIDS

Since the first broadcast, children's programs have always been on the schedule, because we recognize the necessity of reaching children. Children are the hope for a better tomorrow. They learn quickly and are open to new ideas. And children and television have always gone hand in hand!

Yet producing strong children's programming has always been difficult, because most adults do not think like children. They struggle to intuitively make programming that is relevant and attractive for children while, at the same time, teaching Christian truth and values. It is also difficult to manage because children are not easy to work with. As the saying in Hollywood goes, "Never work with animals or children!"

Over the years, though, SAT-7's children's programming expanded dramatically and quickly won the trust of Christian and non-Christian parents across the Arab World.

We began by making programs in a cramped, rented space in a Lebanese production company, with two rented cameras. There were no props, teleprompter, script, mixer for the cameras, or people to go in front of the cameras who had any previous experience in television. It took five hours to record the fifteen-minute children's segment for SAT-7's first two-hour weekly broadcast.

Rita, that first children's segment presenter, had previously worked in Christian radio, where she could just read her script. But on television, she had to memorize the script, pay attention to the lighting, as well as concentrate on how and where she moved, and how she looked at the camera. Lots to pay attention to! She often heard the director say, "No!"—"No, repeat that sentence"; "No, you didn't smile"; "No, you were supposed to be walking toward the camera as you said that." It was a hard way to learn.

But after our Swedish partner TV-Inter invited Rita to record her program in their studios in Linköping, providing her with professional facilities and a committed and sympathetic production crew, things really began to grow. She added new characters to *AsSanabel*, including the mischievous Sanbool the Clown, Angelo the Alien, and Bahoor the Sailor of the Seven Seas. Each few months everyone would fly to Sweden for ten days of shooting. The early morning starts and disciplined European style of working helped Rita and those who traveled with her to learn to work efficiently and productively—something they would perhaps never have learned through on-the-job training in the Middle East.

By 2000, *AsSanabel* was on air with new programs five days a week. And while the show was aimed at five-to-ten-year-olds, research indicated that this was only half the actual viewership. The other half were in the eleven-to-twenty-year-old age range, not to mention the parents and grandparents sitting with their kids as they watched!

Excitingly, but for reasons unknown, the largest single viewership was in Algeria. Viewership grew still further after an Algerian newspaper, *Afaq*, published an article warning parents and teachers about *AsSanabel*. It lamented the fact that the program received so many letters and drawings from Algerian children, and warned of its bad Christian influence. The article went on to share research that the paper had carried out in schools, showing that 60 percent of students admitted to watching the program at least once, 30 percent admitted to watching at least once a week, and 2 percent indicated that they had sent a letter to the program's address in Lebanon.

While most of our children's programs were more easily produced in our studios in Egypt or Lebanon, in 2000, the *AsSanabel* team traveled to record in Jordan and Tunisia. And then, in August of that year, they went on to record programs with Iraqi refugee children in Istanbul, taking them to the main tourist sights and on a boat ride across the Bosphorus—the strait that forms the boundary between Europe and Asia. Though the Arab World consists of many different cultures and accents, the special feeling viewers have in watching songs or clips in their own local dialects of Arabic help them feel that the programs, and the beliefs being taught through them, are not foreign.

In 2002, the production work in Sweden, together with all the sets, was moved to KKR-TV's studios in Copenhagen. In addition, more and more programs were being made in Egypt and Lebanon, inside and outside the studios, especially during the long summer holidays when kids were not in school. This enabled us to move to daily programs for children and, by 2004, to one hour of new kids' programming per day, with two repeats.

We were able to now broadcast these new one-hour blocks for children with their own on-screen *SAT-7 KIDS* logo. Apart from the flagship program, *AsSanabel*, with its new treehouse set and yet more on-screen characters, these SAT-7 KIDS programming blocks now included animation, puppet shows, children's films, music, storytelling, and arts and crafts. In addition we produced *Message from a Sunday School*, which we recorded in different churches across the region; *From the Lab*, in which Professor Naji performed science experiments with a moral lesson; and *The Professions*, which profiled new careers that children could aspire to follow.

Early on during her time at SAT-7, Rita had held to a dream to establish a dedicated Arabic channel for children, though she largely kept it to herself. The few times she mentioned it to any of her colleagues, eyes would roll at the apparent impossibility of the idea.

"How?" they would argue. "We cannot even fill a single twenty-four-hour Arabic channel with good programs, and you want to start another channel, for kids? And how will we pay for it?"

I quietly supported this vision, not only because children are important to our ministry, and not just because we were getting amazing responses from children and their parents. For me, there were two additional compelling reasons to launch such a channel. While there were now a growing number of other Christian channels in Arabic, very few of the programs were for children, mostly because these channels were operating from outside the region, in places where few immigrant children still spoke Arabic. And, on the other hand, there were at least six other Arabic-language channels targeting children, some purveying anti-Christian ideas and attitudes and some glorifying martyrdom, even by children themselves!

The second and most important reason was the issue of scheduling. Our broadcasts covered some four or five time zones, depending on whether it was summer or winter. So when the children in Morocco were just getting home from school, the children in the Gulf countries had already gone to bed! This made it very hard to schedule a good time on the current Arabic channel for the children's shows, whether in the morning or the evening.

Having a twenty-four-hour-per-day schedule would make programming available around the clock to the more than 100 million Arab children under the age of fifteen, whatever their time zone. In addition, we knew that children are happy to watch a program multiple times, and the startup of a new kids' channel would require us to rerun many programs in order to fill the schedule.

At this time, half of these Arabic-speaking children, or 50 million kids, had satellite television at home. If these 50 million were a country, it would be in the top thirty most populous countries in the world. Didn't they deserve their own Christian television channel?

Around this time, I made another trip to Bethlehem in the West Bank, following up on partnerships we had with Bethlehem Bible

College, the Evangelical Lutheran Church, and others in the Holy Land. Because of the political restrictions on any of our Lebanese or Egyptian staff traveling into the area, these were visits only I could make.

At the end of one long day there, I needed to return to my hotel in East Jerusalem. It was already dark when I reached the border crossing, with its massive concrete "barrier" separating the West Bank from Jerusalem, and I had to pass through a maze of metal gates to reach the security office. No one was around to point me to the one unlocked gate to use and I could find no signage in English or Arabic, so I began rattling each of the many gates to try and find one that would open.

As I was doing this, a spritely eighty-year-old nun appeared from behind me and snapped, "Follow me." She made this crossing several times a week and knew the ropes. So I followed her through all the different gates, feeling as though I was leaving a high-security prison! We eventually emerged onto the Israeli side of the wall and waited for a bus to take us to the central bus station in East Jerusalem.

We struck up a conversation and she explained that she was Sister Claire from Kraków, Poland, and had been living in the area for most of her life. The nuns ran an orphanage in Bethlehem as well as one in East Jerusalem, where she lived. As I began to share who I was and about SAT-7, her mood changed, and she became almost aggressive.

"SAT-7!" she exclaimed. "I hate this channel! Every time I come home and want to watch the news, the children are watching your children's programs and refuse to let me change the channel!"

By mid-2006, the one-hour program blocks for children had expanded to two hours on the weekends, and Rita felt she was ready to launch "SAT-7 KIDS" as a stand-alone channel by the end of the year. At this point, we were also set to launch SAT-7 PARS, the Persian service of SAT-7 (which we'll talk about a bit later). However, we did not have enough funding or organizational bandwidth to go from one to three channels all in one go, especially when we were also looking at expanding our studio space in Lebanon, relocating our international office, and possibly securing an additional channel on the Egyptian-owned satellite Nilesat, something that had been a long-term dream and could greatly increase our potential viewing audience.

Rita, who was now the director of all Arabic programming, understood this and graciously agreed to postpone the launch of her SAT-7 KIDS channel for another year, allowing SAT-7 PARS to launch as a separate, new channel on December 18.

The Turkish-language programming also moved with the Farsi programs to the new PARS channel, allowing our Turkish colleagues to expand their programming from just four hours a week to four hours a day. It also made their programming more accessible to the 30 million Azari speakers in Iran—Turkic-speaking people who mostly understood both Farsi and Turkish. This migration of non-Arabic programs to the new PARS channel suddenly made available more time on the Arabic channel and allowed for an aggressive ramp-up of children's programming, in preparation for the much-anticipated launch of SAT-7 KIDS at the end of 2007.

The new year began with more street violence in Lebanon, this time between local political groups. We also had our satellite broadcasts jammed for twenty-four hours by, according to Eutelsat, "an unknown Arab country." Then a SAT-7 crew recording a documentary on the history of the church got caught in the crossfire between rival tribes at a remote archeological site in Egypt's western desert. Though no one was injured, all these things reminded us that we were never far from yet another crisis and needed to depend on God for both the ministry's continuance and the staff's safety.

In May, SAT-7 rolled out new corporate branding, with new corporate colors and a beautiful new logo for SAT-7 KIDS.

By now the children's programming had expanded to two hours a day on the Arabic channel, with one repeat each day.

In September, we opened a new studio space in Lebanon for SAT-7 KIDS, where the team was also working hard on promotional clips for the new channel, to be launched in December. Many new children's programs were now in production in Egypt as well as Jordan, to complement those we were producing in Lebanon.

Advertisements for the new channel began to run on the Arabic channel, now called SAT-7 ARABIC, and people started working late nights in preparation for the launch of the new channel, which would be in time for all the special Christmas programs for children, which were also in production.

The big day finally arrived. A few seconds after midnight on the morning of December 10, the SAT-7 KIDS logo appeared on screen, followed by promos, and then the start of programming to welcome young viewers as they woke up. As Rita watched the start of broadcasts, she had tears in her eyes. Her seemingly impossible decade-long dream to launch such a channel was coming true, and with programming more creative, attractive, and varied than she could ever have imagined back when she made her first program.

Rita later wrote to some of our supporters, "I was so happy to see SAT-7 KIDS finally on the air! It is amazing to see it, and equally amazing that God can use imperfect servants like us to bring about something like this. I truly believe that if you want to change the face of Arab society, you have to start with a child. And I truly believe that a child who has grown up with SAT-7 KIDS, and had their life influenced by the channel, will one day become the leader of a nation in our region."

The initial schedule for the channel comprised a new four-hour daily block of programming, repeated four times, plus four hours of songs, promos, and reruns of older programming, which even found an audience among older kids, keen to watch programs they had enjoyed years before. As time went by, we began staggering the repeats in such a way as to broadcast four hours of new programming to all who watched at the same time every day, and almost a whole day of new programming to those who could watch only one or two days a week.

The initial responses were overwhelming, with kids and parents from all over the Arab World writing to thank us for the new service. A father from Cairo wrote, "As numerous as the stars in the sky and the grains of sand on the beach are my congratulations to the new SAT-7 KIDS channel." We also heard stories of churches rushing out to buy a satellite dish for the first time, so they could make the new channel available to their kindergartens and Sunday schools.

Still, not everyone was happy. More than one lady wrote to complain that her child would not allow others in the family to change the channel from SAT-7 KIDS! With a visible smile on my face, I could not but help think of Sister Claire in East Jerusalem and how much more she was going to dislike me now that the kids in her orphanage had a twenty-four-hour channel to watch! What chance did she now have of changing the channel to get her news?

A foundation in the United States helpfully launched a matching grant fund for the new channel, offering to match any gifts for SAT-7 KIDS, up to a total of $1 million. Without this, the life of the new channel could have been cut short!

Local support for SAT-7 KIDS was also encouraging. One day I opened an envelope that contained an $800 check from Victor, a friend and pastor in Jordan. He had just been on a ministry trip to Iraq and had stayed with a family whose children were avid viewers of SAT-7 KIDS. Even though SAT-7 never asks for funds from its viewers, the father felt he should send money to the station but did not know how. They were not a wealthy family and had no bank account, and, in any case, Iraqi dinars were not a currency that could be exported. He asked Victor if he would be willing to take a gift of dinars from him, to use in Iraq, and then send the equivalent in American dollars to SAT-7. He told Victor, "This channel is vital for our children, and I want to help it continue!"

By the end of the next year, audience responses had tripled and, just before Christmas, SAT-7 KIDS broadcast its first live program, with Rita, Naji the Scientist, and "Mr. Know" from Egypt. The theme revolved around Santa (a well-known but secular figure in the Arab World) being upset because everyone had forgotten the real meaning of Christmas, the celebration of the birth of Christ. The show was an amazing success, and the phones did not stop ringing. People were even texting to complain that they could not get through to speak to the show's hosts. The obvious enthusiasm of kids and their parents to engage in this way, despite the expense of making international calls, accelerated plans for regular live call-in programs, which started early in the new year.

The TEACH Project

The on-air seminary project continued to move slowly. It was almost as if theologians and television people were from different planets. They just thought in different ways and even seemed to have different definitions of basic words like *teaching*, *program*, and *deadlines*. Some of our staff had almost given up trying, with one even sadly circulating a joke about, "How many theologians does it take to change a lightbulb?"

Despite the uneasy relationship between those from an academic environment and those in television, I still felt developing a televised or online video course that could take people through the basic syllabus of a seminary was important, even key to delivering theological training to the thousands of new believers in the region who were never going to get to a seminary. I had even given the project a new name, *TEACH*, an acronym for *Theological Education for Arab Christians at Home.*

In 2004, Jim, an American supporter, became interested in the project. He was already committed to theological training, even in the Arab World. Over the following years, he introduced us to the Overseas Council, which he also supported, and which was based in Indiana. Through them, he worked to rebuild trust between SAT-7 and the different evangelical seminaries in the Middle East.

In May 2006, we cohosted a significant meeting in Cyprus to discuss a potential curriculum. But it was another two years before the Overseas Council and the Middle East Association of Theological Education signed a formal agreement with SAT-7, and then formed an executive committee and a curriculum development team.

We broke down the curriculum into key programming areas: the Christian Life; Family Life; Leadership and Ministry Skills; the Christian's Contribution to Society; the Bible; and the Church. Over five years, we planned to produce 430 programs, or more than three hundred hours of attractive programming at the cost of about $3 million.

Television is, of course, a very different experience to teaching in a classroom. There is no immediate feedback, no eye contact between teacher and student, no informal conversations during coffee breaks. But in the world of television, there is one cardinal sin: being boring! This was our challenge: how could we take complex theological or dry academic concepts and make them work on television? Fortunately, our creative staff found many ways to do this, using different genres of programming, such as game shows, documentaries, poetry, drama, animated series, and talk shows.

To ensure that we included all the key teaching elements in a program, we created an instructional design team under the leadership of Elie Haddad at ABTS, the Arab Baptist Theological Seminary in Beirut. Their job was to receive commissioned manuscripts from leading theologians in the region on subjects in the curriculum and then break these down, clearly identifying the key elements that viewers needed to understand. This made things much easier for our scriptwriters and producers, and helped make program evaluations more objective.

Angel from Hezbollah

A few weeks after the TEACH meetings in Cyprus, Rita was again in Beirut to oversee production work when there was a serious escalation in the street clashes between pro-government and opposition militias, which included Hezbollah. This clash was sparked by a government move to shut down Hezbollah's private telecommunications network and remove Beirut airport's head of security after they discovered a hidden remote-controlled camera monitoring one of the airport's runways.

On May 7–8, Hezbollah-led opposition fighters seized control of several West Beirut neighborhoods and quickly blocked the main highway to the airport with massive earth barriers. This was during the time Rita was scheduled to return to Cyprus. Upon hearing that the airport road was blocked, she was unfazed, presuming it would be over in a few hours. After all, we had seen many such standoffs in the past years and most were over in a few hours.

As the day went on, however, the air became heavy with the smell of smoke, and the airwaves were full of hatred and talk of a resumption of the country's civil war. By midday, *all* the roads leading out of Lebanon were also closed.

Rita did not want to delay her return to Cyprus, especially since it now seemed that this blockade might continue for weeks, even months. This scene brought back memories of the civil war she had experienced as a child. Feeling trapped, she set her mind on getting home any way she could. She made calls to people who were considered better aware of what was really going on in the country and decided to try and travel overland to neighboring Syria and fly home from there. She called half a dozen taxi services, but none would risk such a journey. Eventually she found a driver who, for an obscene amount of money, was willing to take her to Damascus.

As Rita said goodbye to everyone at the studios, offering hugs and kisses mixed with tears, she was bombarded with advice for the journey: "Do not carry too much money!"; "Do not let anyone see your jewelry!"; "Take enough food for the trip!"; "Do not answer anyone who asks you which political party are you for!"

As the taxi headed out of Beirut, many of the roads seemed worryingly empty . . . so empty that Rita started to question if she had made the right decision. After driving for an hour and a half, Lebanese army tanks blocked the road and told her that the road to Damascus was too dangerous and she had to return to Beirut. Rita argued in vain with the tank commander. They would not allow her to pass.

She called the SAT-7 office to let them know what had happened and that she was returning. The staff were all waiting for her, greeting her as if she had just returned from a long, dangerous trip to the moon! They kissed and hugged, celebrating everyone's safety.

Just before 4:00 p.m., the staff gathered around the television monitors in the office to hear the Hezbollah leader Sheikh Hassan

Nasrallah's much-anticipated speech. He called the government's decision to close the organization's telecommunications network illegal and a declaration of war on the movement.

As they were trying to digest the implications of this broadcast, the office director, Naji Daoud, called Rita to his computer to show her that Middle East Airlines flights were leaving from Beirut that night, including one to Cyprus. Though the main purpose of their flights was to get their aircraft out of danger, should the current fighting escalate, they were offering to carry passengers if they could get to the airport.

That was the only challenge—getting to the airport! But Rita was determined to try.

Naji called Adel, a taxi driver who worked for SAT-7 and was a long-time friend of Rita's family. He agreed to take Rita as near to the airport as he could but pointed out that this still may be two to three miles from the departure terminal. Rita insisted that she was ready to walk the rest of the way, going through burning tires and climbing over the earth barricades if need be! Adel reluctantly agreed, wondering aloud how, if he could not get through to the airport, he would bring himself to leave her in such a dangerous situation to complete the journey alone.

Again, there were hugs and kisses, mixed with shouted advice: "Do not wear high heels!"; "Do you really need to take your suitcase?"; "Are you crazy? Wait until tomorrow!" But she was determined to leave.

The road to the airport, just as the other road had been, was deserted and scary, and there were frequent checkpoints manned by the Lebanese army. At each, they urged Adel to turn his taxi around, but Rita interfered, insisting that she needed to get to the airport right then! When they saw how stubborn she was, they reluctantly agreed to let her pass, giving advice to Adel on the safest route, but cautioning them again about the great danger.

As they continued, Rita asked Adel if he was scared. "No," he replied, though Rita wondered if he said that in total honesty. But she felt honored that he was ready to take such risks for her sake. They finally reached the main road to the airport. Mountains of sand and dirt completely blocked the highway in both directions.

"I am sorry," Adel confessed. "There is no way for me to go farther."

She summoned her bravest voice. "Well, I guess I will walk from here."

"I do not like this idea that you are going alone into this Shia, Hezbollah-controlled area, Rita." But after he saw her determination, he sighed. "May God be with you!"

As Rita opened the car door, she saw a dozen Hezbollah teenagers rushing toward them, several on motor scooters. "Get back in the car and leave immediately!" they urged.

"No, I am not leaving," she announced. "I am going to the airport!"

"But it's very dangerous," one of them said.

Again, Rita insisted that she had a flight to catch and was ready to take the risks because she needed to leave the country that day.

"She is from Baalbek!" Adel yelled to them, referring to a town in the Bekaa Valley known as the birthplace of Hezbollah. "You cannot touch her. In fact, you need to help her!"

"From Baalbek? Really?" one of the young men said. "But it is not safe." He paused in thought. "Well, I could take you on my scooter. But you will need to pay me ten thousand Lebanese lire."

Rita knew that equaled only about six dollars. "Deal," she said.

He put her suitcase in front of him on the scooter, and invited Rita to climb on behind him.

With a farewell wave to Adel, off they went.

They drove between the piles of dirt, sand, garbage, and smoking tires blocking the road, all the time with the young man assuring her that she would be safe with him.

They soon came to a Hezbollah checkpoint where they were stopped. He told the commander that Rita was his cousin from Baalbek, and he was taking her to the airport. Rita held her breath and prayed. The guards let them pass.

After five hundred yards, they came upon another Hezbollah checkpoint and were again stopped. This time the man insisted that the "sheikh" at the first checkpoint had given them permission to go. They were again allowed to pass.

When they reached the airport, the young man insisted on carrying Rita's bag and making sure she got into the terminal and the care of airport security. Rita was relieved to have arrived safely, but did not know how to thank her escort enough. Instead of the promised ten thousand Lebanese lire, she pulled out twenty Euros, about three times the agreed amount, and gave it to him.

With wide eyes, he leaned in and kissed Rita on the cheek. "Thank you. Be safe. My name is Hassan Fawaz, and I am always ready to help you, ma'am. Just call." He then gave Rita his number and left.

Rita stood in the check-in area, shaking. She could not believe what had just happened, and the risks she had taken, and was amazed at God's grace and protection over her. She reflected on Hassan, a Shia Muslim who would normally be considered a threat, even an enemy. But for twenty minutes, he had taken amazing care of her.

Apart from a few transit passengers, the flight to Cyprus was empty and the crew were enthralled to hear Rita's story of how she got to the airport. As she arrived at passport control in Larnaca, the immigration officer asked, "Coming from Beirut?"

Rita nodded.

"Welcome to your second home, Cyprus!" the officer said.

It would be another two weeks before the Arab League brokered the Doha Agreement, bringing an end to the eighteen-month political feud that exploded into fighting in May and nearly drove the country back into civil war.

The Growth in Social Media

In 2008 our audience responses doubled (a three-fold increase from kids or their parents). Most of the growth was in SMS text messaging, and there was still virtually no engagement with audiences through social media, which was still fairly new.

In mid-May, I attended an international conference in Monaco, which focused on the future of television. This was an important topic, since the internet was transitioning from being a source of information to social networking. Mobile television was still the fastest growing part of the market, even though there were fewer than 100 million users at the time.

While much of the conference was helpful, even prophetic, some of the virtual universe platforms they were excited about, such as My Space and Second Life, hardly exist today. And the future of video on demand (VOD) was seriously underestimated, mostly because few could then see the enormous potential there was for increasing the capacity of the internet to stream video. Nevertheless, the conference helped me to better see the potential of social media for our future engagement with audiences in sometimes-difficult regions, where traditional means of communication were still insecure, expensive, and at times slow.

But, for now, the main opportunity was the broadcast of uncensored satellite television programming into the region, and that was our first priority.

Getting onto an Arab-Owned Satellite

Until 2008, we had been broadcasting on the popular Eutelsat-owned HotBird satellite. It carried a good number of Arabic channels as well as French channels, which were of interest to viewers in North Africa and Syria. They also carried some more risqué channels, which were popular with many but of concern to conservative parents.

Ever since we started in 1996, our dream was to be on a satellite that had the most Arab viewers, where most of the channels were in Arabic. This was because of the nature of satellite television, which allowed dish owners to see only channels being broadcast from a single satellite, unless people invested in multiple dishes or the very impractical movable dishes, which were easily blown out of alignment by a strong wind.

Two rival satellite systems emerged as favorites with Arab audiences: the Saudi-owned Arabsat and the even-more-popular Egyptian-owned Nilesat. Both had made it clear to us that they would not allow a Christian channel onto the satellite.

At a trade fair in Dubai in 2005, I had met the sales manager for Arabsat. I introduced myself as the CEO of SAT-7, and he was very welcoming. "My children love your channel and watch it every night," he said, then raised his hand. "But don't even ask!" He knew exactly what I was going to ask him, and he made it clear that SAT-7 would never be welcome on a Saudi-owned satellite!

The Egypt-based Nilesat organization were more subtle in their rejection, citing our need to be registered and based in their new "Media City" out in the desert and to have a broadcast license from the Egyptian government, in addition to several other demands. All things that put access out of reach.

In early 2008, I took several steps to break the boycott. One was to approach the United States Department of State to see if they could intercede on our behalf with the authorities in Egypt. The second was to approach several broadcasters in Jordan to see if we could get a channel on one of their channel bouquets on Nilesat, or at least a few hours a day on one of their channels. One channel, Watan TV (WTV) promised to help, if we could make a prepayment of about $70,000 to help them with a cash-flow problem. This popular music channel on Nilesat was owned and operated by Ra'ed, a Jordanian from a Christian background who appeared to be sympathetic with our mission. It seemed a good way to get started.

That April, we signed a contract with WTV that would give us eight hours of airtime each day, starting a month later, on May 31, the twelfth anniversary of the start of SAT-7 broadcasts. Promotions began to run on WTV for the new broadcasts but, as the days went by, Ra'ed appeared to get cold feet and began to raise new conditions and cite new problems. In the end we never got on air! It also took us a long time to get our prepayment back.

Around this time, Nilesat needed more capacity but lacked the needed capital and entered into discussions with Eutelsat about a joint venture to launch an Egyptian-European-owned satellite. This would be co-located with the other Nilesat satellites at the assigned Egyptian orbital slot at 7 degrees west. That meant that the current viewers of Nilesat would also be able to see all the channels on the new satellite. In the end, Nilesat could not come up with their share of the launch costs and so the satellite became a 100-percent-owned Eutelsat project.

Eutelsat was then allowed to sell its channels to a wider range of clientele, so long as this did not include any of the soft-porn teaser channels running on other Eutelsat satellites. This opened the door for SAT-7 to finally begin broadcasts to the Nilesat audience, even though we were technically not on an official Nilesat satellite, but one co-located with them. On October 1, 2009, both SAT-7 ARABIC and SAT-7 KIDS began broadcasting on the new satellite and the audiences dramatically expanded overnight.

The rest of 2009 also went very well. In October, I had my first and only taste of traveling by private jet in North America. Our generous supporter, Jim, used his jet to help me and some of the American staff visit supporters and potential supporters in multiple US cities in a matter of days. No check in, no TSA security, no waiting for bags . . . we just drove into the airport and up to the plane, where the pilot loaded our bags, and we were off. It made the reality of returning to economy travel very tough!

Then in November, SAT-7 was awarded the Christian Broadcasting Council of the United Kingdom's Gold Exploits award. It was of course gratifying to get such recognition from peers in the industry but, more than this, it was an award that helped establish our credibility and visibility with potential supporters in the UK.

At the start of 2010, Andrew Hart, a British volunteer, took a year's leave of absence from IBM to, among other things, help us rationalize our broadcast operations. Having grown from a single channel to a network of three channels, with plans to launch a fourth, a Turkish-language channel, we either had to invest heavily in expanding our small master control room (MCR) in Nicosia or outsource everything to a specialized playout and uplink provider. We explored such centers in the UK, Germany, and other countries, and eventually contracted with STN, a new facility in Slovenia.

We were now able to move most of our programs around over the internet or by satellite and, at the same time, could remotely control scheduling—so the move made a lot of logistical and economic sense. At the end of that year, we began by moving the SAT-7 PARS service to STN, and eventually all the channels followed as we phased out our own MCR in Cyprus.

By now we had been on the new Nilesat satellite for a year without interruption or interference and felt confident to turn off at least the SAT-7 KIDS channel still running on HotBird. However, because we still had many viewers, including children, with dishes pointed at HotBird, we decided to retain the SAT-7 ARABIC channel there, renaming it SAT-7 PLUS in December 2010. This new channel on our old HotBird frequency had its own schedule, a mix of programs from both SAT-7 ARABIC and SAT-7 KIDS.

We were now truly a network and felt excited as we set our eyes to further expanding our reach and even adding new channels.

Chapter 7

The Lands of Persia

The people of Iran have always been part of the vision for SAT-7. After the Iranian Revolution swept through the country in 1979, it had seemed an impossible place for any kind of open Christian witness. However, in the early 1990s we began to hear exciting reports trickling out of a growing house-church movement in the country. But alongside these reports, we were also hearing heartbreaking stories of severe persecution and martyrdom.

The year 1994 was an especially dark time with multiple assassinations. It began with the murder of forty-nine-year-old Bishop Haik Hovsepian-Mehr, a Christian of Armenian descent and the superintendent of the Assemblies of God churches and chair of the Council of Protestant Ministers in Iran. In this latter role, Bishop Haik had acted as an advocate for the Christian community in front of various state departments, especially the minority affairs section of the Ministry of Islamic Guidance. In late 1993 he was involved in an international advocacy campaign on behalf of Pastor Mehdi Dibaj, who had already spent nine years in prison and, on December 23 of that year, was sentenced to death for apostasy. Following Bishop Haik's efforts and the resulting international pressure on Iran, the sixty-year-old Mehdi was released on January 16, 1994.

Three days later, on January 19, Bishop Haik disappeared while on his way to meet a visitor arriving at Tehran International Airport.

Human rights organizations later collected evidence that his car was seen inside the infamous Evin Prison around 9:00 that morning. It is widely believed that Bishop Haik met his death in Evin, between the hours of 9:00 and 10:00 a.m.

Eleven days later the Tehran Office of Investigation informed his family that his body had been found on January 20, about thirty miles west of Tehran, and, in the absence of any identification on the body, he had been buried in Beheshte Zahra (Muslim) Cemetery.

His family immediately applied for a court order to exhume the body so they could give him a Christian burial. Two weeks after his disappearance, his body was returned. But only two people from the church were given brief access to him, for ceremonial washing. Two contingents of Iran's Islamic Revolutionary Guard Corps (IRGC) or "Revolutionary Guards" accompanied the body on its way to the cemetery and a permanent police guard was placed on the grave for three months following the burial on February 3. The body appeared to have undergone an autopsy, though no official report was ever released, and no death certificate issued. Eyewitnesses who saw the body, including Haik's nineteen-year-old son Joseph, counted more than twenty stab wounds and noted that the fingers on one hand had been crushed. All photographs and videos from the funeral were confiscated by Revolutionary Guards.

Sadly, the newly freed Pastor Mehdi Dibaj also disappeared the following June. Police found his body in a shallow grave outside the capital some twelve days later. He had also died of stab wounds and, again, the body was released by the police only about two hours before burial, making any proper, independent forensic examination impossible.

Other martyrs followed that summer, including sixty-two-year-old Pastor Tateos Michaelian, the senior pastor at St John's (Presbyterian) Church in Tehran, who was shot in the head and his body dismembered.

Bishop Haik's wife, Takoosh, and their four children—Joseph, Gilbert, Andre, and Rebecca—emigrated soon after the awful events of that year, and eventually settled in the United States.

As we heard these believers' stories, we knew we needed somehow to help and perhaps even broadcast into Iran one day.

While we continued to contemplate our options, my executive assistant at Middle East Media, Mark Harvey, got caught up with the issue of advocacy and left to head up a new agency, Middle East Concern (MEC). MEC was an interagency partnership with a mandate to help Christians in the region who were facing persecution. I enthusiastically became a founding member of the board, acting as its first vice-chair.

My time on the board was a short-lived responsibility, however. Because of my earlier deportation from Egypt over human rights issues, the SAT-7 international board asked me to step away from all such activities, which could potentially aggravate relations with regional governments at this sensitive time of SAT-7's start up. I reluctantly complied.

The Dream of Persian Broadcasts

Initially, SAT-7's Arabic broadcasts consumed all our attention and resources, but the vision to include Farsi-language programming remained. At the end of the 1990s, my administrative assistant, Fred Farrokh, helped me to keep Iran on the agenda. His father was from there and he was also enthusiastic to see something happen.

Around the turn of the century, I had many fruitful discussions with people who also had a vision for broadcasting to Iran, which resulted in nine of us meeting in London on April 19–20, 2001. We came together from Iran, the UK, France, Holland, and the USA to explore the vision and potential for a satellite television service to broadcast into Iran. Over the two-day meeting we carried out a Strengths, Weaknesses, Opportunities, and Threats (SWOT) analysis, reviewed the needs of our potential audiences, studied the best approach to programming, and set the main goals for future broadcasts.

Initially, we had little discussion about the organizational structure we intended to create. But I was happy to enter into such a joint venture, with SAT-7 being an equal partner in the new initiative, and providing a broadcast platform to get the initial programs on-air. We shared the other responsibilities within the group for programming, production, facilities, dubbing, licensing, talent recruitment, audience relations, research, finances, and fundraising. All the parties agreed to adopt the current SAT-7 programming and other policy documents as a starting point, with the chair of the new working group, Lazarus, being responsible for coordinating revisions.

Our first goal was to produce a one-hour pilot broadcast tape by the end of July, in time for review at our next meeting, which would be held in the United States in late September 2001.

Joseph, martyr Haik Hovsepian-Mehr's son, had become interested in media at the age of seventeen, when he worked with the audio-visual department of the Evangelical Church in Iran. After his father's murder, he moved to the UK to study film and video, going on to both produce and direct short films, commercials, and music videos. He then moved to the United States in 2000, where he founded JFA Productions in California. He seemed the perfect person to help with the initial program production. In addition, he and his family could add to the programming by sharing their personal stories and painful struggle to find the grace to fully forgive those who took their father from them.

The steering committee agreed on a provisional six-month budget—with all members responsible to help raise the $100,000 we needed. We also approved a name, agreeing to work together under the banner of Iranian Christian Broadcasting, or ICB.

The committee's next meeting was scheduled for September 22–24, in California. It nearly did not happen, with all the uncertainties and disruption of 9/11 that month and the sudden restriction on visas for people from the Middle East. Fortunately, seven of the eight steering committee members did make it.

At this meeting we discussed the theological content of the new channel—a difficult conversation given the wide range of positions around the table, ranging from very charismatic to conservative evangelical. We discussed in-depth issues of healing, the prosperity gospel, and the power of the spoken word. And we thrashed out where red lines needed to be drawn. These included not telling our viewers that they would *always* be healed or saved from difficult situations if they only had enough faith. In the end, I was relieved to see everyone agree and sign up to the existing SAT-7 programming policy as a set of guidelines acceptable to all.

The group then reviewed the pilot broadcast tape but expressed a lot of criticism for its shortcomings, both technical and content. The proposed programming did not come across as coherent, mostly because of the decentralized nature of the work—with different program segments coming from Iran, Holland, Lebanon, and California. We tasked Armond, an Iranian Christian of Armenian descent, and his team with providing continuity and assembling these programs onto broadcast tapes at the small television studio he had set up in Santa Ana, California. An impressive feat given that he did this in parallel to running a company that distributed nutritional healthcare products across the United States.

As I listened during the meeting, I felt the real priority was to ensure that we produced as many programs as possible in Iran, despite the obvious risks involved. I worried that programs coming from Western countries would be too obviously foreign looking, and perhaps slightly out of touch with the day-to-day concerns and contemporary language of Iranians. To undertake production work in Iran, we had already secured Sony DVCAM cameras and editing equipment for the team there. However, the need to hand carry into the country all programs for dubbing, and then hand carry out the finished tapes, together with new, locally made programs was slowing everything down.

To help speed things up, we also sought an operations director to coordinate international logistics. We interviewed several West Coast Iranian Americans. However, the only potential candidate was unwilling to accept the salary we were able to offer. Armond kindly agreed to take on the responsibility part-time and on a volunteer basis.

We ended the three days of meetings on a positive note with our chair, Lazarus, reminding us that, after all the discussions, we were able to rejoice in our differences and the balance these differences brought to the ministry. Iranian Christians from different backgrounds had not worked together in this way before!

The steering committee met again in Holland in February 2002. At these meetings the steering committee became the ICB board and approved and registered a logo for ICB. We agreed that the initial broadcasts should focus on youth—their felt needs and interests. We explored new potential production centers and also agreed to go ahead with a Farsi version of our popular children's program *AsSanabel*, recording it in parallel to the Arabic production, on the same sets at KKR-TV in Denmark, but with Iranian actors working from adapted Farsi translations of the same scripts.

We decided that more training of expatriate Iranians in Europe would help us expand the program output of the production centers. However, children's programming presented a special challenge. If we were going to produce outside of Iran, it would prove difficult to find children who still spoke good Farsi, as expatriate children quickly lost their fluency or gained an accent from where they now lived . . . and I feared that we might end up having to work mostly with adults presenting programs for kids.

By now, some of the steering committee members were beginning to express a growing frustration over the repeated delays. Many of them just wanted to see Farsi programs get on-air! We had hoped to begin regular broadcasts the previous month, in January 2002, but the delays caused by all the international logistics, especially getting the drama segments from Iran, continued to slow things down. Some, like Armond, wanted to start buying time for experimental programs on one of the Iranian opposition channels broadcasting from California. But if ICB programs or presenters went on such a channel, perhaps this would create a negative backlash due to the other content on these channels, which would then make it even more difficult to continue with the production and dubbing work in Iran. Eventually we found a formula that would allow Armond, and later others, to put specially made programs on such channels, using different on-screen talent, and in a way that would hopefully not jeopardize the team in Tehran.

At this meeting we were also being advised by Pastor Vruir, an Armenian Iranian who was a popular singer and musician before becoming a committed Christian and eventually an ordained minister in the Assemblies of God church. Vruir was optimistic about the potential of producing programs in Iran and reported a growing interest and support from the leaders of all churches in the country, some of whom were already familiar with SAT-7's Arabic broadcasts. However, he expressed the expectation that the leaders of the Armenian Orthodox, Catholic, and other traditional churches would need to avoid any formal links with SAT-7 and, of course, ICB, because it would put their churches at greater risk of problems with the government authorities.

We held the next meeting of the new ICB board in California in early June 2002. Again, members scrutinized yet another pilot broadcast tape, put together in Armond's studios. However, Vruir was unable to come from Iran, so we were again missing the important drama segments from the team there, which we had also wanted to review at this meeting.

Some on the board again voiced their impatience to get programs on-air, aiming for that to happen before the Iranian pastors' conference to be held in Hamburg, Germany, at the end of July. We had arranged for the SAT-7 ARABIC channel to carry the initial ICB programs. Online responses from the audience would go to FarsiNet. com, while phone calls and fax messages would be handled in Holland and the United States. It was all a little scattered, but at least we had a plan.

The board met again in Hamburg at the end of July, even though we were still not on-air. Again, several board members expressed frustration at the delays, with those from Holland and Iran feeling that their capacity to make programs was being underutilized. At this meeting, we did eventually get to see some programs from Iran, but we also learned that the presenter in one of the programs had changed his mind and did not want his face used on-air.

This new challenge led us into a long discussion about what types of programs could safely be made in Iran. We decided to focus on dramas, music videos, and collecting general footage of the country, which we could then use in other programs.

Vruir was to take a six-month sabbatical from his pastoral responsibilities in order to build a production team in Tehran, where he already had five full-time staff and some fifteen part-timers undergoing media training.

In a follow-up teleconference a week or two later, the board agreed to commence broadcasts on September 12, doing "whatever it takes" to keep to that deadline.

On this conference call, we also finalized the plans for my August visit to Iran and agreed that I would hand carry in some master tapes of programs for dubbing in the country. Even though I understood the potential problems, I agreed to the decision, and was glad that my host for the visit would be Pastor Vruir.

The idea of making and dubbing programs in Iran, while risky in 2002, was not unrealistic. But this window of opportunity was not to last very long.

Visiting Tehran

The visa application process in 2002 was a long one. After I got the necessary forms from the Iranian embassy in Nicosia, completed them, and assembled all the required documents, I returned to the embassy, only to be told I needed to bring additional, notarized documents. On my third visit, I was asked to go to the bank, pay for the visa, and take the receipt back to the embassy. On my fourth visit, in early June, with the bank receipt in hand, I found the embassy guard asleep in his air-conditioned police box outside the gate and so walked through into the compound, unchallenged. I rang the doorbell to the embassy, but no one answered. Upon pushing the door, it opened, and I entered but found no one in sight.

"Hello, is anyone here?" I called out in a loud voice.

Someone eventually came, who in turn went and got the person dealing with visas. No one seemed especially happy about getting a customer in the heat of summer.

The official found my file and attached the bank receipt to it. I stood there feeling hopeful that I would now receive my visa.

"Now you need a letter from your employer," the man told me.

"But this is not a business trip," I protested, trying to keep my voice from giving away my frustration. "I've applied to travel on a tourist visa."

No matter how much I tried to explain, the official refused to budge. "You still need a letter to prove that you work in Cyprus and can therefore apply to the embassy here rather than in your home country."

I left, worried that a letter from SAT-7 would raise concerns over my application. Two days later, and six weeks after my first visit, I returned once again to the embassy. The outside guard was predictably sleeping in the heat of the day. I entered and presented my letter.

The officer on duty, who was in his late thirties, took it, looked at it for a second, and then his eyes lit up. "Ah, SAT-7! That is a very nice channel. I watch it with my family," he said and proceeded to issue my visa.

I arrived in Tehran late in the evening of August 15, 2002. My flight from Beirut had been delayed eight hours for technical reasons, but Pastor Vruir was patiently waiting for me as I left the arrivals hall and drove me to his apartment near the city center. There were many things that surprised me about Tehran, which had changed beyond recognition since my last visit in 1974, when the shah was still in power.

I was struck by the sight of women walking down the street with their headscarves worn as far back on their heads as was possible without them actually falling off, as if to say, *I have to wear this in public, but I will not-wear-it as much as I can, and so let you see my hair, and my colorful slacks and ankles under my shortened chador!*

I visited coffee shops with couples cuddling in the darkened corners. I smelled the ever-pervasive aroma of hashish being smoked, even in public places. I saw DVDs of western movies on sale. I even found, and bought, a Farsi version of The Jesus Film produced by Cru, complete with an epilogue by a dubbed Dr. Bill Bright asking Iranian viewers to give their lives to Christ. Almost everywhere I went in Tehran, I felt welcomed as a foreigner and witnessed a real affinity for the United States, with many telling of relatives there and many wanting to visit. Apart from movies, people also seemed to love American music, clothes, and food, with many look-alike American-type clothing and food outlets.

I was also surprised by complete strangers coming up to me in stores or bookshops and discreetly asking me if I had a spare copy of the Holy Bible. Even one taxi driver had, in big letters across his back windscreen, "God Loves You." He used to give passengers his Christian testimony, printed copies of which he kept in his glove compartment, in Farsi, Armenian, and English.

Perhaps the biggest surprise was when I attended a so-called "secret" house church, meeting on the third floor of an apartment in a Tehran suburb. About sixteen or seventeen people squeezed together in the living room and, despite the fact that the windows were all open to cope with the summer heat, they were singing Christian worship songs at the top of their voices. The whole neighborhood must have been aware of what was going on in apartment 302!

Through a translator, I asked people in the room about their spiritual journeys and, specifically, "What have been the most difficult things for you to deal with since becoming a Christian?"

While there were many different responses, one clear theme that emerged was the disappointment they felt by the behavior of other believers. I suppose that this should not have been surprising when I considered that most of the new believers in Iran were and, to a lesser extent still are, mostly spiritually immature and undiscipled. But it did flag up to me the importance of providing more foundational programming on the teachings of the Christian faith to support and build up the many new believers in the country and the relatively young leaders of this "new church."

It was also a blessing to meet with many of the leaders of the official churches in Tehran, to learn more of their trials, hopes, and opportunities, and to better understand how our broadcasts into the country might better serve them and the kingdom of God. I was especially impressed by the bold witness and creativity of a seventy-year-old French Jesuit priest and long-time resident in Iran who had set up a small studio and was ready to work with Pastor Vruir on producing programs for ICB!

During one of my last days in Iran, I was on a downtown street, looking up at one of the many political murals painted on the sides of multistory buildings. It depicted burning American and Israeli flags. The words on it declared, in Farsi and English, "Death to the Great Satan." But in a metaphor for the divided country, along came a young man, walking under the same mural, wearing a T-shirt on which was written "I ♥ New York." Oh, that I had possessed a camera at the time!

I returned to Cyprus feeling enthused and with a clearer sense of what we needed to provide in order to serve Iranian believers.

Farsi-Language Broadcasts Begin

True to our commitment to the steering committee, we were able to start our first broadcast on schedule on September 12, 2002. We were able to produce only one hour of new programming each week, which we then repeated several times. But it was a start!

Even with our limited broadcast hours, we received responses. One enthusiastic new viewer wrote to say that he was fixated by the broadcasts and tuned in ICB every Friday without fail, recording the programs on VHS tapes to share with his friends. He said that the testimonies, the music, and the teaching all ministered to his soul.

Another viewer wrote, "Tonight is the most beautiful night in my life, because I have just discovered your channel. I am so happy; I cannot express the joy I have. The words from the Bible bring me rest and peace."

An Iranian pastor called us to explain that there is a widely held belief in Iran that the church is unwilling or unable to answer people's questions or engage in any public discourse. He was thrilled that many people were now seeing a different picture of the church—one that was welcoming . . . and reaching out to all homes with messages of hope, love, and faith.

The team and I wondered how many people were watching and how people would discover the programs, especially insomuch as they were on a mostly Arabic-language channel. But, as we had seen in the Arab World, people were discovering these broadcasts by chance or from one another. This viewer response was typical: "I saw your channel at a friend's home. I like it so much. I felt a deep peace within me as I watched. Thank you!"

By June 2003, the SAT-7 ARABIC channel was carrying six hours a week of Farsi programming—a one-hour general block on Thursday, including segments for children and women, music, Bible readings, some drama, and Bible teaching, which we then repeated on Friday and Sunday evenings. Each Thursday we also broadcast a one-hour block of programs for youth, which we repeated on Friday and Saturday.

However, the work was still dogged by a lack of centralized leadership and coordination. With so many different program or segment contributors, a decentralized audience response team, a lack of clarity on decision making, poor funding (up to this point most of the start-up funds had come through SAT-7 supporters, and partly at the expense of support for the SAT-7 ARABIC channel), a lack of clarity on the rights of members to use their different productions on other channels, and with many potential and actual conflicts of interest, it was time for a more centralized coordination of operations. So in April 2003, and until we could find and hire a full-time executive director, I took on the role of acting ICB executive director, working closely with Armond, who was still the part-time programming director.

Things were looking up—or at least we thought they were. A new challenge hit soon after I took on the responsibility: the situation for Christians was becoming more difficult in Iran and we had to suspend drama production and instead focus on dubbing work, as well as music clips and some children's program productions. Recurring overhead costs were also high at the production center in Iran, which was concerning given how increasingly little we were actually able to do there.

During the following months responses from our audience, especially by phone, began to grow—but so did the opposition. The Republican Guard was deployed to confiscate satellite dishes, often being guided to different buildings by helicopter crews hovering above the city, especially in the suburbs known for their lack of support for the regime. And from the Iranian Embassy in Cuba, the government began jamming Iranian opposition television channels broadcasting from California on the Telstar satellite.

Our audience also reported many incidents of intimidation. One man called us from Tehran to tell us how he had been summoned to the police station, where he was shown his recent, itemized phone bill and told that if he were to call the ICB number again, he would face charges. So he went home and called our number again to tell us!

We also discovered that sometimes those who called the ICB helpline later turned out to be government agents.

Those early days occurred before social media took off, and even email was still a new way for Iranians to communicate, with some not fully understanding how it worked. One man phoned SAT-7 from Kerman in Iran to request a New Testament. When we said we could email him the text, he gave us his email address and then asked if we also needed his password!

The team itself also faced growing challenges. In April 2004, Vruir needed to undergo heart surgery in neighboring Armenia. There was already a backlog of more than two hundred programs we wanted to dub in Iran, but it was not just Vruir's health delaying things; it was also funding.

The Risks of Believing

Sara Afshari joined the ministry in the summer of 2002, moving from the UK to Cyprus in September, the same month as we went on-air with our first Farsi programs. She was from Iran and had gone through difficult times as a young believer there. The leaders of her small but growing church in a small town in southeastern Iran had been arrested and imprisoned. Sara then became one of the leaders of the mostly young congregation as the church was closed and its members went underground.

Sara and several others had come to faith when Jesus appeared to them in a dream. All of them experienced their families' rejection. "We had no one to turn to except each other," she shared with me. "We had no pastors or teachers to instruct us in how to be followers of Jesus. There were not enough Bibles for everyone. And, of course, there were no SAT-7 Persian-language broadcasts then."

Exhausted from living in hiding and knowing that her family's home was being watched by the secret police, Sara boldly went to the officials who were seeking her. She knew the risks and their reputation. Passing through those doors, she knew she might never get out alive. They bound and blindfolded her and began to threaten her.

"You know who we are," they told her. "Do you know what we can do to you? Whatever we like! If you disappear, no one will know."

For eight hours they continued the questioning and threats. Incredibly, Sara eventually began to laugh. "You don't know who *I* am," she told them. "I have nothing to lose. The only thing I have—Jesus— you cannot take from me. Your threats don't work on me!"

Her captors demanded, "Do you believe Jesus is the Son of God?"

Without any formal theological training, she testified to her interrogators about Jesus' divinity. Eventually, they fell silent. Sara was leading the conversation! All the while, she had the sense that the Holy Spirit was in her every word. Her memory was so sharp she was able to remember and share everything she had read and come to understand about Jesus.

Finally, the interrogation ended. Amazingly, the officer in charge told Sara, "It seems you have found a faith that's right for you. Your testimony, all you have said, has touched my heart. We were going to keep you here for three months, but I'm going to release you tonight, because of what you've shared. Stay in your faith, for no one here can answer your questions."

In time, Sara felt led to leave Iran and undertake a theology course at Trinity College Bristol in the UK. After finishing, she received several job offers in the UK but, with the encouragement of a good friend and the support of the Church Mission Society (CMS), she agreed to join SAT-7 in Cyprus.

Sadly, as a woman and a convert, she almost immediately faced resistance from some of the Iranians on the ICB board who were from a Christian background. They were especially concerned as to whether she could be trusted with issues of theological content within programs. She even initially faced discrimination from our Arab staff and board members—people who had grown up hearing only negative things about Persians in their school history classes, in political speeches, and through Arab media.

It is one of the great blessings of SAT-7 that these different groups could eventually find and love each other as brothers and sisters in Christ and coworkers in the same ministry.

Initially, Sara's title was "ICB liaison officer" and she acted as a local coordinator for the Farsi-language programs broadcast on SAT-7's Arabic channel. By 2004, as still the only full-time ICB employee, Sara had become the main point-person for logistics and coordinating the channel's activities. She also took new initiatives in scheduling and programming. At the end of the year, she proposed that we move to two-hour blocks of programming on SAT-7 ARABIC, allowing for the channel to include Farsi movies or other programs that were more than sixty minutes in length. She also proposed that the weekly assembly of the broadcast tapes be moved from California to Cyprus, starting in 2005. The board accepted these recommendations and appointed her to the new position of "ICB program coordinator."

Admittedly, our first attempts at dubbing programs in Iran were amateurish. Sara firmly believed that no one would watch such programs as they had become accustomed to very professionally dubbed films on Iranian television. People expected higher standards.

Our solution came in an unusual way. Around this time one of our viewers, Reza Ghambari, who worked in the Iranian television industry, got in touch. Although a Muslim, he was fascinated that we were "broadcasting Christianity," saying that he had never seen anything like this before.

Sara followed up on him and eventually confided that we were looking for someone to dub our Christian movies into Farsi, respecting the conservative values of Persian culture. He agreed to undertake some dubbing for us and so Sara sent him a selection of films and cartoons for children, to see how well he could do. Both Sara and the ICB chair, Lazarus, were impressed with the results, which were far better than our team in Tehran had achieved to date.

Initially, everything went smoothly. Sara deliberately chose to send Reza movies and stories that were not overtly evangelistic, and his team were happy to work with those. Reza even came to visit us at the SAT-7 international office in Cyprus. But then we sent him a documentary talking about Jesus Christ as the Son of God and discussing the Trinity. Reza called Sara and said that they could not continue their work.

"This program says that Jesus Christ is the Son of God and promotes other ideas that we don't believe in. It is too dangerous, and we can't continue," he said.

"Don't worry," Sara told him. "I will send someone to explain to you what these things mean." She quickly got in touch with an Anglican priest she knew in Tehran, Father Ibrahim, and asked him to visit Reza's team, to give them some orientation on the teachings of the Bible, explaining what the programs were all about.

After Father Ibrahim made a few visits, Reza called Sara back. "Now that we understand what these things mean, of course we will continue." Reza's team dubbed more and more of our programs, and Father Ibrahim continued to visit each week to review and correct the translations before the actual dubbing took place. In the process, he shared more with the team about the Christian faith and, eventually, the whole team gave their lives to Jesus.

Unfortunately, there were repercussions. Many of Reza's dubbing team were famous actors in the Iranian television industry and, over time, the Iranian Education Department received multiple complaints from school teachers in Iran saying, "As a result of these programs, our children keep asking about Jesus. They are becoming more interested in learning about Christianity than our own religion!" The education department passed the complaints to Herasat, one of the two main intelligence networks in the country.

Herasat branches had been established inside every civilian organization and university in the country and were tasked with identifying potential security threats. Herasat officials reportedly monitor employees, act as informants, and influence hiring and firing practices. One of their roles is to protect the Republic's Islamic values, and so, when our programs were brought to their attention, and they recognized the voices of the actors, they immediately took action. They quickly identified Reza's dubbing house, raided it, and took all the computers away. Some of the staff were briefly detained, and we lost many hours of programs. One of the actors was not only a dubbing voice for us but also had his own weekly program on the Iranian national Channel 3. Herasat ensured that he was removed from that position.

As a result, our dubbing in Iran virtually stopped. However, Reza eventually managed to put together a new team, with less high-profile people, who then began producing children's programs, along with songs and other clips.

Sara also passionately wanted to produce a program in Iran on Iranian church history. Ninos, an Assyrian pastor in Tehran, had written a great script, and we commissioned Reza's team to film it, traveling to a number of biblical and historic locations within Iran. But while they were recording at one such location, members of the Revolutionary Guard realized what they were doing and confiscated their equipment, along with all their footage. Amazingly the team were still determined to continue. They managed to recover the equipment and went back to reshoot, but again members of the Revolutionary Guard seized all the equipment and footage, and sadly, this time, some of the team were detained. They were held for a few days, threatened, and made to sign a declaration that they were Muslims, and they had been obligated to do this filming as part of their commercial work.

Eventually, like so many believers who faced continual harassment, most of these brothers and sisters moved out of Iran.

Reza himself spent some time working out of Abu Dhabi. After he thought that things had cooled down in Iran, he returned to the country, but the government again confiscated all his equipment. His wife and children were very stressed by the insecurity and they all moved to Norway, and eventually back to the UAE again but, by then, Reza's production team had dispersed, and he had lost all motivation. This took a toll on Reza's marriage, and he and his wife eventually divorced. He returned to Iran. But suffering from depression, he tragically died from a heart attack a few years later.

One of the last to leave Iran was Mahyar. He had been part of Reza's team from the beginning, initially working as an editor and then developing his animation skills. Leila, Sara's sister, also went to work with the team, specializing in animation. The two became friends and, four years later, Mahyar and Leila married.

Following Reza's death, Mahyar took over leadership of what was left of the team. They continued to create new children's programs and sent us lots of library footage of Iran to use in programs and music clips that were being recorded outside the country. Mahyar was also working with Iranian national television as the producer of a one-hour weekly overview of events in Parliament, as well as a soap opera.

But the team experienced further incidents of equipment and programming seizures. The Revolutionary Guard again confiscated programs from the studio, returning only those intended for use on Iranian television. None of our programs were ever returned.

Several years later, Mahyar bought a drone to use in filming and obtained the proper license from the Iranian Television Authority. Near where he lived, there was a park that was popular for flying toy airplanes and drones. One day Mahyar received a phone call from someone he trusted.

"We are all going to fly our drones in the park today," the man said. "Come, and bring your drone."

So Mahyar went, taking his son with him. Almost as soon as he got there, and as he was taking out his equipment, members of the Revolutionary Guard surrounded him. He was arrested and taken with his son to the police station. Under the pretext that the home of a high-ranking military officer was in that region, they accused Mahyar of taking his drone there to film it. Sara's sister had to go and collect their son from the police station later that day while Mahyar remained in detention. This was the last straw for them as a couple and, with the court case against Mahyar still pending, they left the country to seek asylum overseas.

The Broadcasts and Responses Increase

In the years following my visit to Iran, things became more difficult in the country, with all Farsi-speaking church meetings being stopped and new believers again being harassed. Despite the challenges, ICB was now broadcasting two hours per day on SAT-7's Arabic channel and we continued to receive amazing testimonies from our viewers.

Sahar hated her husband, Koorosh. He beat her nearly every day, and she could do nothing about it. One of Sahar's few joys was watching ICB, especially because a relative worked for the channel and she would occasionally see him on the programs. For some reason he could never explain, Koorosh also began to watch the channel. One day, while watching an on-air pastor, God touched Koorosh's heart. He was struck by the weight of his sin and his need for a savior. That day, he embraced Christ and his life totally changed. Sahar later reported that the beatings stopped, and their relationship was renewed.

Another viewer, Hamid, began calling the channel's counseling line. He described himself as a gangster, a thief, and a drug dealer (Iran had and still has one of the world's worst drug-addiction problems). He shared that, one night, he was flipping through the channels when he happened upon ICB, and it started him thinking. He and his young daughter eventually gave their lives to Christ. Again, God totally turned Hamid's life around. He was able to say no to huge sums of money offered to him for his part in the drug trade. "Although I needed the money," Hamid told the counselor, "I refused it because I knew that Christ would not be happy." Hamid's wife, who was not a Christian, also called the counselor to express her thanks for the change she had seen in her husband.

Many others shared how they had visions and dreams, things that made sense to them only after watching one of our programs. Broadcasting Cru's The Jesus Film in Farsi was especially effective. It always provoked many responses and requests for more information about Christ and His teachings.

Even with all the challenges, equipment seizures, and detainments, our team and I knew that the work we were doing was definitely making a difference in the lives of our Iranian viewers. And that gave us the motivation to keep going.

Chapter 8

SAT-7 PARS

By 2005, our endeavors to reach the Persian-speaking world were bringing more challenges than we were prepared for. We struggled under financial constraints, and our combined fundraising efforts weren't bringing in the funds we desperately needed. Even though SAT-7 was providing free airtime, as well as raising most of the funds, we needed much more to help cover the growing costs of salaries, equipment, and the expenses of acquiring or making new programs. In addition, we received little reporting back from the production team in Iran. And then we had continuing difficulties with the board. Half of the original ICB board had resigned. Some were asked to leave because of conflicts of interest. And some had theological or cultural differences with other board members, including understanding what the role of those from a non-Christian Iranian background should or could be.

Two weeks before Christmas, we held a make-or-break board meeting in Armenia. The capital, Yerevan, was very cold and gloomy in December, with virtually no street lighting. Even the airport seemed on the verge of collapse. The guest house where we all stayed was so cold that I had to think long and hard about whether I really wanted to make a trip to the bathroom in the middle of the night. This was so different from my impression during an earlier visit in the 1970s, when the streets were bright and alive, and a visit to the Yerevan Opera House was the highlight of the weekend.

But the doom and gloom did not end with the environment. It pervaded the atmosphere of the two-day board meeting. We read letters from some of the former board members who had either resigned or been asked to leave. In each letter, the ex-member raised concerns about the process the board had followed and highlighted conflicts of interest, some of which still existed within the remaining board. Though the concerns and accusations were difficult to hear, we all agreed that we must address each in detail and reply to all those who had taken the time to write.

Next we turned our attention to new officer elections. We appointed Rev. Tat Stewart the new chair of ICB. Tat was the son of missionary parents and had grown up in Iran, where he had learned to speak Farsi fluently. He later returned to Iran, a few months after the Islamic Revolution, to serve as the pastor of the Community Church of Tehran. He was there during the 1979 US embassy hostage crisis. The ICB board felt confident that Tat would bring years of wisdom and an understanding of Iran that few foreigners possessed, as well as healing to the board. He did and remained the board chair for the next decade.

When I returned to Cyprus after the meetings, I felt that we were making progress. And I was right. The next board meeting, which we held in sunny Cyprus six months later, could not have been more different. Though we now had a much smaller board, the atmosphere was undeniably and overwhelmingly positive. They were clear that they were there to support the staff and the vision in a fresh way. A new chapter was starting for ICB, and it was a joy to see.

Their support was especially obvious toward Sara. The year before, Sara had taken time out to do a communications course at the Oxford Center for Mission Studies (OCMS). The title for her final dissertation was *A New Strategic Plan for ICB*. This plan called for us to begin producing two hours a day of new programming in 2006, enabling ICB to move to its own 24/7 channel by the end of the year. Sara presented her plan and budget at the board meeting. Not only did they approve it; they unanimously voted her in as the first ICB executive director.

Sara pressed ahead with her plan, recruiting Eileen Ghali as the channel's program coordinator, as well as hiring one or two people to work on the channel's graphics, scheduling, and anticipated technical services. In light of the tight budget, her actions seemed foolish to some of the staff. For me, it was just another small step of faith.

Hard Choices

We were taking bold steps to grow ICB into an independent channel and organization. But, if it were to move out from under the legal umbrella of SAT-7, it would need to set up its own fundraising offices in key territories; it would need its own legal status in order to secure satellite contracts and a broadcast license, and it would have to rehire the existing ICB staff currently employed by SAT-7. In addition, it would need to develop its own HR, accounting, IT, broadcast and other support services. So much to consider and plan for.

Sara strongly favored taking all the necessary actions to make this happen. Her decisions ran deeply cultural and personal. For decades Iran had suffered under Western imperialism. Additionally, it had struggled for centuries against discord and rivalry between Persia and the Arab World. And, more recently, she had personally witnessed the awkwardness of ICB being accepted by the Arab-dominated SAT-7 international board. She remembered when ICB was first introduced to the SAT-7 board and how some of its members reacted. They had made it clear that they did not want to take responsibility for broadcasts in a language they did not understand, especially in light of Iran's radical political and religious regime.

Sara feared that ICB would always be treated as the unwanted stepchild of SAT-7, always struggling for its share of attention from the board and support offices and the resources it would need. And, given the centuries of conflict between Arabs and Persians, she was also rightly fearful of the optics—the political perception of Arabs supporting a Christian channel for Iran.

In September 2006, I invited Sara to attend the SAT-7 United States office's tenth-year anniversary event for supporters, which we were holding at the Reagan Library in California. We gave ICB and its potential new channel a high profile during the event's program, and Sara had a number of successful meetings with both individual supporters and foundations during the weekend, resulting in almost $2 million in pledges to the new channel. We were extremely encouraged, though it raised concerns among some senior SAT-7 staff and international board members, many of whom feared that this support would be at the expense of income for the Arabic channel. Sadly, I even received criticism for bringing Sara to the event and allowing our key supporters to get a vision for ICB, especially if, as Sara was planning, ICB would become a separate organization in the near future. While understandable, this criticism was not in the spirit of partnership or building the kingdom of God. In any case, we did not "own" any of our donors.

During the program in California, the SAT-7 international board's executive committee held a meeting and invited Sara to discuss the future relationship of ICB with SAT-7. Some wanted ICB to continue as a separate ministry, while others wanted to see the new channel as part of a larger SAT-7. I strongly supported those on the executive committee who felt it was important that ICB, for its own sake, needed to take its place as a distinct and important member of the SAT-7 family, reminding all present that Iran had always been a part of the vision and mission statements for SAT-7's ministry.

I also believed that Sara's idea to build a parallel international organizational infrastructure for ICB would be a senseless duplication of effort. How long would it take and how much would it cost her to incorporate and set up support-raising entities in different countries and her own legal and administrative structures in the region? All this would seriously delay any channel launch.

However, when confronted with these concerns in the meeting, Sara reacted angrily. "Do you know what I hear? I hear a colonial voice."

"What do you mean?" I said, feeling genuinely surprised. "You mean Arabs colonizing Iran?"

"No! English colonizing all of us."

I was taken back—especially given that I am English—and didn't know what to say. This was so far from my heart and so against everything SAT-7 stood for. Both Sara and I left the meeting to calm down. It wasn't exactly a fruitful discussion, but later we were able to talk through the issues in a less heated way.

Sara felt passionately that we at least needed to allow ICB to become stronger before it officially joined SAT-7. She was concerned that the board was still weak but believed ICB had the potential to become strong. "Then we will join you, as equals."

Our debate continued through to the next meeting of the SAT-7 international board, a month later. At that meeting the board decided to extend an invitation to ICB to officially come under the legal umbrella of SAT-7 and its international fellowship of support offices and production and broadcast centers. It recognized that the response to this invitation needed to come from the ICB board itself. Sara remained angry with me and submitted a letter of resignation. In fact, during this period she attempted to resign several times.

But I made it clear to Sara that if she resigned, I would not continue to seek the integration of ICB into SAT-7, since I believed that it would not work without her as the executive director. She was clearly unhappy with the situation, but thankfully she was blessed by having discerning friends to whom she could turn for counsel. One of these was Robert, a former supervisor from Trinity College Bristol, where she had studied theology.

After listening to her concerns, he wisely asked her, "If you start this television channel, what will happen?"

"There is real potential that lots of people will hear the name of Christ and many people will become Christians. It will strengthen Christianity in Iran."

"So if you resign and none of these things happen, does that mean that you are stopping God's plan?"

That's all it took. She realized that her resignation was perhaps driven by her own ambition. Thankfully, after this, she decided to stay. This is not to say that this was the end of the heated discussions! We had plenty more, and they gave me greater insight into how difficult the whole thing was for her. Her experiences up to this point meant that she really didn't believe that the channel would succeed in the way she wanted it to.

It was a difficult process but nothing important comes easily. However, out of this painful journey, SAT-7 PARS (*PARS* meaning Persian or things related to Persia) was birthed and has borne fruit beyond all our expectations ever since.

When the ICB board met again at the end of November 2006 in Dubai, without exception, they felt that the best, if not the only, practical solution was for ICB to be formally adopted into the SAT-7 family, as a semi-autonomous division within the ministry. They therefore voted to move ahead with the merger and change its organizational and channel name from Iranian Christian Broadcasting to SAT-7 PARS, in time for the launch of the channel in less than three weeks, on December 18, 2006.

Making History

In the weeks leading up to the launch of the new channel, staff worked tirelessly to produce new promotional videos and spots, as well as new weekly programs for youth and women, new Christian music and Bible teaching programs, and three new children's shows. In addition, production partners in the United States and Europe produced new evangelistic and teaching program series. This was to enable SAT-7 PARS to start its new channel with four hours of new programming each day, which we would then repeat at a different time of day on each of the following three days.

The new channel would also carry four hours a day of Turkish programming for what would eventually become SAT-7 TÜRK. This Turkish programming was moved from the Arabic channel both to enable it to have more airtime on the new channel each day and because millions of people in Iran spoke both Farsi and Azeri, a language close enough to Turkish to allow them to also follow the Turkish programs.

The big day came at last. SAT-7 PARS began as a separate Christian television channel for the people of Iran, Afghanistan, and Tajikistan, broadcasting from the HotBird 6 satellite. For me and many of the staff and SAT-7 PARS board members, this was a dream come true. Over the past years I had come to realize that, if satellite television was strategic for the Arab World, it was much more so for Iran. Why? Because after thirty years of rule by the mullahs, most Iranians had lost trust in their leaders and in the religion that was so often used to oppress them. They were hungry for authenticity, for truth, and for meaning. And even from the earliest Farsi broadcasts, we could see that we were meeting a deep spiritual need and offering hope to the many who had none.

Within a couple weeks of the new channel starting, the number of letters and emails increased four-fold and a new telephone hotline began getting dozens of calls each day. One call came from Aleen, a lady who wanted to know how she could accept Jesus as her own personal Savior. The SAT-7 PARS' counselor spoke with her and explained the simple gospel message and the woman prayed with her. Then, just thirty minutes later, Aleen called again but, this time, there were loud voices in the background.

"What is happening?" the counselor asked anxiously.

"My mother-in-law also wants to give her life to Jesus," Aleen replied.

The counselor carefully explained the way of salvation to Aleen's mother-in-law, and she too prayed to receive Christ as has Lord and Savior.

As the year went on, it became increasingly obvious that nearly all mail from Iran was being intercepted, and so people were limited to emails, text messages, and phone calls. But even the phone calls were being blocked, so we had to begin changing the phone numbers every week, just to stay ahead of the Iranian authorities. And with the launch of a new SAT-7 PARS website in September 2007, viewers began using the chat rooms to get answers to their questions about Christianity and to share with us and each other personal stories of how they were able to live as believers in an increasingly oppressive Iran.

Growth and Opposition

In early 2008, the growing SAT-7 PARS team in Nicosia moved to a larger rented flat in the same building as the international office, while all local production work moved to a converted villa fifty miles away in Limassol, where most of the Iranians in Cyprus seemed to live. The layout of the villa was not perfect, insomuch as the best space for recording was right in front of the main door out to the street! But it also had a quiet basement, and some shooting could even take place in the large kitchen area. And, as a bonus, the villa also came with its own small swimming pool!

At the same time, the team recognized that many of Iran's exiled Bible teachers and church leaders were now based in the UK, so they felt it strategic to set up a small studio in West London. Initially this was in a business center on the North Circular Road, but a year later, they moved the studio to a larger, more suitable space in a nearby industrial complex.

These new studio spaces allowed the team to double the hours of new programming they produced in 2008. In the same year we also began moving all our programs to the broadcast center over the internet, instead of the time-consuming and more costly method of shipping them to the center on professional broadcast tapes. This also opened the door for the team to plan for their first live broadcasts in 2009, starting from the London studio.

The live shows brought a whole new dynamic to the channel, just at a time of renewed unrest and street violence in Iran following the elections. Disillusioned and hurting people called in with personal or theological questions, which our program presenters and guest Bible teachers answered live on-air. Most of these questions represented the questions in the minds of thousands of others, triggering them to join in the conversation, on-air or online. There was a new sense of authenticity and transparency in this kind of live programming, and it touched people in a way that prerecorded programs could not.

In November, SAT-7's Annual Day of Prayer helpfully focused on the people of Iran and the growing challenges faced by the new believers there.

And in 2010, the weekly live shows expanded to four, but our efforts to constantly change our phone numbers for live shows was not keeping up with the government's ability to block our lines. Fortunately, this was the era when many new social media platforms were becoming available internationally, with Iranians among the early adopters. Increasingly, audiences began interacting with us through Facebook, Twitter, Messenger, and Skype.

During 2011 we were able to commission an independent marketing company to conduct a survey, calling Iranian households from outside the country. One thing about the survey we were sure of before we started was that the numbers would not be a true indication of the actual viewership. The survey questionnaire began by asking the head of the household if they had a satellite dish. Since this was illegal and since the person receiving the call did not really know just who was calling, many would have just said that they did not have a dish, and the survey would have ended there. The next questions asked them about the number of people in their household and the channels they watched. Again, with the uncertainty of who was calling them, we did not expect a lot of people to admit they watched a Christian channel, but an amazing number did.

The results showed that we had at least two million adult viewers in Iran, and potentially the same number again of children. Bearing in mind the uncertainty about millions more actual viewers, the numbers were very encouraging indeed.

At this time, a man started to call a private line operated by the SAT-7 PARS counseling team in Cyprus, a number that was not advertised on-air.

"How did you get this number?" asked the counselor, suspecting that the authorities had perhaps discovered it.

"A relative gave it to me, the same one who gave me a Bible and helped me find Christ," the man said. He went on to share that he was actually calling from a prison.

"How are you able to call us?" asked the counselor, still unsure about the caller's trustworthiness.

"I have my own phone card that I am allowed to use occasionally."

Over the following weeks, the man called regularly, and the counselor answered his many questions about the Bible and church history, as well as about how to live as a Christian. The man explained that he shared the answers with others in the prison who were also followers of Jesus.

He eventually confided that he had been a drug smuggler and was now on death row, but that he had asked God for forgiveness. He also expressed his amazement that God had kept him alive until now. "I'm telling everyone about Jesus, the only one who matters. And I tell all my friends who contact me here in the prison to watch SAT-7 PARS!"

In July 2012, we closed the London studios for major remodeling—essentially to make better use of the space we were renting and to improve the sound insulation for the studio. Being in the middle of an industrial complex and under the flight path into London Heathrow Airport meant that we often had to re-record material due to unexpected outside noises. But as the remodeling proceeded, we found problems with the basic structure of the building and much of the electrical wiring. The project became even more complicated with changes needed to comply with new fire regulations and then the need to provide a disabled persons' toilet. In the end, the work was some 200 percent over budget!

To protect our investments in the building, Sara secured a ten-year extension on the lease, without increases in the monthly rent. The idea of investing in such a facility in London still seemed alien to me. I believed strongly in making programs in-country, but it was obvious that this was no longer an option for us when it came to Iran. However, I believed then, and continue to believe, that it is only a question of time before things change there, and we will be able to set up a studio and ministry center in Tehran.

For now, things were still moving in the wrong direction in Iran and the government again stepped up its surveillance, as well as blocking websites and social media, and even selectively jamming satellite channels, especially international news and Iranian opposition channels broadcasting from the United States and Europe. This came to a head in October 2012 when Eutelsat shut down all Iranian channels on their HotBird and other satellites, at the same time as the European Union increased sanctions against the Islamic Republic. All nineteen state-owned television and radio channels were switched off. It was not until nearly two years later, and after promises from Iran to end its jamming of foreign-owned satellite systems, that these channels were allowed back onto European satellites.

Despite the government's efforts to censor us, SAT-7 PARS continued to expand. The following year, the Turkish programming moved off the SAT-7 PARS channel altogether, giving more airtime each day to expand the Farsi programs on what was now a 24/7 Persian-language service. The extra time was soon used for new programs, including a new weekly live and interactive youth program, *What's Up?* and a new teaching program on the essentials of the Christian faith, *Living Faith.*

On November 20, 2013, International Children's Day, the popular weekly show *Carousel* made its first live broadcast. Parastoo, the host, was by then already well known to young viewers in Iran, and this first live show received more than two hundred calls in the first five minutes of being on-air! This was soon followed by two other new programs for children—a one-hour weekly live show called *Smile* and a humor-filled puppet show that showed how Persian proverbs and literature resonated with passages from the Bible.

Other new shows were to follow including one in the Dari language, *Secret of Life.* Dari is a Persian dialect spoken widely in Afghanistan, allowing viewers in Iran to understand the program while attracting new audiences in Afghanistan. Christian Afghans now living in Canada produced this weekly show. From its beginning, it had a special focus on forgiveness, showing it as not a single act but as a way of life. In one episode the program's host, Shoaib, used the Lord's Prayer to demonstrate that, as God has forgiven us, we should also forgive others. This is a message that is especially important in war-weary Afghanistan where grudges can often turn into decades-long family or tribal feuds. The show eventually went live, attracting many phone calls each week.

New Leadership, New Opportunities

After twelve years of amazing work, in 2014 the time came for Sara to move on. She had long wanted to continue her academic interests and felt the time was right for her to pursue her doctoral studies fulltime at the University of Edinburgh. She would be a hard act to follow.

The SAT-7 PARS board chose Rev. Mansour Khajehpour to succeed her. A Princeton graduate, Mansour moved with his family from the United States to Cyprus that summer. His arrival was followed by a number of changes, with a new audience relations team being appointed, more live shows going out each week, new programs by women for women, and a new weekly broadcast in the Azeri language. We also began a new series of programs dealing with issues of persecution under the title *The Suffering Church*.

In the year following, the telephone counseling hotline expanded from a few hours a day to a globally connected 24/7 service, and the team began to make use of new, secure social media platforms like Telegram. By now, Telegram had 20 million users in Iran, and many used this as a secure way to message us as well as to download parts of the Bible, program clips, and other Christian resources in Farsi.

And as the stream of refugees from Iran and Afghanistan passing through Turkey to Greece grew, PARS sent a team to join them on their dangerous journey, recording the challenges they faced, as well as interviewing them about their hopes and fears for the future. Freelance producer Petros Mohseini led the production team, who described their experience as "humbling." They also recorded interviews with migrating Christians, brothers and sisters fleeing persecution because of their new faith in Jesus. The resulting documentary premiered on SAT-7's Day of Prayer in November 2015.

In October, SAT-7 PARS hosted its fourth Teachers' Conference in the UK. This brought together thirty leaders from the different Iranian churches to develop the channel's biblical and theological strategy—helping us deliver relevant and needed theological content to our viewers. The conferences also acted as a great networking opportunity, strengthening relationships between the different Iranian churches of the diaspora.

At the end of 2015, our research showed that a new satellite, launched by a company based in the United Arab Emirates (UAE) in the Gulf, was gaining a significant audience in Iran and Afghanistan. One of the features that made this satellite so attractive to Iranians was the fact that it was broadcasting a very focused, high-power beam over Iran and the countries immediately adjacent to it, meaning that a viewer needed only a very small satellite dish, about two feet or less in diameter to pick up a good signal. And in a country where satellite dishes were still illegal, a small dish was easier to install and then keep concealed! Another attraction of this satellite system was the growing number of popular, free-to-view Persian news and entertainment channels it carried, many being in high definition.

In January 2016, SAT7 PARS filed a formal application for a channel on this satellite. After trying to follow up on the application for more than six months, we eventually learned that our application had been rejected, on the basis that our "channel did not comply with the broadcast regulations in the UAE." However, when we asked for more specifics, concerning which regulations or laws we were not in compliance with, the correspondence stopped.

The SAT-7 PARS team and broadcast staff felt discouraged by the rejection and were now beginning to explore another satellite, which also offered some potential to increase our audiences in Iran and Afghanistan, but not to the same extent as the UAE-based satellite.

I felt God wanted us to keep trying to secure a channel on this strategic satellite. I had seen the importance of persevering as we'd sought to get onto the Egyptian and Turkish regulated satellites in past years.

Ten months after submitting our original application, in early October, I decided to directly call Mohammed Omar, the satellite's chief operating officer in the UAE. He recognized the name of SAT-7 PARS and immediately became defensive. I tried to put him at ease by telling him that I understood his concerns and that, operating from and broadcasting to Muslim-majority countries, he had every right to be fearful of giving a satellite channel to an obviously Christian channel. "But," I challenged him, "would you mind if I told you a bit about SAT-7?"

He politely acquiesced, and so I told him in detail about how we had broadcast licenses from the UK, were currently broadcasting on the Egyptian- and Turkish-regulated satellites, had registered offices in Egypt, Lebanon, and Turkey, worked with all the different churches in the region, had a program policy that prohibited the criticism of any other religion, and so on.

Mohammed respectfully listened to my monologue without interruption. When I finished, and without any commitments other than to run this by his board, he asked me to put everything I had told him in writing. The next day, I sent him a six-page briefing paper, complete with details of our licences and legal registrations, and even a photo of our international board. Mohammed immediately acknowledged the email and said he would get back to me shortly.

After four weeks of patiently waiting, I followed up on my email, stressing that it would be helpful to hear back from him soon as our own board planned to meet in the near future and would like to be briefed on the situation. Again I received a polite reply, explaining that things were taking longer than he had expected, but that he would get back to me as soon as he could. And again, weeks went by in which I heard nothing.

The new year arrived, and I put out another reminder. The response was the same: they needed more time. I followed up again in February, with the same result. I was now losing hope, and we began to look for other options. I gave it one more try in mid-March.

To my surprise, Mohammed replied, asking if we could meet at CABSAT 2017—the region's cable and satellite trade fair in Dubai—at the end of the month. I had been to this event several times in the past, but was already committed to other meetings this year, so I asked our chief operations officer, Andrew Hart, to go and meet with Mohammed.

Andrew returned from Dubai with the news that the meeting had gone well, but it was unclear about what had brought them to their current openness. In any case, they agreed in principle that they would carry SAT-7 PARS on the new satellite, beginning in May.

We were thrilled and immediately entered into technical discussions concerning how we would deliver the signal to them in the Gulf. These discussions went right through to early May, with all parties signing the agreements a mere four days before we went on-air with a full 24/7 schedule on May 15.

Our prayers and perseverance had paid off. We doubled our potential viewing audience overnight.

However, we were unsure whether or not SAT-7 PARS would encounter a political reaction, since it was the only Christian channel on this Arab-owned satellite, so we delayed any publicity about it for several weeks. New viewers soon found us anyway and began publicly congratulating us for being on the new satellite platform. In fact, the number of viewer responses doubled over the following twelve months, with a ten-fold increase in responses coming from Afghanistan!

One of our new viewers called from Iran. He lived in a village where they performed something like a Passion play each year. In their tradition they had an annual parade where people from the village dressed up as prophets of Islam and paraded through the streets. For many years this caller had dressed up as *Isa*, or as we would call him, Jesus, and had carried a giant cross through the town.

This year, after the parade finished, he had a dream in which he met a man dressed in dazzling white who said to him, "All these years you have acted as Me, don't you want to know Me?"

The next morning when he awoke, he started flicking through television channels and came across SAT-7 PARS. Immediately he knew this was the place where he would get to know the man from his dream. A few days later he phoned our audience relations team to learn more.

More Space, More Programs

With an increasing number of shows now coming from the small studio in Limassol each week, we had begun to run out of space for sets, creative camera angles, makeup and changing rooms, and editing suites. So in parallel to the negotiations for the new satellite, we also began exploring our options for a larger studio space. We eventually found a suitable unit in a remote industrial estate on the outskirts of Limassol, and in August 2016, I signed a lease agreement. The space was huge—sixty thousand square feet—which gave each show its own permanent set, saving us hours in taking down and rebuilding sets each week. The only drawback was that the new place was hard for studio guests, and even staff, to find.

At this time, we also underwent yet another change in leadership, with the appointment of Panayiotis Keenan as SAT-7 PARS's new executive director. Although not Iranian, he had a strong television production background, which we desperately needed. He also had dual British-Cypriot nationality, allowing him free movement between our two main production centers in Limassol and London. His first responsibility was to get the new studio space in Cyprus up and running in time for our special live Christmas programs.

Many new programs launched over the coming months and years, and not just from our own studios in Cyprus and London, but also from those of our valued partners in Helsinki, Paris, California, Ontario, and other locations. The programs included: Tajik programs; *Signal*, a live call-in show for youth where many viewers share powerful testimonies and prayers; *Heavenly Worship*, for Christian viewers to watch as their church service or with their house church; *Safe Home*, a comedy-drama series charting the highs and lows of a newly married couple who are both new believers, with a well-known Iranian actress playing a lead role; *The Sound of Hope*, addressing the problem of drug addiction, which directly or indirectly affects the lives of an estimated 6 million Iranians; *Insiders,* a live chat show dealing with the challenges facing girls and women in Iran and sensitively tackling difficult subjects not discussed elsewhere in the media; *Café Bahar*, a youth drama series shot in Paris, addressing daily problems faced by young people everywhere; and *A Girl's World*, aimed at teen females in Iran.

We also launched a new website with an extensive library of programs and other Christian resources, as well as live streaming services.

And we continued to hear from viewers.

One longer-term viewer called in to share her story. Elmira's family had forced her to marry when she was just eleven years old. By her fifteenth birthday, she had two children. Sadly, her husband was a drug addict, and he forced her into prostitution to fund his habit.

"Being a woman in my world hurt so much," she said. Over the next fourteen years, Elmira became HIV positive and lived as a virtual slave. Even though she did not know what the future held, Elmira eventually found the courage to run away. Broken and depressed, she came across SAT-7 PARS.

"I felt like I was nothing, lost! I didn't know how anyone would reach me, but then one day I heard on your television service that I really was loved. That God could help me with everything. I wish my life had been different, but what I heard on your program that day changed everything. I continued to watch your channel and learned that God loves me—despite all that I had done. I gave my heart to Jesus."

Watching the channel changed Elmira's whole future. At the guidance of our counselors, she began attending a local house church, where she also met and eventually married a Christian man. "He loves me and treats me with respect," she shared.

Predicting the Future

We can only guess at what the future will be for the church in Iran. But a recent study of fifty thousand Iranians has given us new insights into what is happening in the country. The study, "Iranians' Attitudes toward Religion: A 2020 Survey Report," conducted by the Netherlands-based "Group for Analyzing and Measuring Attitudes in Iran" (GAMAAN), showed that approximately half of Iran's population of 84 million reported "losing their religion." Eight percent of the total population self-identified as being atheist; and 1.5 percent, or 1.25 million people, identified as being Christian. At least 90 percent of these Christians are people who had made the decision to convert to Christianity.[1]

God is clearly at work in Iran, and we should remember in prayer our brothers and sisters in this new and still emerging church. It has been a great privilege for me and my colleagues to be a small part of what our Lord is doing in this ancient and important nation.

1. Maleki and Arab, "Iranian's Attitudes toward Religion."

The SAT-7 international board, July 2004.

Satellite dishes on a building in Casablanca, 2006.

Hormoz, Vruir, and Joseph during time-out at an ICB board meeting, April 2001.

Sara Afshari, the first executive director of SAT-7 PARS, November 2007.

Kenan Araz, the Turkish brother with three kidneys and a big smile, circa 1973.

In Istanbul with MEM founder, John E. Ferwerda, winter 1993.

SAT-7 TÜRK executive director, Melih Ekener and chair, Tamar Karasu at a board meeting in Istanbul, January 2015.

Posing with me as *Charlie's Angels* during a break at Network meetings: Turkish programming manager, Gülsüm; SAT-7 PARS executive director, Sara; and Arabic programming director, Rita, November 2009.

Gavin at a press conference in London with his surgeons, holding the pellet they had removed from his left eye after he was shot in Tahrir Square, Cairo, at the start of the Arab Spring, April 2011.

Members of the SAT-7 international board celebrating SAT-7's fifteenth anniversary of being on-air. Lebanon, June 2011.

Mar Gregorios Yohanna Ibrahim, the Syrian Orthodox Archbishop of Aleppo speaking at Network 2013, just four weeks before being abducted in northern Syria on April 22.

Giving the international keynote address at the National Religious Broadcasters' 2013 convention in Nashville, Tennessee.

Joining me: SAT-7 ARABIC's programming manager, George Makeen; SAT-7 Egypt's executive director, Farid Samir; and Father Joseph, in Baghdad the week before the rise of the so-called Islamic State in Iraq and Syria (ISIS), June 2014.

Maronite Patriarch Bechara Boutros Al-Raii, together with SAT-7 international council chair, Rev. Dr. Habib Badr, at the official opening of the new SAT-7 studios in Lebanon, November 2014.

SAT-7's international management team meeting in Lebanon, July 2015.

Rita El-Mounayer visiting Syrian refugee children in the Bekaa Valley, Lebanon in
November 2015, as plans were being made to launch SAT-7 ACADEMY.

The SAT-7 executive board and international management team, meeting in Cairo, November 2019.

Chapter 9

Into Turkey

My first experience of Turkey came at the end of a long and cautious drive from Vienna along snow-covered roads in the early spring of 1973. After having spent several months working as couriers taking Bibles into Eastern Europe, Jackie and I were now driving overland to Beirut, Lebanon, where we would be taking up our next assignment and, in the process, delivering a reconditioned Volkswagen station wagon to the director of the work there.

As we entered Istanbul the snow abruptly cleared, and the traffic was suddenly moving at a pace I had not seen before. This was my baptism by fire into Middle East driving. To make matters worse, there on the highway into the capital was a Turk with his car stationary in the fast lane while he changed a flat tire!

Our hosts for our first visit to Turkey were Kenan and Jenny Araz. Kenan was a Turkish believer who always wore a radiant smile. He would tell everyone about his "Big Father," the one who had saved him and shown Kenan His love in extraordinary ways.[1]

Kenan and I had a number of things in common: We had both studied civil engineering; we were both involved in Christian publishing; and we had both married during the previous autumn, within ten days of each other and in the same city. But, otherwise, we could not have come from more different backgrounds.

1. Farnham, *My Big Father.*

Kenan was born Amanuel, the oldest son to an upper-middle-class Assyrian family in the city of Midyat, which lies in the southeast of Turkey, near the Syrian border. He grew up speaking Assyrian, Kurdish, Arabic, and Turkish. He later changed his obviously Christian name by deed poll to Kenan, a more distinctively Turkish name. He was proud to be a Turkish Christian, which seemed like an oxymoron for the many who have always equated being Turkish with being Muslim.

His family sent Kenan to boarding school in Istanbul when he was seventeen, and it was there, in the mid-1960s, that he met other believers and committed his life to Christ. From his early days as an active believer, he got involved in helping publish different Christian books and pamphlets to support the witness of the very small but growing Protestant community in the city.

On our first evening in Istanbul, Kenan shared more of his story. In 1970, he became seriously ill and was in danger of dying from kidney failure. Through a series of miraculous interventions, he ended up in a London hospital for a kidney transplant, which his mother donated. Upon his return to Turkey, he would introduce himself to strangers with the question, "Have you ever heard of a man with three kidneys?" And from there, the conversation became his testimony to all that God had done for him.

It was while in that London hospital that he reconnected with Jenny, who had previously volunteered with Operation Mobilization in Turkey. Two years later they were married and setting up home in Istanbul, a home that was always welcoming guests and people passing through, such as Jackie and me.

The next morning, Kenan showed us around Istanbul. It was a cold and dirty city. Even the snow piled at the sides of the road was filthy, mostly as a result of the smoke from the many coal fireplaces that were choking the atmosphere. At that time, Istanbul was on a par with Cairo—a big, noisy, overpopulated city with an exhausted infrastructure. But to compare the two cities today would be like comparing night and day; Turkey has developed much more, especially since the turn of the century.

After a brief stay with Kenan and Jenny, we needed to continue on our journey to Lebanon, which would take us across the Bosphorus—the busy waterway that divides the city, separating Europe from Asia and connecting the Black Sea to the Mediterranean. In the spring of 1973, the first suspension bridge was being built across the water. But since the bridge would not be opened for another six months, we had to take the car ferry.

On the ferry I got out of the car to take photos of the bridge. Having spent the last few years working in a bridge design office, I was intrigued by the beauty and sheer scale of this structure, with its amazing more than half-a-mile span. Jackie decided to join me on the upper deck and carefully locked the car as she got out, not noticing that I had left the keys in the ignition switch. As the ferry entered the port on the Asian side, we suddenly realized we were locked out and blocking others from moving off the ferry as well. Fortuitously, a local appeared, sheepishly offering help. Within thirty seconds he had skillfully managed to get into the car through the quarter-light window and had opened the door. His easily and quickly managed entrance presented a shock to us as all our worldly possessions were in this station wagon, and until now, we had trusted that it was secure!

Over the coming two decades, I returned many times to Istanbul. In 1974, Kenan and I began working together on the Turkish version of *The Living Bible.* One of my roles at that time was as the Middle East production coordinator for Living Bibles International (LBI). We then opened a book distribution company, and eventually I got to share with the churches there many of the other new media initiatives we were taking in the Arab World, like getting Christian literature out on the newsstands and into secular bookstores and, eventually, producing Christian television programs for an audience outside the Christian community.

Turkey's Christian community at that time, including new believers and those born into traditionally Christian families, was and remains far less than 1 percent of its total population, making it difficult to believe that this was once the center of the Christian World. It was in Antioch in south-central Turkey that the followers of Christ were first given the name Christians. And it was in AD 313, from his throne in Constantinople (now Istanbul), that the Emperor Constantine mandated tolerance for Christianity in the Roman Empire.

Modern Turkey also encompasses many sites that were central to the development of the early Christian church—Sardis, Laodicea, Galatia, and Cappadocia. People come from around the world to pray, study, and learn at the ruins of ancient Ephesus and the other six churches mentioned in the book of Revelation. And yet, today, Turkey is a country with the smallest percentage of Christians in the world.

A Vision for This Ancient Biblical Land

In the late 1990s, Merle Hochstetler, manager of Middle East Media's (MEM) book publishing work in Istanbul, closed down the work, and then opened a new company with a wider media brief, VIA İletişim. VIA was an acronym for Video, Internet, and Audio. This company also became the legal umbrella for a wider consortium of churches, agencies, and individuals interested in media of all kinds—publishing, radio broadcasts, video, television, and the performing arts—which met under the banner of Asia Minor Communications, AMC.

Merle invited me to present SAT-7 at an AMC meeting in Kuşadası on the west coast of Turkey, near İzmir. I arrived on November 29, 2000, the second day of Ramadan, and found my way to the hotel—a beautiful holiday destination that offered steeply discounted group rates out of season. Several dozen people attended the seminar but most remained skeptical about the possibilities of being able to do something like SAT-7 in Turkey, where there were so few believers relative to the Arab World. But at least, as some admitted to me later, it opened their eyes to the opportunity.

During its early years AMC was involved in a wide range of media activities, but by early 2002, it became more focused on television, having recognized that this was one area where they could make a unique contribution. They again tried to get some traction by inviting a range of agencies and churches to a consultation in May to discuss a potential broadcast television initiative for Turkey. Since their aim was to model it on the SAT-7 ministry and work in partnership with SAT-7, they extended another invitation to me so that I could again present the SAT-7 story. I enthusiastically agreed to go, but based on my many previous visits to the country, I was not expecting anything to happen quickly.

We met for two days in the Istanbul suburb of Kadikoy, in one of those gloomy, windowless, underground meeting rooms that budget hotels in Turkey seem to specialize in. After my detailed presentation, Pastor Ihsan spoke passionately about the potential of Christian television in Turkey, followed by a question-and-answer time and discussion.

The second day included a series of workshops and ended with us establishing a working group to consider next steps.

After the conference, Merle went on a year-long furlough to the United States, leaving the consultation follow-up responsibilities with the small AMC team: Fatma from Turkey, Kari Vitikainen from Finland, Kirk DeVries from the United States, and David Middleton, from Northern Ireland, who was also a trained architect.

David had not planned to get involved in media when he first went to Turkey with his wife, Ruth, in 1999. But a year later, after someone from AMC saw his publicity design work for a live theater play in Istanbul about the life of Jesus, he was invited to join the organization.

I promised the working group that I and other SAT-7 staff would remain available to help as we could, with both advice and training.

During Merle's absence, AMC staff became increasingly frustrated over the lack of communication between him, the AMC team, and the television working group in Turkey. That frustration continued to grow following another television consultation in April 2003, which also included representatives from local and international media agencies.

Over the course of the two days, it became clear that the existing AMC structure was not going to be an attractive way to engage a wider partnership—mainly because it was not legally incorporated and its operating company VIA İletişim was privately owned by Merle and one other individual. To discern the best next steps, it was agreed to set up a study group that could consider the best future partnership structure and report back to the potential partners as soon as possible.

I was one of those appointed to the group, and of course I brought my own ideas and experience on what had worked well and not so well in the SAT-7 model. As in the case of ICB, I respected the independence of this Turkish initiative and saw the great value in the believers of Turkey "owning" it. It would not work in the best way if outside parties controlled it, no matter how well intentioned they might be. My role now was just to ensure that SAT-7 resources and experience would be available if and as needed to support this important start-up.

Introducing TURK-7

Over the following months, the study group met several times, and agreed on a new partnership structure, which they circulated to potential partners for an entity that we were now calling TURK-7. Two of the team members, Fatma and David, handled a lot of behind-the-scenes diplomacy and church presentations to pave the way for the founding TURK-7 partnership meeting, which we held in central Istanbul on October 8, 2003. Some eleven local churches and the same number of international agencies were represented, with fourteen of these having already committed to being partners in the project. Willy Svahn from Sweden was elected as the facilitating chair for the meeting.

During the meeting we discussed, tweaked, and adopted the proposed new TURK-7 constitution and bylaws, and we elected a founding board of seven persons, including myself. The group unanimously elected Kamil, a Protestant minister in Izmir, to serve as the chair of the new board. We were excited about the prospects of this new television channel, and felt that our meeting was a good beginning.

I attended the first meeting of the new TURK-7 board a few weeks later, on November 17, in Istanbul. David Middleton was formally appointed as the channel's first executive director and Fatma as its operations director. Fatma had been the accountant for the original MEM book publishing ministry and during the formation of TURK-7 had worked closely with the Turkish churches and partners in particular, playing a key role in developing and building the fledgling partnership.

With the exception of this one-day TURK-7 board meeting, my main purpose for being in Istanbul was to take part in several days of meetings with Iranian Christians, being held in yet another subterranean conference hall, this time at the Grace Hotel. This was an annual international meeting of Iranian Christians and ministries focused on Iran, and they happened to be meeting in Istanbul in 2003. I was therefore staying at the Grace Hotel, in a room overlooking the grounds of the British embassy. I had to leave one day before the meetings finished in order to attend other meetings in Beirut before the public holidays to mark the end of Ramadan began.

At 11:00 a.m. on the last morning of the meetings, while the Iranians were still in their basement hall, a massive truck bomb went off right in front of the embassy, blowing in all the hotel windows, and even the door of their underground meeting room. This explosion was one in a series of four carried out that week by a militant Turkish group linked to Al-Qaeda. Sixteen people were killed in this incident, and several hundred more were injured, some very seriously.

The Iranian brothers and sisters still in the hotel were of course shaken up, but I was amazed and delighted to hear that none of them was seriously injured. This was God's protection on all those in the meeting. Had anyone been in one of the guest rooms when the bomb went off, they would most certainly not have survived. It took several hours for those who had not yet checked out of the hotel to get back to their damaged rooms and disentangle their personal effects from the metal window frames that had been completely blown into the rooms, scattering glass and dust everywhere. While the hotel was thankfully still standing, it was structurally damaged and had to be demolished in the following days.

Sadly, a total of 60 people were killed in the Istanbul bombings that week and another 750 were injured.

In December that year, a television production "Discovery Day" was held with training sessions that MEM's Wayne Larson led. Thirty people from local churches attended with many showing interest in further training and signing up for twelve-day workshops in script-writing, single camera production, and basic editing, to be held early the following year.

One of the people who attended the training was Debora, a Chaldean Christian who had grown up in a believing family.

In January 2004, her pastor received an advertisement for the workshops and insisted that Debora participate. So, with the support of her family, she attended the training and proved to be a quick learner. She enjoyed meeting new friends and was excited to get involved with this new ministry. She began by taking on small roles in the production team and joined the team full-time the following year. She worked in many areas, starting with holding reflectors and microphone booms, then acting as a camerawoman and later as an editor. She eventually became a program director and then the editing director. From the beginning, Debora enjoyed working with people from different cultures and backgrounds, calling them her family, and she passionately believed in the wider vision to broadcast the gospel to her people.

A Clash of Cultures

By May 2004, the team had begun to grow, with it being a mix of local believers and foreign staff on loan to TURK-7. They had produced several programs, including a pilot magazine-format show, a Christmas program, a documentary on the concept of sacrifice (*kurban*), and some children's programs—original shows and dubbed animation. Everyone hoped that we could sell some of this programming to a secular Turkish channel, pending the opportunity to launch our own TURK-7 channel.

In the summer of 2004, an opportunity seemed to open up for future broadcasting. Eurasiasat, a satellite co-located with Türksat, and that could therefore be viewed by the same audience, was offering to let Christian programs go on its platform despite the fact that this was 75 percent owned by Türk Telekom. The company was based in Monaco. Our chair, Kamil, and the then-representative of our Swedish partner TV-Inter, Arne Winerdal, encouraged us to try for a channel, even though we were not yet anywhere near ready to operate a 24/7 satellite channel in Turkish, either in terms of being able to produce the volume of programming needed or being able to find the $250,000 a year to lease such a channel.

By the spring of 2005, we learned through third parties that our chair was in separate, undisclosed discussions with different Scandinavian and American organizations, some of whom were partners with TURK-7, concerning the launch of a separate Turkish channel. The attraction was that this would get on-air sooner than TURK-7 by following the more typical funding model for Christian television, relying mostly on sponsored, dubbed programming from Pentecostal preachers in the West. The channel also planned to carry some polemic programming of the kind that would not be acceptable to the TURK-7 board.

That May, the TURK-7 board determined it best to replace the chair, and elected pastor Carlos to take over the role. They also decided to end the formal partnership with the TURK-7 partners from Sweden who were involved in this new initiative and who would then go on to launch the only other Christian channel in Turkish today, Eurasia Christian TV (ECTV, later renamed Kanal Hayat). This was unexpected and discouraging for the board and team, after all the work we had accomplished.

ECTV was to start broadcasts on Eurasiasat in October 2006, but before broadcasts could begin, the company in Monaco went into liquidation and their satellite system was absorbed by the Turkish government controlled Türksat Organization, closing the door to such a Christian channel. Instead ECTV began broadcasting in March 2007 on the European HotBird satellite.

We later held talks with ECTV's management to explore ways in which we could possibly work together. But their US sponsors felt we were "not faithfully presenting the gospel" if we failed to explicitly point out to our viewers the errors in their religion.

I could not understand the theology or the logic of such a position. Challenging the authenticity of another person's religion would not win their trust or interest in what we wanted to tell them about our own. And offending potential viewers in this way would certainly not open the door for them to then encourage their families and friends to watch our programming.

Furthermore, such an approach would not endear us to the authorities in the Middle East, so we would end up broadcasting from outside the region, with on-air presenters from outside the region—people who would be increasingly out of touch with the daily life and changing opinions in their country.

Sadly, their position reminded me of my earlier reservations about Christian television and closed the door on future discussions and collaboration. They were far from the SAT-7 model and strategy that we had spent years developing with church leaders from the region, and which TURK-7 had also adopted. We confidently stood by our strategy to positively present the Christian faith through an authentic local witness, highlighting the difference that knowing Christ makes, rather than questioning the beliefs of others.

For TURK-7 to maintain its vision of being an independent voice for the Christians of Turkey, it would need to see a lot more funding come in—more than could be expected from the combined efforts of the local and international partners. David had already begun to make exploratory fundraising trips, but without dedicated people to help with this in the West, especially in the United States, funding would continue to be a major challenge.

The 2005–2006 strategic plan we envisaged began with a regular two hours per week of broadcasts on any available channel, in much the same way as SAT-7 ARABIC had started in 1996. But which satellite to use? None of the Turkish broadcasters on the government-regulated Türksat satellite showed any interest in carrying any of our programming—not even the children's programs or dubbed cartoons! But given the fact that these channels did not carry any Islamic religious programs either, their response was not totally surprising.

Broadcasts Begin

Eventually the TURK-7 board asked SAT-7 if they could begin their broadcasts on the SAT-7 channel. At that time, we were still broadcasting on the HotBird satellite, which covered Turkey as well and was the second most popular satellite in Turkey after Türksat, with a potential viewing audience of 16 million and many more in Western Europe. We agreed. After we commissioned the new SAT-7 Nicosia broadcast center, TURK-7 would begin broadcasting in early 2006.

SAT-7 ARABIC was going to need a link-satellite in 2006 to carry its signal from the new control room in Cyprus to our HotBird uplink provider in London. Remembering our earlier conversation with Arne Winerdal of TV-Inter, we applied to Eurasiasat for this satellite capacity, strategically thinking that any Turkish programming on this satellite would then become available to all the Turkish-speaking viewers of Eurasiasat. We began the negotiations in the summer of 2005, and all seemed to be going well. We reached agreement on a capacity, a price, and a start time, and all that was left was the final written contract. But in early November, just two months before we were to start, Euraisasat stopped answering emails or taking our calls.

What we did not fully understand at the time was that Türksat, as mentioned earlier, was in the process of taking over full control of Eurasiasat. Eventually their contract negotiator informally told us that they were no longer in a position to carry a Christian channel. With the support of the Fellowship of European Broadcasters (FEB), several members of the European Parliament appealed this decision. These eventually resulted in a letter from the chair of Türksat, saying that he knew nothing of our application and that, in any case, they no longer had spare capacity on the satellite.

During this period, I was flying to Istanbul three to four times a year, mostly to attend TURK-7 board or partner meetings. One of the other board members, Willy Svahn, was the representative of one of the founding partners of SAT-7, InterAct. Based in Limassol, Cyprus, Willy had chaired the founding meeting of TURK-7. He'd held many professional roles in the past, including being on the boards of different ministries and churches, and the chair of one of Sweden's biggest estate agencies. I enjoyed his great sense of humor and his collection of bizarre signs—road, restaurant, warning, direction, and others—that contained humorous mistakes or double meanings. I remember how he was always the last one to board our flights to Istanbul. I used to joke that he was so late for most flights that I was already settling into my seat on the plane and opening my newspaper as Willy "Lastminute.com" Svahn was arriving at check-in. But somehow he never seemed to miss a flight!

The first Turkish programs began broadcasting on the SAT-7 Arabic channel on January 10, 2006, and a week later, Willy and I again traveled together to Istanbul for a TURK-7 board meeting, arriving in the middle of a snowstorm. We stood in line for forty-five minutes waiting for a taxi to take us from the airport to downtown, wondering how and if we would be able to complete the journey on the icy roads and with the blinding snow. No problem! Our taxi driver had infrared vision and was able to drive at nearly fifty miles per hour on the almost-deserted and barely visible highway. It was one of my more horrifying taxi rides!

Everyone was delighted and thanking God that we were finally on-air with programs, though I wondered how long it would take our potential viewers to find two hours a week of Turkish programming on an Arabic channel, which, by then, was also carrying a daily two-hour block of Farsi programs. But people did find us, and the Turkish press gave us huge publicity—out of all proportion to the scope of the initial broadcasts. This helped people discover the programs, and the phones began to ring with positive, as well as a few negative, calls from viewers. We also received emails from all over Turkey, and from the many Turks living and working in Germany.

One viewer, Berk, sent us a message saying that he had recently been released from prison. While he was there, he'd made friends with a few Christians. "I started reading the Bible," he said. "After some time I decided that Christ is credible and close to my heart. When I was reading the Bible . . . I can't describe the feelings I experienced. Since then, I consider myself a follower of Jesus. But outside of prison, I haven't found a Bible, and I don't have anyone to talk to about these things. While changing channels I came across your wonderful programs. I started watching them and wanted to write you. Maybe you can help me learn more about Christ? Also, could you please guide me to someone I could talk to here? I would be so glad. There aren't many churches in this area of Turkey, so I really appreciate your help."

In an effort to boost awareness of the new broadcasts, we took out ads in several national newspapers and tried to get press coverage where possible, with some news agencies even interviewing David and Fatma. And though we were overjoyed by the response we received, we still had the very-real challenge of finances to contend with. Some of the TURK-7 partners, including SAT-7, were channeling gifts as they came. And, of course, SAT-7 was also providing the satellite time free of charge for these early transmissions. But much more was needed if we were to produce the kind of attractive programs that would grow our audiences in Turkey.

It was interesting to see that many of the initial responses to the broadcasts came from Azeri speakers in Iran, who understood Turkish and Farsi and had already been watching the PARS programs on the channel. This helped us see the added value of later moving all the TURK-7 programs from SAT-7 ARABIC to the new SAT-7 PARS channel when it launched in December 2006. The SAT-7 PARS channel, because it too was in a startup phase, was able to give the TURK-7 team a generous four hours per day of airtime. As wonderful as that was, it had its program production challenges, and meant a lot more work for the still small TURK-7 team!

Until this point, the team had handled much of the production in confined spaces inside the TURK-7 offices or in rented third-party studios and church buildings. However, at the end of the year, another apartment became available in the same building as the Istanbul office, so we quickly rented it and dedicated it as studio space. This was still far from a proper studio, with no professional sound insulation, no high ceilings for the best positioning of lights, and so on, but it was ten times better than the team had had to work with until then. Even with this new space, we still needed to undertake some of the production in partner studios in Europe, and much of the dubbing work for Christian films, documentaries, and children's programs continued to be contracted out to local studios in Istanbul.

Apart from now making news, testimony, church history, teaching, and children's programs, the team chose to dub some of the Christian Arabic dramas, which SAT-7 ARABIC had produced in Lebanon—including *AsSabil* (*The Way*), a seventy-two-part soap opera coproduced with the Lebanese Broadcasting Corporation (LBC).

The Malatya Martyrs

Just before the 2007 TURK-7 Annual General Meeting in Istanbul, a shocking event took place in Malatya, a Turkish province a few hundred miles northeast of Antioch, the city where believers were first called Christians.

On April 18, five assailants entered the Zirve Publishing House in Malatya and brutally tortured to death three of its employees: Christian converts Uğur Yüksel and Necati Aydın and German national Tilman Geske. Necati was an actor who played the role of Jesus in a theater production that TURK-7 had recorded in front of a live audience of more than two thousand people and aired over the Easter holidays only a few days earlier.

Gökhan Talas, the chief witness, who years later became the SAT-7 TÜRK broadcast manager, came with his wife to the Zirve office that morning. The door was locked from inside, which was unusual. Suspecting that something had happened, he called Uğur Yüksel, not knowing that he was inside tied to a chair. Under pressure, Uğur replied that they were in a hotel for a meeting. But Gökhan

heard someone crying in the background during the call and decided
to phone the police, who arrived soon thereafter.

The five perpetrators were caught at the scene of the crime and
had actually video recorded everything on their cell phones. In total, eleven suspects were apprehended after the attack. The apparent
ringleader, Yunus Emre Günaydın, was treated for serious wounds
after he attempted to jump out of a window to escape police. All of
the alleged killers were between nineteen and twenty years old.

When apprehended, the suspects were carrying a note that said
in part, "We did it for our country. They are trying to take our country away, take our religion away."

The responses to what soon became known by Turkish media
as the "missionary massacres" were mixed. The then prime minister,
Recep Tayyip Erdoğan, denounced the killings "as savagery" but the
justice ministry statutes directorate general manager, Niyazi Güney,
reportedly declared, "Missionary work is even more dangerous than
terrorism and unfortunately is not considered a crime in Turkey."

The complex process of prosecution went on for another decade,
with the case being linked to shadowy groups and the trials of other
ultranationalists, and the lawyers for the victims being threatened
and intimidated.

It was not until September 28, 2016, that the First Criminal
Court in Malatya finally sentenced each of the five perpetrators to
three consecutive life sentences for murder. The defendants appealed
the case but on July 18, 2017, the Third Criminal Chamber of Ga-
ziantep District Court upheld the sentences, and this seems to be the
end of the matter.

Aydın was survived by his wife, Şemse, and a son and daughter,
both preschool age. Geske was survived by his wife, Susanne, and
three children ages eight to thirteen. Yüksel was engaged.

Other Attacks

These ugly murders reminded me of other similar incidents in modern Turkey, where committed followers of Jesus, leaders in the small

Christian community, had their lives cut short through murder or disease. Was this a spiritual battle that was going on in what Operation World has long called "the most unevangelized country in the world"? Was that too what our team at TURK-7 was potentially facing?

The year before the Malatya murders, in 2006, a priest was shot dead in the Black Sea province of Trabzon, which coincided with worldwide protests over the Danish cartoons of the Prophet Muhammad. Two other priests were also attacked that year.

Then earlier in 2007, the Armenian-Turkish editor Hrant Dink was also murdered by an ultranationalist, which prompted us to take extra security measures for our own staff. Dink was also from Malatya.

And then there was Archbishop Mesrob II Mutafyan, the Armenian patriarch of Constantinople. David and I had the privilege of meeting with him several times in 2005. The patriarch was a very educated man who had grown up in Germany and gone on to study philosophy and sociology in the United States. He was ordained to the priesthood in 1979, taking the name Mesrob and continuing his theological studies in Jerusalem, and later in Rome.

He began his ministry as a pastor on one of the Princes' Islands in the Sea of Marmara just outside Istanbul, and seven years later became a bishop, coordinating the ecumenical relationships of the Armenian Patriarchate.

In 1993, he was elevated to the rank of archbishop and, following the death of Patriarch Karekin II, Mutafyan was elected the eighty-fourth Armenian Patriarch of Constantinople on October 14, 1998.

Archbishop Mesrob was especially excited about the potential of TURK-7 to touch the lives of the estimated four million Turks who are the descendants of mixed marriages, having some Armenian heritage. He gave me his personal email and asked me to help him with sourcing some books dealing with apologetics, so he could prepare a series of talks for TURK-7 aimed at presenting the logic of the Christian faith. He also made an interview to be broadcast the following Armenian Orthodox Christmas, during our first broadcasts.

In May 2005, a few weeks after one visit, the patriach wrote us the following letter:

> Gentlemen,
>
> Thank you for your recent letter, enclosing details of the TURK-7 television service and inviting the Armenian church and community to consider formally joining in partnership with this ministry, which you shared with me at our meeting last month.
>
> In reply, first I wish to say that we fully support and appreciate the genuine desire to involve all the churches of Turkey in this project. We are pleased to note that the structure for the ministry described in the documents you have given us enables individual partnering churches to have a real voice and a sense of ownership of the project.
>
> Furthermore we believe that such a ministry could help to sustain and encourage members of the Armenian church in Turkey in their faith and service to Christ. With this in mind we are pleased to inform you we wish to enter into further discussions to agree the precise nature of our churches' involvement and how we can best contribute to the project.
>
> We wish you to consider this letter a preagreement to partnership, being subject to the outcome of these discussions and the subsequent approval of our respective governing bodies.
>
> We look forward to hearing from you.
>
> Yours Sincerely,
> MESROB II
> Armenian Patriarch of Istanbul and All Turkey

We were thrilled by this response. So it came as a great shock for me to learn, just a year or two later, that Archbishop Mesrob, still in his early fifties, was suffering from the early onset of Alzheimer's. He was obliged to withdraw from all his duties and from public life, even though he officially remained patriarch and archbishop in name. He sadly passed away a decade later. Though it wasn't a deadly attack by another person, his death from disease was a severe loss to the church in Turkey—and to TURK-7—just the same.

Another enthusiastic supporter of TURK-7 was Bishop Luigi Padovese who, in 2004, was appointed as the bishop of Monteverde and the vicar apostolic of Anatolia in Turkey.

On May 22, 2010, he wrote to us (translated from the Turkish):

Dear Board and Partners,

Due to my not being in Turkey on the day of your annual general meeting, I am writing to send you all greetings on behalf of the Council of Catholic Bishops in Turkey. I want to thank you for accepting us into the partnership and, on behalf of other bishops in Turkey, to say that we appreciate the ecumenical ethos of this joint project.

For a long time now, our churches have gone their separate ways in life. We have been like small streams, never a single, strong river.

May this cooperation strengthen the faith of our brothers and sisters and may our lives in this world demonstrate that we are disciples of one Master. I understand this to be the will of our heavenly Father.

I am pleading with our Lord that this meeting will have a positive outcome and bring real blessing. May the peace of the Lord be with you.

Respectfully,
Luigi Padovese

Tragically, just twelve days later, on June 3, sixty-three-year-old Bishop Padovese was fatally stabbed at his summer residence in southern Turkey. Witnesses claim that the perpetrator shouted "Allahu Akbar" ("God is great") during the assault, then severed the bishop's head.

For the previous four-and-a-half years, Bishop Padovese's driver, Murat Altun, had been receiving treatment for psychological disorders and was detained the same day by Turkish police. He confessed that he had killed the bishop on a "revelation" that identified him as the antichrist. Turkish police believe the murder was not politically motivated.

Two months before his murder, Bishop Padovese had written a letter to nuns in the Monastery of St. Clare of Camerino, Italy, asking for them to pray for the "martyred lands" in the region. His letter read, "The Churches of the Middle East have endured situations of great tribulation for years, which often culminate in acts of real persecution, as happens, sadly, every day in Iraq and in other countries. . . . The fruitfulness of forgiveness, as opposed to the sterility of hatred and vengeance, is the key to peace in the Middle East."

Bishop Padovese's death was, like so many others before, a terrible loss to the church in Turkey. People began to wonder just how many more such losses could the Christian community bear?

For me, it reinforced the importance of a Turkish-language Christian television channel that could address the many misconceptions Turks have about Christians and Christianity; a channel that could present the gospel, making God's love visible to millions who might never otherwise hear.

Chapter 10

SAT-7 TÜRK

The death of the three believers in Malatya cast a somber mood over the TURK-7 partnership meetings in Istanbul in May 2007. There was a feeling of vulnerability, and questions consumed people's minds concerning whether it was really appropriate to broadcast Christian programs into the country at a time of such extremism. Was it not just too provocative?

But for others, it was a time to stand up and be salt and light, to show the power of forgiveness—as the grieving families in Malatya had so powerfully and publicly expressed. So instead of retreating, the tone of the meetings became one of resolutely moving forward toward having a dedicated Turkish Christian channel on Türksat.

However, funding was still slow in coming in, and we had yet to find a full-time fundraiser in the United States. So David Middleton, the executive director, floated the idea that he might move back to the UK with his family in a year's time to help strengthen the development work, visiting the Istanbul office every six weeks. We certainly needed to see more income if we were to double the hours of new production in 2008, from the projected one hundred hours in 2007, and begin new weekly programs for women and for children.

Early in 2008, we appointed a new program chief, Serkan, to oversee all program production, as well as a full-time US director.

During this time several secular Turkish channels began streaming their programs on the internet, a new phenomenon in those days. The TURK-7 team started exploring the potential of this option as a test environment until we had our own satellite channel. We soon signed a contract with the subscription online provider, JUMP-TV, and we registered TURK-7 as a channel on YouTube. We also re-launched the TURK-7 website at the end of 2008, with pages to better support such web-streaming services.

But by year's end, we realized that some of the new initiatives in the United States to raise funds were not working out, and TURK-7 was facing major challenges in developing as an independent entity, especially in the areas of fund development, communications, and international legal and financial affairs. If TURK-7 was to remain viable, something had to be done soon.

Merging TURK-7 with SAT-7

One month later, at the January 2009 board meeting, David proposed a merger between SAT-7 and TURK-7.

That put me in a difficult position. While such a merger would remove some of the ambiguity about the relationship between SAT-7 and TURK-7, the timing was terrible. The world was in the midst of an acute recession, right after the mortgage scandals in the US and the collapse of banks on Wall Street. In addition, despite the fact that the SAT-7 vision had always included Turkey, we had not seen the same interest in Turkey by our supporters as they had shown over the past decade for our work in the Arab World or Iran. And I knew I would face resistance to such a merger from the SAT-7 board, our support offices, and some staff.

Finally, I was concerned that, with David now based back in Northern Ireland, there was no local or national leadership for the work in Turkey. David had assured us that he was working with the board to find a new, locally based executive director for TURK-7, even though the first round of interviews had failed to find a suitable candidate.

I emphasized to the TURK-7 board that, should such a merger go ahead, it would be important—for religious, cultural, and political reasons—that the work in Turkey retain its own responsible, independent board of directors and, where possible, its existing local and international partners. Since I was the CEO of SAT-7, I felt it best for me to leave the meeting at this point to allow the board to freely discuss the proposal without any potential sway from me.

They debated the pros and cons, recognizing the similarities between the two entities, such as policies, ethos, and strategy. However, the fact that SAT-7 was based in Cyprus, a land that remained in contention with Turkey over their 1974 intervention in the north of the country, raised some political concerns. After much deliberation, they agreed that the ultimate decision makers on such a big step should be the TURK-7 partners. So the board wrote to them laying out the options and to let them know it would be on the agenda at the May 2009 Annual General Meeting. If the partners supported such a merger, then the conversation would move to the SAT-7 international board the following month.

Before the May meeting, twenty-five of the twenty-seven partners indicated being in favor of pursuing a merger with SAT-7, though they still had questions. The partners met on May 26 in Istanbul. After receiving reports from David Middleton and the board chair, Carlos, most of the rest of the meeting focused on the proposed merger.

They discussed the advantages: the display of Christian unity—showing Arab, Iranian, and Turkish believers working together; the cost-efficiency of sharing support office costs and of jointly acquiring new Christian films, documentaries, and animation for dubbing into Arabic, Farsi, and Turkish; and sharing organizational experience and other resources such as training and software. Then they considered the concerns, in particular the potential loss of autonomy.

After lengthy debate, the partners voted unanimously, with three abstentions, to proceed with a merger. Next, the proposal moved to SAT-7's international board.

Carlos attended that meeting the following month, held in Ain Saadeh, Lebanon, where he explained the background to TURK-7 and their desire to merge with SAT-7. After his presentation, I took the floor and passionately reminded the board how, in addition to the Arab World and Iran, Turkey had always been part of SAT-7's founding vision. I reminded them that TURK-7's ethos and policies had been modeled on SAT-7's, making this merger not only strategic but a relatively simple process.

Then the discussion began. Some members were concerned over the potential danger of losing some of TURK-7's existing partners, exacerbating the lack of financial support for the channel. This was especially important, because SAT-7 also needed to consider the financial feasibility of taking on yet another channel at a time of severe global recession. Others again expressed worries about the political implications for SAT-7, as a Cypriot-based organization getting involved in Turkey.

Ziya, one of the international board members from Turkey and a political commentator, spoke about how such a collaboration between Arab, Iranian, and Turkish Christians would help bring the Turkish church into a wider regional fellowship, one that would enrich the whole church.

Again, after much deliberation, the board ultimately voted unanimously to support the merger.

In September, the TURK-7 board met for the last time as an independent entity. They finalized the proposed needed changes to their own constitution and bylaws and agreed on the new channel name—SAT-7 TÜRK—effective January 1, 2010. They were joining the SAT-7 family of channels, which now also included SAT-7 ARABIC, SAT-7 KIDS, and SAT-7 PARS.

In January 2010 the new SAT-7 TÜRK board met for the first time. I was thrilled by the strong sense of optimism everyone felt.

We needed that optimism. Fatma had been trying hard to find airtime on any Türksat channel but nothing was opening up, even on shopping channels. Following government permission for a Kurdish channel, and rumors that the popular cable operator Digitürk was open to the idea, we made a strategic effort to approach some of the public broadcasters to see if we could negotiate airtime for and on behalf of the churches. We formed a broadcast subcommittee in May 2010 to take the matter forward.

In addition, we needed to build a strong staff who could handle the job and remain true to SAT-7's vision, policies, and procedures.

Building a Staff

Gülsüm was one of our first hires. She had grown up in Istanbul as the middle child of three. Her father was often in trouble and, while she was used to her father's frequent absences and her parents' arguments, nothing prepared her for the day when her parents got divorced and her father left home for the last time. Like many Turkish women, her mother had never worked before, and the meager wages she now began to earn were not enough to pay the rent. They lost their home and spent a year staying with relatives.

"We were not a religious family, but I remember praying to God every day in those hard times," Gülsüm told me. "But nothing was going well. God was not answering my prayers, and I decided it was up to me to fix my life. I focused on school and studying and gave up praying."

Gülsüm's hard work at school and then at university paid off. In 2001, she graduated with a bachelor of arts in television and cinema. That same year she moved to New York City to continue her education—working three jobs to pay her fees. In 2006, now clutching a master's degree in media arts from a university in New York, she started work in the media, something she hoped would bring the security and fulfilment she was looking for.

A year later, she returned to Turkey and started working as an editor in TURK-7. "It was either a big coincidence or a part of God's plan!" Gülsüm said. Her cousin, who had come to Christ years before, told her about the channel, and his wife sent Gülsüm's resumé to us.

"I heard about Jesus for the first time there," Gülsüm said. "I even drafted scripts for Christian TV shows and read the Bible." Working on a thirteen-part documentary series called *The Living Church* gave her a great introduction to the rich history and teachings of the different churches in Turkey. Despite all this, she admitted, "My eyes were totally closed." She also struggled with a belief her university professors instilled in her: that media and religion do not mix. "Though I heard the Good News, all I was thinking about was my career," Gülsüm confessed.

After nine months with TURK-7, she left and subsequently worked for several other production companies. But she was not happy. "There were so many problems in the cut-throat media sector," she said. "I was entering my thirties and I felt things still weren't working out the way I'd hoped. Despite my master's degree and getting a dream job working on Turkish versions of *Sesame Street* children's programs, I was not enjoying my work."

Gülsüm started to compare the competitive culture she found in secular media with her experience at TURK-7. "The way people treated each other in TURK-7 was very special," she explained to me. "Everyone was working and serving as one body."

As she was trying to figure out her next move, she decided to take a break and, at the last minute, joined her mom and aunt on a short holiday in Cappadocia. This picturesque region of Turkey is famous for its strange pillar-like rock formations and rock-cut homes and underground cities. Here, from the fourth century, Christians sheltered from persecution and later came to live in monastic communities.

Gülsüm and her family visited some of the preserved, centuries-old churches and chapels and also watched the renowned local potters, whose every pot is unique.

While in Cappadocia Gülsüm sensed God speaking to her. "I had a short dream or vision," she said. "I saw myself in a church and I was praying and making the sign of the cross with my hand. I felt so relieved and peaceful at that moment. It was a feeling I had never felt before."

After the trip Gülsüm immediately visited her cousin's wife, who had earlier helped her get the job at TURK-7. This cousin-in-law invited Gülsüm to visit the church she attended with her husband, and challenged her: "Before you go, ask God one of the most important questions of your life. I am sure he will answer."

So she did. The day before she visited the church, she asked God, "Why does nothing go well in my life? Don't you love me?"

Soon into the service, she realized God had heard her. The sermon started with the question she had asked God. The preacher said, "Much of the time we ask God, 'God, don't you love me?' But God treats us like a potter does the clay pots, shaping us, sometimes painfully, to the unique shape of a useful pot."

As the preacher began to read the passage from Jeremiah 18 in which the Lord tells the prophet to visit the potter's house and see him shape the clay, Gülsüm was gripped. "I saw that God was trying to communicate with me."

After that day, she went home and started to read the Bible again—"but this time with a changed heart." During that year, she committed her life to Christ. With this decision came a desire to again join the ministry of TURK-7. However, the discussions had already begun concerning the merger with SAT-7, which meant I was personally involved in the interview process, especially as Gülsüm was being considered for a key programming position.

Though we had met briefly during Gülsüm's first time working with TURK-7, we did not know each other well. In fact, the only thing Gülsüm remembered from our first meeting in 2008 was me asking her if she was a Christian. When she said no, but she believed in God, my dry response was, "Well, that's better than being an atheist, I suppose!"

During the 2009 TURK-7 Annual General Meeting in Istanbul, I interviewed her for the position. I remained poker-faced during the interview and, according to Gülsüm, interjected long "hmms" between her answers and my next question.

"Are you now a Christian?" I asked.

She confirmed that she was.

"Have you been baptized yet?"

"No."

"Hmm. Well, that might be a problem."

But by the end of the interview, I felt confident that she was the right person for the job.

Shortly later, we offered her the position with TURK-7, soon to become SAT-7 TÜRK. In accepting the job, she admitted that her interview with me was the most difficult one she had ever had, and the only one where she left not knowing if she had gotten the job. She was baptized that September!

After years of seeking, she had found God as her good Father, and fulfilment in her new role with SAT-7 TÜRK, a channel that uniquely enabled her to share God's love with others in her culture.

With our new programming manager now in place, we turned our attention to other hires, but we were struggling to find Christian staff with television skills, and often had to take people who were at least sympathetic toward Christians and try to work with them. Gülsah was one such person, whom we hired to present Bible stories for children. However, whenever she mentioned God, whether she was reading an Old or New Testament story, she would always say His name in a fearful and dramatic way. Gülsüm challenged her on this interpretation, asking her why she made God sound so scary to our young viewers.

"Because He *is* scary!" Gülsah told her.

That conversation led to them discussing the issue in more depth, trying to address the image of God that Gülsah and many of her friends had grown up with in Turkey. Dozens of other such conversations took place in different departments as the team sought to be a witness not only on-air but also to its own staff.

The team slowly grew—but without a Turkish leader. We still had not found a new, local executive director, although we had interviewed several candidates. Finally, we found the right person in Melih Ekener. He agreed to start in January 2012.

Melih's Nagging Question

Melih was born in Üsküdar, referred to in ancient Greek literature as the "Golden City." Today it is a large and densely populated district of Istanbul, on the Asian side of the Bosphorus.

Melih's family were Orthodox Christians who, for political reasons, had converted to Islam after migrating from Albania during the Ottoman era. Growing up, Melih was a hard-working student and, according to his teachers, "hungry for knowledge," with a "grand imagination." From early on, he had the dream to become an academic at a university, helping humanity by introducing his country to new innovations from around the world.

But this dream ended at age fifteen, after the school system was disrupted by the 1980 military coup, which led to massive inflation and the arrest of five hundred thousand people, many of whom were teachers. Unable to continue at school, but having discovered a talent for acting as a member of the school's theater group, Melih applied and was accepted to study at the Istanbul Municipality Conservatoire.

In Melih's first year at the conservatoire, at the suggestion of a friend, he visited one of the oldest Latin Catholic churches in Istanbul, the Saint Antoine Church. His goal was to observe, for acting purposes, all that went on. But something deeper drew him in. He began to attend the church's weekly Bible study lessons, as an introduction to Christianity. It was here that Melih encountered the real Jesus Christ, one so different from the Christ he had been told about when growing up.

He had always been someone, even from an early age, who asked the difficult, existential questions of life. He had continuously been seeking answers. Though he had explored many beliefs before, in Christianity he felt he had discovered the real history of God on earth. From that point on, it became impossible for him not to believe. But Melih being Melih, he still had a lot of questions about the Christian faith! And it took a few years for him to get all the answers, as God spoke to him through His Word and through those He brought into Melih's life.

In fact, it took more than a decade after giving his life to Christ for Melih to feel ready to take the big step of being baptized. It was then that he had to go through the distressing police investigations and the legal harassment meted out to those who converted to a different belief in Turkey at that time.

His conversion also affected his ability to work. As an actor, he struggled to find a job in the industry. But God answered his prayers and opened doors for him, and he began to play leading roles in some of the best theaters in Turkey. Then followed the opportunity to act in long-running dramas on major television networks, often with huge audiences. Gradually his work grew to include producing and directing programs, and finally Melih moved into the world of cinema where he played leading roles in many of the country's most popular movies.

But a nagging question always seemed to follow him: "Why is it that I waste my time with fame and earthly riches, and get caught up in the plans of the evil one, when all I want to do is to walk the path that leads to God?"

When the fledgling TURK-7 team began making Christian programs in the small apartment in Kadikoy, they invited Melih to present a children's program. Melih's wife, Senem, had graduated from the University of California—Los Angeles, with a degree in cinema and television, and was to direct the show. While TURK-7's offer was a modest television role for Melih, he felt it was a strong, bold step to identify in such a way with a Christian television service. It was during this time that I first met Melih.

Now many years later, as we were considering potential candidates to the fill the role of executive director for the new SAT-7 TÜRK, I thought of Melih. So in September 2011, with the support of Senem and the board, I asked to meet with Melih. As we discussed the position, Melih immediately saw God's hand in preparing him for this moment. During the previous six months most of his demanding acting jobs in television, cinema, and radio had mysteriously ended, leaving him a little demoralized and without a regular income. Melih saw this as God clearing his schedule in order to consider the new role we were now offering him!

He and Senem took time to fast and pray about the offer, and eventually felt God leading him to accept the position, effective January 2012. Interestingly, right after he accepted the job and signed the contract, new theater, cinema, and radio acting opportunities started to once again present themselves. But Melih's commitment to Christian ministry was made and he felt that God had at last answered the nagging question that he had carried for so long.

But as he started with his new responsibilities, he faced a lot of seemingly impossible challenges. How could we become a 24/7 Christian Turkish channel when we had only a tiny studio with no space to expand? Or when we had only a few out-of-date cameras and no professional lighting? Or when we had a technical team of only four people? Not to mention how would we ever get all the needed permissions to get onto a Turkish government-regulated satellite?

There was an answer to those challenges. One I'd seen over and over: we had something that no other start-up television had—and that was faith!

Miracles at Work

Within the first four months of being on the job, Melih moved the whole operation to a massive basement under a supermarket in Kadikoy. The space had been used as a paintball gaming area but was inexpensively converted into two huge new studios with high ceilings to facilitate professional lighting. It also held ideal spaces for a control room, edit suites, changing rooms, set storage, and a green-screen recording area. The only downside was the fact that all the available offices were also underground, which administrative staff found difficult. There was also the not-insignificant challenge of equipping the new studio spaces with lighting and new professional cameras, some of which had to be rented until we could raise the needed funds to buy them.

This, however, did not slow down the production of several new, innovative programs addressing contemporary trends in Turkish culture. Or recording some fifty testimonies from new believers across Turkey. Or even adding a new teaching program that used the game of chess as a model to convey important Christian principles.

We also launched a new SAT-7 TÜRK website in 2012, with its own news service to help dispel misconceptions about Christianity and the church. And that October, we started a 24/7 web TV service. This would not only make programming more available online to Turks everywhere but also give the Turkish authorities an opportunity to better monitor and evaluate the nature of our programming as we began the seemingly impossible process of seeking a channel on Türksat.

The following year, in May 2013, I attended the annual SAT-7 TÜRK partner meetings in Istanbul and agreed with the local Bible Society to carry a number of Turkish Bibles back to Cyprus for use in the north of the island. As I was in our office, trying to cut down the boxes of Bibles to fit in my luggage, my hand slipped and the box cutter slit my left wrist, squirting blood everywhere. It was an alarming sight but looked much worse than it felt. Fatma and Buğra, Melih's assistant, rushed me to the local hospital emergency room where I got half a dozen stitches from a doctor who obviously suspected that I had just tried to commit suicide and, in Turkish, quietly urged my friends not to leave me alone!

I felt well enough to leave for the airport that evening for my scheduled flight back to Nicosia. But as I was putting my heavy bags on the scale at check-in, two of the stitches in my wrist tore, and I began bleeding again. The Istanbul airport medical staff said that they could call a doctor but that it would cost me several hundred dollars and they did not know how long he would take to get to the airport. I wasn't about to potentially miss my flight! So I had them tape up the wrist tightly and hurried off to the gate for my flight, leaving a trail of blood drips, much to the horror of other passengers. I still occasionally remind the Bible Society staff in Turkey that I "shed my blood in support of their good work!"

By that summer, the studios were fully equipped, enabling the team to produce new programs and get ready for the start of regular live programs in 2014. Even as everyone continued to work, we still had received no response to our application for a broadcast licence from the Turkish government, and the daily broadcasts were still limited to four hours per day on the SAT-7 PARS HotBird satellite channel.

At our meetings in January 2014, the TÜRK team and board were growing evermore impatient to begin their own channel. I continued to call for patience, believing that the door would open in God's time. But they were ready to compromise, giving up waiting for a response from the Turkish authorities and signing a contract for a European HotBird channel, even though it had a much smaller viewership of Turkish-speaking people than Türksat.

In April, and with some prompting from the deputy prime minister's office, the Radio and Television Supreme Council, RTÜK, at last invited us to submit a formal application for a Türksat broadcast license. The process involved two phases: (1) a study of the legal entity applying for the licence; and (2) an assessment of the company's technical capability.

Over the coming weeks, RTÜK requested more and more documents, which we complied with. By July 7, they passed our company through phase one and were ready to move to phase 2, the technical assessment. This was great news, although they wanted us to pre-pay the ten-year broadcast licence fees before proceeding to the second phase. This was the equivalent of just over $100,000!

In faith, we pulled together the finances and made the payment, and the technical inspectors came to our premises on August 6. Despite the fact that the power went out during their visit, and some of the audio equipment did not work as required, the inspectors left us with the impression that they would file a positive report, which would then go to the following week's meeting of the RTÜK board.

Exactly one week later we received the news that our license would be issued within two or three weeks. Everyone was ecstatic and we thanked God for this long-hoped-for moment. We were also conscious of and grateful for the openness of the Turkish authorities to engage with Christians and accept our application, opening the door for us to secure a frequency on the official Turkish satellite.

On September 15 the ten-year broadcasting license was delivered, with a start date of five days earlier, September 10, 2014.

The next day, September 16, Melih met with Türksat. They immediately offered us a channel on the Türksat 2A satellite. But just an hour after the meeting, they called Melih back to say that they could give us a better channel on the new Türksat 4A satellite, which had recently been launched and which was to begin broadcast operations the following day—to a potential audience of 50 million people. They asked us for our SAT-7 TÜRK logo to put on-screen with an announcement that we would begin broadcasts shortly on that channel. Things just kept getting better and better.

Türksat had asked for a cash prepayment equivalent to three months of airtime, which was almost immediately covered by a "love gift" from the Trinity Christian Center in Singapore. Everyone could see God working miracles.

All the staff were galvanized into action—working on schedules, promotional clips, press releases, and technical and playout issues.

The contract from Türksat arrived the next day, September 17. With great excitement, Melih signed it and sent it back with a courier, together with the receipt from the bank, which showed that we had sent to their account the initial three month's fees of the contract. Later in the day, Melih checked to see if they received the contract. They confirmed they had, and everything was in order. By the early evening our channel logo appeared on the frequency allocated to us, with a message saying that the channel would begin soon. It was a dream come true!

The next day, we made an agreement with Türk Telekom to deliver our signal to Türksat. Everything was ready for the channel to begin broadcasting two days later, during the weekend.

Then, without warning, the SAT-7 TÜRK logo disapeared from the screen. We received an email from Türksat explaining that our payment had arrived in their account too late and they had therefore cancelled the contract and given our channel to another broadcaster. We were shocked!

The next day officials at Türksat informed Melih that they did not have another channel available but would add our name to their waiting list. They said that they would return our money. There was nothing more we could do with Türksat at that point.

Armed with our RTÜK broadcast licence, Melih began contacting other broadcasters on Türksat to see if they could sublease us a single channel from the ones they had. The Power Group had extra capacity, warmly received Melih, and happily made an agreement with him. But only an hour after agreeing on everything, Melih got a call to say that they could not give him a channel after all, "for technical reasons."

Melih tried other broadcast companies—the Oflaz Group, the Doğan Group, the Planet Group, and others—but the same thing happened with each. Initial enthusiasm, followed by a phone call to say it was not possible.

Türksat returned our money at the end of October.

Months passed and all options of getting onto Türksat seemed blocked. And no one, including those who had helped us secure our RTÜK licence, seemed able or willing to help us. People even began refusing to take our calls or respond to messages. The team became very discouraged. (We later learned that one influential person inside the Türksat organization was hostile to such a channel and used his position to block us from getting on-air.)

By December I again came under pressure from the SAT-7 TÜRK staff and board to pursue a channel on the European HotBird satellite. I had felt so strongly that God was leading us to go in the direction we had been pursuing, but had I made a mistake? I asked God, "Why were we given a ten-year broadcast license?" And why did God let us pay all that money for it if this was how it was going to end? I pushed off any decision about HotBird until SAT-7 TÜRK board's January meeting.

In the meantime, Melih felt strongly that we were in spiritual warfare and that he also should not give up. So he resumed his conversations with potential channel providers.

A few days before Christmas, he revisited The Power Group. To his delight, they agreed to try again to give us a channel. This time there were no "technical problems" raised by Türksat and they agreed to a new contract to get us on-air with test broadcasts a few hours before the end of the year.

We were all thrilled at this development, but understandably cautious! This time we made no immediate plans to announce the launch, we created no press releases, and we alerted only SAT-7 staff and board members. Having been so disappointed once, we were just waiting to see how long we remained on-air.

For weeks, the last thing Melih did before going to bed and the first thing he did in the morning was to nervously check the signal—just to make sure the channel was still on-air! It was not until six weeks later, on February 14, 2015, that we introduced a full daily schedule of programs and had the confidence to begin an aggressive promotion of the channel, both in Turkey and to our supporters around the world.

The new channel achieved wall-to-wall coverage in the Turkish press and the SAT-7 TÜRK website received more than one hundred thousand visits after a prime-time interview on CNN Türk, which was the first television channel to interview Melih live on-air. Conscious of the suspicion Christians often faced in Turkey, Melih explained in his interview that "SAT-7 TÜRK is a place where Christians can correct misunderstandings that exist about the Christian faith, and address the many questions people have about it."

In an interview with Christian media, Tamar Karasu, the executive secretary of the Turkish Bible Society and the new chair of the SAT-7 TÜRK board, exclaimed, "It's like a miracle, and you can feel that God is with us. It's amazing!" She went on to share how Turkey is changing and how people are more open, even to Christians. "It was good that SAT-7 TÜRK was ready with its programs, staff, and support, because we do not have any other way to explain our faith, one by one, to 75 million people. It is like a dream come true."

Even before we publicly announced the new channel, the number of calls as a result of people watching us on Türksat went up tenfold overnight. A man in the town of Burdur called to say, "I have been praying secretly like a Christian for twelve years but I have never met any Christians at all. Now I watch you and I can't believe my eyes. I praise God! Please help me to meet with other local Christians."

A woman from nearby Azerbaijan called to share how she had seen Jesus in a dream, in which He called her to follow Him. But she had been scared and felt confused about which religion was right for her to follow. She thanked us for the new channel and the peace and stability it gave her.

As the channel viewership grew, one of the most exciting and encouraging developments we saw was that viewers started to ask more challenging questions. Cem Erçin, pastor of Istanbul Immanuel Protestant Church and a SAT-7 TÜRK presenter, told me, "We used to get common questions, such as 'Has the Bible been changed?' but now viewers are researching the Bible, they are comparing verses, they are engaging with the programs, and their questions are becoming more difficult. This is a huge encouragement to us."

By the end of 2015, the SAT-7 TÜRK staff had grown to twenty, though this was still very small for a 24/7 satellite television channel, and many people were working several jobs within the ministry. And 2015 was not without its other challenges. We encountered hacks on the SAT-7 TÜRK website, local churches received threatening emails, and our studio flooded when some water pipes broke.

One day, after an international leadership team meeting, Melih and I were walking down a street in Kyrenia, in the northern, Turkish-speaking part of Cyprus. I was trying to discuss something important with him, but we were continually interupted by people who recognized Melih from the movies and soap operas he had played in, people who wanted a selfie with the famous actor. When we were eventually alone, Melih began to share with me how, after getting onto Türksat, he thought that his job was done. But I looked at him in disbelief and made it clear that, no, the job had only just begun! So after spending time with his team, he came back with a new personal and audacious goal: For "SAT-7 TÜRK to become one of the ten most-watched private TV channels in Turkey."

The next year, on July 15, 2016, there was a failed military coup in Turkey, which resulted in the imposition of a state of emergency. In its wake, more than three hundred media agencies were shut down. But we give thanks to God that SAT-7 TÜRK broadcasts continued uninterupted. In fact, by August, many more live shows had begun and we also started broadcasting on D-Smart, a digital subscription channel that made our programs accessible to an additional 4 to 5 million people.

Though we may not yet have reached Melih's goal to be one of the ten most-watched private television channels in Turkey, SAT-7 TÜRK is doing well and continues to reach many with the Good News.

Chapter 11

The Arab Spring

Returning to the events that had been taking place in the Arab World during this time, the Arab Spring was the big story. The commonly accepted date for the start of the Arab Spring is December 17, 2010, when Tarek el-Tayeb Mohamed Bouazizi, a twenty-six-year-old Tunisian street vendor, set himself on fire. His self-immolation was in response to a municipal official and her aides confiscating his wares and harassing and humiliating him.

Simmering public anger over high unemployment, rising prices, and perceived political corruption intensified in Tunisia following Bouazizi's death, leading the country's president, Zine El Abidine Ben Ali, to step down on January 14, 2011—after twenty-three years in power. The success of the Tunisian protests inspired protests in other Arab countries, ultimately also resulting in regime change in Libya, Egypt, and Yemen, as well as civil unrest in Syria, Bahrain, Sudan, and elsewhere.

Before the Arab Spring could gain traction in Egypt, however, a large Coptic Orthodox church in Alexandria, the Church of the Two Saints, was hit by a car bomb, just as worshipers were leaving a New Year service in the early hours of January 1. It was the worst attack on Copts in a decade and resulted in twenty-three deaths and nearly one hundred injuries.

The Egyptian government issued a statement blaming "foreign elements" for carrying out the bombing. In a televised address, President Hosni Mubarak promised to pursue the perpetrators. But based on the government's response to similar recent attacks on Christians, most doubted that anyone would be pursued.

However, the attack was also condemned by Al-Azhar, Sunni Islam's main institution. And the Egyptian Muslim Brotherhood even called upon Muslims to protect Christian churches. On January 6, the eve of the Coptic Christmas, Egyptian Muslims boldly showed up at churches before the liturgy, offering to serve as "human shields" against any possible further attacks.

So when the Arab Spring protests and strikes began in Egypt on January 25 (National Police Day), many Christians, despite a lack of support for the protests from their religious leaders in Egypt, felt no qualms about joining with Muslims in the demonstrations. In fact, these brought together not just Muslims and Christians but a wide cross section of Egyptian society, including secularists, feminists, Islamists, anti-capitalists, and many others, but, remarkably, with no centralized leadership. They all shared a concern for the widespread political and economic corruption, the censorship imposed under the state-of-emergency laws, high unemployment, rising food prices, and the increasing police brutality witnessed in the country. People wanted change!

Things get Personal

The protests began on a Tuesday, now referred to as the January 25 Revolution, but it was anticipated that the main demonstrations would take place at the weekend. My son Gavin, the one born during the war in Lebanon, was teaching at a private English-language school in a suburb of Cairo. All the schools and universities had been instructed to stay open during the unrest—the government having learned valuable lessons from the situation in Tunis, where the authorities had closed all the universities, and so released thousands of students to swell the street demonstrations. However, the schools had already begun closing early each day out of concern for the increasing breakdown in public order. And there was mounting anticipation of a major demonstration on the Friday, which also marked the start of the two-week, mid-year break for the universities. Would the army intervene? That was a key question that everyone was wondering, and which still had no answer.

YouTube, Twitter, and Facebook were awash with comments and video clips of street demonstrations—until Thursday night when it all stopped. The government shut down all social media and blocked access to the internet. Even the cell phone network was shut down for many hours. Though we lost contact with Gavin, Jackie and I believed he would be okay. He had lived in Egypt most of his life, spoke fluent Arabic, and was streetwise enough to keep himself safe.

The Friday morning church services were cut short and people sent home. Gavin spent several hours watching events unfold on Al Jazeera, as national television was showing little of what was really going on downtown or at the epicenter, Tahrir Square. By 7:30 p.m. the army had begun to move into the city, calming tensions at key intersections. Gavin longed to be part of what seemed like a moment of historic change, and to perhaps help in a positive way, to show kindness in what was an intrinsically violent and confrontational situation. But what to do? As a foreigner, by joining the ranks of stone-throwers or chanting slogans he could help the government claim that the unrest was the result of foreign interference. By 8:00 p.m. he had loaded his car with water bottles and had resolved to distribute these to all who needed them—demonstrators or police officers.

On the highway into the center of Cairo he encountered several military checkpoints, but was just waved through. However, each time, he stopped and offered the soldiers bottles of water, which they gratefully accepted. On the outskirts of the city center, a mob armed with clubs and swords who had just burned down the local police station blocked his way. After ensuring that Gavin had nothing to do with the police, they allowed him to pass.

He reached the October 6 Bridge, which was deserted except for a large convoy of slow-moving tanks and armoured personnel carriers also heading for Tahrir Square. After passing them, he stopped at a point overlooking Ramses Square, where the army was trying to restore order as the nearby Al Azbekia police station burned. A local Secret Service officer approached him for a light, but Gavin did not smoke and couldn't help. The man admitted that he was terrified of what was going on and quickly hurried on.

As Gavin approached Tahrir Square, a group of demonstrators stopped his car, warning him that people ahead were burning vehicles and, indeed, the air was acrid with smoke. Gavin handed out more water bottles to the exhausted-looking demonstrators.

After several more attempts to get nearer to Tahrir Square, and having nearly depleted his water supply, Gavin decided to join others walking on one of the Nile bridges, overlooking events below, in and around Tahrir Square. It was now 10:00 p.m., four hours after the curfew had supposedly started, though it seemed as if the whole city was out on the streets. The nearby headquarters of the President's National Democratic Party, next to the Egyptian Museum, was now engulfed in flames. Below in the square, the people had fought back the police and were walking around in pride and amazement at their successes. Armed groups of demonstrators were attacking looters, especially those who were stealing furniture from the burning NDP building. They shouted at them, "We are a national revolution, we are not thieves!" Another, larger group was protecting the museum with its amazing collection of ancient Egyptian treasures and artifacts.

Gavin slowly made his way to Tahrir Square, where clashes were still going on between the police guarding the parliament and the demonstrators. His eyes were stinging from his first taste of tear gas. It was unclear what was really going on.

Why is the crowd attacking the police? he wondered. *Is it to remove the last of them from the downtown area . . . or to actually set fire to the parliament building?* Gavin certainly didn't approve of the latter.

The police seemed to be fighting for their lives and were firing rubber bullets into the crowd. Some of these shattered on impact, and Gavin's clothes were soon covered in fragments of plastic.

At this point, dozens of army tanks and armoured support vehicles appeared. The crowd cheered them on as they rolled past in front of the Egyptian Museum.

But some protestors were still uncertain about the army. "Are you with us or with the police?" they shouted.

"We are with the people. We are here to defend you," one officer replied.

So people from the crowd began climbing on the tanks for selfies with the crews.

In the meantime, the police who had been defending the parliament forced their way back into the square and were heading toward the crowd near the tanks, hurling tear gas and firing shots. The army assured the crowd not to worry and dispatched an armoured vehicle in the direction of the oncoming police unit. The crowd cheered and even began following after the army vehicle.

An expected confrontation was about to take place between the police and the army—and Gavin just had to see it! But then shots rang out and the crowd turned to run, shouting, "The army is with them!"

The army vehicle had indeed turned around and was now shoulder to shoulder with the police. While initially at the back of the crowd, Gavin now found himself on the front line. He looked around to check out his options. While turning back to see where the advancing forces were, he heard a loud crack. His glasses shattered. Immediately he felt a terrible pain in his left eye and collapsed to the ground. He was barely conscious as some strangers quickly picked him up and carried him away with the fleeing crowd.

"Ambulance, we need an ambulance!" his rescuers cried out.

Gavin was in a state of shock. He tried to reach up to touch his bleeding eye, but his eye felt numb.

"Please! You can put me down. I can walk," he begged his rescuers. But the moment they stood him up, he collapsed again. So they continued to carry him down the road, still crying out and looking desperately for an ambulance.

Two young men got Gavin onto a motorcycle, sandwiching him between them and driving as fast as they could to a local hospital.

On the journey, Gavin covered his right eye to see what he could with his left, but there was only darkness.

"I can't see. I'm blind!" he cried out in Arabic to his helpers.

How stupid have I been? he thought. *How can I ever tell my dad or my mom? Or my church? Or my school?* He tried to imagine his life with one eye.

"Why, Lord, why?" he prayed. But soon he gathered his thoughts and changed his prayer. "Your will be done, O Lord!" As he prayed, a sense of calm came over him.

Many casualties from the square were already at the hospital. Feeling nauseated and faint, Gavin was led to the ophthalmology department and told to wait for an available doctor.

As he waited, he began to reflect on everything that had happened. The day before, he had finished reading the last chapter of 2 Chronicles, having read the two books of Kings the month before.

Why on earth had those kings of Judea and Israel so often gone off into battle without consulting God, which resulted in their defeat? he had wondered. Now he knew why!

He too had not consulted God before going out this night. No one had asked him to go. He had gone in his own confidence to witness history in the making, to have an exciting story to tell. Yes, he did want to help others, but perhaps on his own terms. He learned a valuable, if costly, lesson that night.

Gavin's two companions stayed with him, waiting for the doctor and offering occasional words of reassurance and encouragement. A physician eventually arrived and asked the nurse to clean up Gavin's eye and administer anaesthetic to enable a proper examination.

When the doctor shone a light into his wounded eye, Gavin could see something, albeit faintly.

"It appears that a rubber bullet bounced off your glasses. It did not penetrate your eye, but it did traumatize it," the doctor told him. "You have a good chance of recovering your sight."

Gavin breathed a sigh of relief. "May I have a mirror to see it?" When the nurse handed one to him, he was horrified by what he saw. The bloodied left eye, though intact, was facing in a different direction from the right eye.

"You're going to needed stitches and an X-ray," the doctor said.

However, the government facility was so overwhelmed that night that nothing was available. So on the doctor's orders, the nurse bandaged Gavin's eye so he could go home and return later the following day.

As she began her work, the Egyptian president, Hosni Mubarak, began a national broadcast. Everyone drifted off toward the television monitor. President Mubarak announced that, in response to the protests, he was going to dissolve his entire government and announce a new one the next day. But to the disappointment and anger of most watching, he confirmed that he would not be stepping down.

It was time to leave. Gavin's faithful companions escorted him back to his car, still parked on the bridge over the Nile where he had left it several hours earlier. He thanked them profusely and gave them the rest of the water bottles he had there. As he climbed into the vehicle, he wondered just how he was going to drive the ten miles back to his home in Maadi.

Not only was he exhausted, in pain, and had one eye bandaged, but his glasses had been lost in the chaos of the square. And his one good eye needed them for driving! It was now 12:30 a.m. but it felt much later as he cautiously moved off with his hazard lights blinking. He could hardly see anything, and then, to make things worse, it began to rain.

He eventually reached home, got cleaned up, took some pain relievers, and collapsed into bed. But the pain was so intense that he could not sleep, so he decided to write his mother and me a long email about the day's events. It was 6:00 a.m. when he finished, but he knew he could not send it until the government decided to restore the internet. His email ended with a request for prayer, that God would somehow take away this disability from him or give him the strength to bear it.

That week I was in London for meetings and was following the news from Egypt with increasing concern for my many friends and colleagues there. I had also been trying to get Gavin on his cell phone, just to see if he was okay, but the networks were all down. On Saturday, I was finally able to reach him.

As he shared the horrific tale of the previous day's events, I was shocked and could not help wondering how his mother in Cyprus would take the news.

"What can I do to help?" I asked.

"Nothing, Dad. My friends are taking good care of me and we're searching for a hospital with actual doctors." He explained that the situation was bad, with many medics unwilling or unable to get to work in the current chaos. And with no police on the streets, looting and carjacking had begun, restrained only by local vigilante groups seeking to protect private and public property.

The next day, Sunday, Gavin managed to get an X-ray, which confirmed that his eye was intact. But it also showed that he had not been hit by a rubber bullet that had just bounced off, but with a metal bullet of some kind that had penetrated his eye socket and was still lodged behind the eye. He would need surgery to have the bullet removed, but no surgeons were available.

When I heard the news, I suggested to Gavin that we try to get him to London. I could stay on to meet him at the airport and help him get the urgent medical care he obviously needed. After one more day of trying but failing to find a surgeon who could help him, Gavin agreed.

But Cairo airport was a mess, with thousands of tourists and foreign businesspeople rushing to get out of the country before things unraveled further. All the flights were totally full. British Airways were adding extra flights, however, and were able to prioritize Gavin as a medical emergency, giving him a seat on a flight out the next morning, Tuesday, February 1.

Gavin's friends got him to the airport in good time, which was just as well, as his flight was not leaving from the usual terminal, and he needed to transfer terminals by himself in the chaos of overbooked flights and crowds of people competing for seats. With one eye still conspicuously bandaged, he arrived at the correct terminal only twenty minutes before the flight's departure. A stranger, apparently also traveling to London, must have noticed Gavin's bandaged eye and his predicament. The man took Gavin by the hand and passed the now-closed check-in desk and through passport control and security. Within fifteen minutes—with five minutes before departure—Gavin made it to his seat on the flight. Gavin's passport had expired a week or so before, but, miraculously, this was not an issue for the airline or the Cairo airport authorities.

Gavin arrived safely in London at 2:30 p.m. My daughter, Mona, and I met Gavin outside baggage claim and, after impromptu interviews with journalists waiting at the airport for news from those arriving from Cairo, we drove Gavin to the world-famous Moorfields Eye Hospital in central London, where Mona herself had had surgery as a baby. But, to our disbelief, they would not admit him, saying Gavin needed neurosurgery, which was not exclusively to do with the eye. They referred us to the Royal London Hospital in a somewhat rundown area of East London.

We arrived at their Accident and Emergency unit at 6:30 p.m., only to have to take a number and wait for what seemed eternity. The small A&E unit was overwhelmed with patients seated or slouched everywhere, some even dripping blood on the floor from nasty wounds. Our turn eventually came. Once inside the treatment area, things began to move quickly. The nurse gave Gavin a morphine shot to alleviate his pain, which made him a much happier person! They then scheduled surgery for the following day, subject to more tests in the morning.

The consultant surgeon, Simon Holmes, examined Gavin. "You are both very lucky and very unlucky," he said. "You are lucky that the bullet has done so little damage going into your eye socket. And it stopped short of going deep enough into your skull to kill you. The bullet must have been a ricochet not to have done more damage."

"And I'm unlucky how?" Gavin asked.

"The bullet is lodged in a critical place—next to the optic nerve. It's in a position that makes it extremely risky to remove it, but we also cannot simply leave it there."

After the specialist left, Mona and I settled the now quite "high" and smiling Gavin into a surgical ward for the night, then I returned with Mona to her home in North London.

The operation went ahead the next day and went as well as it could have. The bullet turned out to be a metal shotgun pellet, only the size of a pea, but with a jagged spike from a ricochet. The very tip of the jagged part broke away during extraction and was left behind—meaning that Gavin will never be able to have an MRI on his head.

Although the muscles under the eye were "shredded" by the pellet, his eye returned to a normal position, and he could already see well enough with his left eye to count the fingers on one hand six feet away.

Dr. Holmes used the word *miraculous* in his written report to describe the incident and how the surgery went. In fact, the whole team was so excited by the success and drama of Gavin's story that, in the operating room, they videoed on the surgeon's cell phone the moment Dr. Holmes dramatically dropped the just-extracted pellet into a metal surgical dish, as if it were a scene from an old John Wayne movie.

Gavin was discharged a day later, but stayed on in London for another two months for follow-up hospital visits. Toward the end of his stay in the UK, Gavin was paraded out at a press conference, organized by the Royal London Hospital, to tell his story—and for the hospital to showcase the skills of their surgeons! The national *Daily Express* ran the story under the headline, "NHS Saved Me from Cairo Bullet Nightmare!"

By the time Gavin returned to Egypt, he was able to see well again and move both eyes left and right, though he was still unable to move the left eye up and down. In a strange way, he was grateful that his recovery was not 100 percent, so that he would always have an impediment to remind him of all God had done for him and taught him through this experience.

The Unrest in Egypt Continues

Back in Cairo, in the days after Gavin's evacuation on February 1, the street demonstrations continued with marches, occupations of plazas, acts of civil disobedience and strikes. Across the country, more than ninety police stations were torched. Millions of protesters, from all walks of life, demanded the overthrow of the Egyptian president. Over the eighteen days of what became known as the Egyptian Revolution, violent clashes between security forces and protesters tragically claimed at least eight hundred lives and injured six thousand.

With my enthusiastic support, SAT-7 programs had covered the unfolding events, beginning with special live programs after the earlier bombing of the Church of the Two Saints in Alexandria. Many of the phone calls to the live shows at that time were angry over the treatment of Christians in the country. The ministers on-air, Pastor Sameh Maurice, Father Samaan and Father Makari Younan, agreed with callers that they had the right to be upset, but also reminded them of our higher calling—to love and forgive. They pointed out that many Muslims were also outraged and that our enemy was not other people but Satan himself.

Later, when the government shut down internet services after the January 25 street demonstrations, SAT-7 had to broadcast all its live shows from our Lebanon studio. In one such live show, our Egypt studio director, Farid Samir, shared how SAT-7's stated goal of being a voice for the Christians of the region had never been more relevant than in these days. But he also made it clear that the station would not be endorsing any specific political agendas. Instead SAT-7 programs continued to urge prayer for the country.

The government finally restored the internet, and social media again became a way for the protestors to organize themselves. But, at the same time, the security forces began to manipulate the crowd with anonymous social media messages. Their tactics included sending people off to join a protest in another part of the city where no demonstrations were being planned or to places that would discredit them or put them in danger. National television also lost credibility by not broadcasting what was actually occurring in different parts of the country at the height of the protests.

But transborder satellite television had shown itself to be the most reliable source of information, especially as viewers could go to different channels to double check statements or news.

Our viewers were especially moved by the Iraqi Christians who called into our live shows to pray for their Egyptian brothers and sisters, after themselves facing difficult years of persecution, death, destruction, and displacement.

As the Egyptian Revolution continued to grow in strength and numbers, the vice president of the Protestant Community of Egypt, Rev. Dr. Andrea Zaki, stressed that the church was with the protestors in calling for increased social and political freedom but cautioned against the use of violence.

Kasr El Dobara Evangelical Church, adjacent to Tahrir Square, was closed but providing first aid to those injured in the demonstrations. On Sunday, February 6, the thirteenth day of the revolution, SAT-7 was able to broadcast a worship service from the square, jointly organized by Kasr El Dobara church and Coptic Orthodox and Catholic believers—a service protected by Muslim clerics from Al-Azhar. The speaker shared with the crowd how Jesus had also stood against and suffered great injustice. Muslims and Christians in the square joined together in reciting the Lord's Prayer. I was truly amazed by this unprecedented event.

One Muslim writer in Tahrir Square, who had previously written negatively about the country's Christians, including lies about them hiding guns in their churches, apologized to one of the Christian leaders present. He later repeated the apology on Al Jazeera and committed to write positively about Christians in the future.

On February 11, 2011, Vice President Omar Suleiman announced that President Hosni Mubarak had resigned as president, turning over power to the Supreme Council of the Armed

Forces (SCAF). That left much uncertainty about what would follow. In a special live show on February 12, Pastor Sameh Maurice sincerely congratulated the Egyptian people for the peaceful change they had brought about, with 15 million people coming out onto the streets the day before the president stepped down. He expressed his condolences on behalf of himself and SAT-7 to the families of the dead and injured, the martyrs of the revolution.

One caller to the live show, Fawzy, shared his experience. As a Christian, he did not feel he could just pray and not join others on the street to call for change. Here he felt a strong bond with other protestors as he witnessed the police beating people and was himself overcome by tear gas. He shook hands with a Muslim cleric and introduced himself as "Brother Fawzi, a church worker." The cleric responded, "I am an imam from Al-Azhar and, from now on, nothing will separate or differentiate between us!" Fawzy spoke of the goodwill and peace there was between people and how they even helped an injured police officer. He felt that the Lord was blessing Egypt through these difficult days.

Fawzy cried as he remembered the death of the hundreds of beautiful young people who had made this day possible, one he had never imagined he would live to see.

On February 13, the military junta announced that the constitution was to be suspended, both houses of parliament dissolved, and that the military would govern until elections could be held.

Even though the president was gone, the emergency regulations were still in place, and the security services were still intact—albeit with a few less police stations—and people remained unsure about how much freedom of speech they really had. On top of this, many people held unrealistic expectations that the new military authorities would immediately create new jobs and increase salaries, as well as ensure that the prices of food, medicine, and fuel would be cut, and free and fair elections would be held in the next few weeks.

At this critical time, SAT-7 called on Christians to pray for national unity and for the new leadership of the country as they led through this period.

The demonstrations continued, and many protesters stayed on in the square for months, to help ensure that all that had been won so far, at such great cost, would not be lost.

The Uprisings Spread . . .

On February 15, 2011, protests broke out in neighboring Libya against Muammar Gaddafi's authoritarian regime.

The Libyan government attempted to jam some satellite broadcasts, which impacted the SAT-7 Arabic channels. Fortunately, the jamming never lasted long before the International Telecommunications Union in Geneva or attacks on the facilities that were performing the jamming stopped it.

The battle for the capital, Tripoli, took place during the last week of August. Rebel forces quickly captured and took control of the city, effectively overthrowing the government. It would be another two months, however, before President Muammar Gaddafi was captured and killed by rebels in the city of Sirte. Gaddafi's son, Saif al-Islam, was finally captured a month later, after hiding in Nigeria.

Meanwhile in Yemen, on June 3, 2011, the country's president, Ali Abdullah Saleh, was injured in a failed assassination attempt. He temporarily made his vice president, Abd Rabbuh Mansur Al-Hadi, the acting president of the nation.

Other protests also took place in Syria, Morocco, and the Arabian Peninsula, while the Syrian uprisings would not take off in a big way until the following year. And the worried monarchs in Morocco and the Gulf found ways to appease the majority of their populations.

While the Arab uprisings raised security issues and disrupted life, many of our SAT-7 activities continued almost as normal. Though we did cancel the May 2011 meeting of the Arabic Media Convention in Lebanon, I was able to attend the Central Asia Consultation in Antalya, Turkey, to talk about satellite television. We also were still able to hold regular SAT-7 management, board, and partner meetings in March and June. And in late July I traveled to Algeria, hopeful that the Arab Spring wasn't going to meet me there.

Algeria: A Country Not Ready for More Instability

Algeria had gone through an ugly civil war in the 1990s and so was in no mood for another period of instability. Their uprising would come much later.

The Algerian war began in December 1991 when the new and enormously popular Islamic Salvation Front (FIS) appeared poised to defeat the ruling National Liberation Front in the national parliamentary elections. The elections were canceled after the first round, and the military effectively took control of the government, forcing pro-reform President Chadli Bendjedid from office. After the FIS was banned and thousands of its members arrested, Islamist guerrillas rapidly emerged and began an armed insurrection against the government and its supporters.

The conflict saw extreme violence and brutality used against civilians, including many children, women, journalists, and foreigners. The total fatalities during the 1990s has been estimated at between one and two hundred thousand.

In 1999, following the election of Abdelaziz Bouteflika as president, violence abated as large numbers of insurgents "repented," taking advantage of a new amnesty law. The remnants of the armed fighters were hunted down over the next two years and any remaining resistance had practically disappeared by 2002.

During the war, many clergy were murdered, including Pierre Claverie, the Catholic bishop of Oran. He was born in 1938 in French Algeria. A scholar of Arabic and a prolific writer, he was also known for his continuous efforts to build bridges between Muslims and Christians. On August 1, 1996, he, his driver, and a Muslim friend were killed in Oran by a bomb.

The Protestant Church of Algeria (EPA, Eglise protestante d'Algérie) had been officially recognized by the government of Algeria in 1974. While the exact number of its members has never been clear, estimates in 2011 were in range of 60,000 to 120,000. Almost all of the membership was not from a Christian tradition, with many of the fifty or so registered churches being in the Berber, Kabyle-speaking regions of the country. Though these believers had faced waves of persecution and church closures, their numbers continued to grow.

The early North African Christian writer, Tertullian, observed, "The blood of the martyrs is the seed of the church." When one considers the dozens of murdered Christian workers in Algeria over the past decades, it is not surprising to know that it hosts the fastest growing church in the Arab World today.

The violence the Islamists committed against Algerian civilians also appears to have been a factor in turning many to Christ. This was graphically illustrated by a drawing a young Algerian girl sent to our children's program, *AsSanabel*. It pictured Jesus on the cross, holding an Algerian flag in each hand. To Christ's left was pictured something that no child should be thinking about: a bearded Islamist cutting the throat of this young artist with a sword. Over this gory part of the picture was a big X, rejecting the behavior. To Christ's right was a happy child holding a cross in one hand and declaring their freedom. And at the bottom of the picture she had written, "They are killing the children, but Jesus was killed for the children."

Rita, who was by then the executive director for SAT-7's Arabic channels (and still the presenter and producer of *AsSanabel*), and I flew into Oran on July 25, 2011. It was a long-postponed trip to strengthen SAT-7's ties with the church and local producers there. Security was tight but friendly. Several of the immigration staff in the airport recognized Rita from her regular programs on SAT-7. This perhaps delayed things a bit, as they seemed anxious over the possibility of us filming in their country. We assured them we would not.

Our first impressions of the city were not that great. For the second largest city in Africa's geographically biggest country, with one of the world's greatest reserves of natural gas, their investment in public services and infrastructure seemed underwhelming. Many of the streets were unpaved, littered with rubbish. And we could find stores selling only the most basic range of local produce. Unemployment was high. Many of the apartment buildings seemed poorly maintained and had no elevators or air-conditioning, despite the stifling summer heat. But they all had satellite dishes!

Our Algerian hosts welcomed us warmly. They clearly had a heart for ministry and for sharing their faith with others in North Africa through SAT-7's broadcasts, especially at a time when half-a-dozen churches in the country had recently been given orders to close. These brothers and sisters had already been recording simple church services and other programs but were obviously in need of both better and more equipment, as well as some advanced training in television production.

Rita questioned if the believers at the church services being recorded minded that their faces would be shown on television, especially given the growing problems for such churches at that time. Youssef, the ministry leader, explained that when they discussed this issue in church, instead of people moving to the back and away from the cameras, many moved to the front to let their faces be seen more clearly!

Rita then asked Samia, both a presenter and a producer of several shows, "Is it not dangerous to show your face on screen?"

"Rita, what are you afraid of?" Samia asked.

"I am not afraid for myself or for SAT-7," replied Rita, "but for your sake."

"Afraid for me?" Samia said. "Persecution is actually a crown that we put on our heads each and every day before going out into the world. Don't take this away from us!"

These are the Christians of North Africa.

As the days went by, and we got to know one another better, our enthusiasm to help these courageous brothers and sisters in Christ grew. We catalogued equipment and techniques that would help them in the days ahead. And before leaving the country, we drafted some proposals that we hoped we could use to raise funds for them in the immediate future. As we left our new friends, we had tears in our eyes and looked forward to a return visit and ongoing fellowship with each of them.

After the summer, I traveled to Lebanon where, on September 3, 2011, we held a ground-breaking ceremony for a new SAT-7 studio. Several hundred guests attended; notable among them was Lebanon's

Minister of Information, with whom I had the privilege of ceremoniously shoveling some topsoil to symbolically mark the beginning of construction. Other VIPs included different church leaders, government officials, and the American donor, Jim, who was generously supporting this major capital investment.

Over the previous fifteen years, we had gradually rented more and more floor space in the building where we had started in Lebanon, but as our options for growth there became exhausted, we began looking for a new, larger facility to rent or buy. At this time, one of our generous friends, Jim, purchased land in the name of a local NGO and allocated a portion of it for the new studio, then funding a local architect to work with us on the studio designs. He was now paying for the significant construction costs of the new facility. Legally, we were to be "tenants." We had a twenty-five-year lease for a total rent payment of one dollar, with an option to buy the building and land during or at the end of the lease period, for $1 million. This was all a little complicated, but within a couple of years, we were going to receive an amazing new production studio and administrative facility. God was continuing to bless us.

A Night to Remember

Back in Egypt, Tahrir Square was still a scene of ongoing protest. People were becoming impatient for real change, for a new constitution, and for free and fair elections.

In early October, Coptic Christians and some supportive Muslims gathered to peacefully protest the government's demolition of a church in Upper Egypt, which, the government claimed, had been built without the appropriate license. Unfortunately, the army responded by attacking the protesters—even using military vehicles to run some over. Dozens were killed and more than two hundred injured. Video footage of the event went viral and further inflamed the situation. Church leaders in Egypt called on their congregations to pray, fast, and forgive those who had carried out what was seen as the most violent and open attack that Christians had experienced in many years. There was a sense of shock and disappointment, and I noticed that many of the staff in our Egypt studio had lost the smile on their faces and the hope in their eyes.

SAT-7 programs from Cairo tried to bring words of comfort, reason, and encouragement. The live program, *Salt of the Earth*, brought together church leaders, Muslim and Christian politicians, Christian young people who had been at the recent protests, and a family who had lost a son in the January 25 Revolution. They discussed issues of citizenship and the current struggle for civil and human rights for all in the country, irrespective of gender, ethnic, or religious background.

November 11, 2011—11/11/11—was an extraordinary day. The churches of Egypt set aside this date for a night of repentance, prayer, and fasting for the Egyptian nation. SAT-7 was to cover this event live, from 6:00 p.m. until 6:00 a.m. the following morning. It was our longest-ever live broadcast—twelve hours.

The venue was the open-air Cave Church, cut into the rockface of the Mokattam hills above Cairo. As many as seventy thousand Christians from Orthodox, Catholic, and Protestant traditions came together for some or all of the event, which included contemporary worship led by choirs and music groups from different churches, all working together in a marvelous show of unity. Priests and pastors from different traditions gave messages on matters of personal repentance and the current needs of the church and the country, and led in prayer. Many of these prayers sought God's blessing on all Egyptians—Muslims and Christians—the authorities, and the forthcoming parliamentary elections.

Farid Samir, the director of SAT-7's work in Egypt at the time, shared with me how moving it was to see the spirit of unity that existed, both in front of and behind the cameras. His SAT-7 crew was not just committed to doing their best during this twelve-hour marathon but were really caught up in the spirit of the event. Eva Botros, a member of the SAT-7 Egypt board, was leading a group of 250 ushers at the event. She also testified to the amazing spirit and helpfulness shown by the SAT-7 crew to others involved—even when there were last-minute changes in the program and what was expected of them.

SAT-7's involvement made it possible not only for participants to follow the proceedings on big screens, but also for literally millions more to share in or witness the event as it was broadcast across the region. Additional audiences were added as a dozen other television channels approached SAT-7 at the last minute asking for our live feed from the event. Al Jazeera and several secular Egyptian channels carried at least some of it, and the local press gave it a favorable write-up the next day.

We received eighty thousand comments on Facebook and hundreds of SMS text messages from viewers. We streamed as many of these as we could across the bottom of the screen throughout the night. Many people outside the region tried watching the live feed through SAT-7's website, eventually overloading and crashing the service.

Without doubt, it was a night that changed the church in Egypt and how that church was seen by those outside it. It restored for many the joy and Christian hope that had been eroded by recent events in the country. God's hand was clearly at work.

All these events seemed a world away when, in December that year, I was privileged to receive an Honorary Doctor of Christian Ministries award from Belhaven University, delivering the commencement address at their graduation exercises in Orlando. But back in the wider Arab World, the Arab Spring was in serious trouble.

Chapter 12

The Arab Winter

The street protests in Egypt continued through the parliamentary elections in November 2011 and into the new year. But on New Year's Eve, a congregation of about five thousand people, including church leaders from all the main denominations, came together at 8:00 p.m. in and on the street outside Kasr El Dubarrah Evangelical Church, adjacent to Tahrir Square. After the first part of the service, which SAT-7 broadcast live, the congregation processed with candles to the already busy square, where many more Christians from all backgrounds joined them. The crowd sang worship songs and then offered prayers for the country, the injured, the sick, the economy, and for peace. Different church leaders gave short messages, and eventually many returned to the church for the final part of the service, which concluded at 3:00 a.m. on New Year's Day.

SAT-7 covered the entire seven hours live, which was a logistical challenge. We had to approach people living in tall buildings around the square and beg them to use their balconies for our camera positions. We had to position cameras not too high or too far from the OB van, lest we lose the wireless connectivity we needed for communications and the live feeds. And it was mostly guesswork, since we were unsure of the timing and exact route the processions would take!

For a community that has always had to conduct its activities behind the walls of the church, this event of celebrating, praying, and singing in Cairo's iconic Tahrir Square was an incredibly liberating experience. To be salt and light and to sing the praises of God in the proverbial marketplace for all to see and hear made this experience, in the words of one SAT-7 staff member, "The best New Year's Eve of my life!"

As wonderful as this time made us all feel, a different kind of change was in the works. The uprising of the Arab Spring was turning into the start of an Arab Winter.

By June 17, Egypt had held its presidential primaries and run-off elections. But the results remained unclear. Rumors began circulating that the Muslim Brotherhood candidate, Mohammed Morsi, had failed to receive the most votes, but that the army was hesitant to announce Ahmed Shafiq, from the former president's political party, as the winner, fearing the Brotherhood would go on a rampage of destruction. Finally, a week later, Egypt's election commission announced that Mohammed Morsi had won, taking 51.7 percent of the vote.

Even the country's Christians seemed willing to give the new president a chance. President Morsi actually added Christians to his initial government, though he failed to honor his pledge to appoint a Christian vice president.

However, the new president seemed unpredictable and dangerous. Several months after his inauguration, in November, he granted himself unlimited powers to "protect" the nation, as well as giving himself the power to legislate without judicial oversight or review of his acts.

When people learned of his new assumption of powers, many hit the streets again. On January 25, 2013, the second anniversary of the 2011 revolution, protests against Mohammed Morsi developed all over Egypt and at least six civilians and one police officer were shot dead in Suez, while almost five hundred others were injured nationwide.

Two weeks later, I found myself in Egypt for the Cairo International Book Fair. I also planned to visit Bishop Mounir at the Anglican Cathedral in Cairo and the Coptic Catholic Pope elect, Bishop Ibrahim Isaac Sidrak in Minya. The visit with Bishop Ibrahim involved a four-hour trip south, mostly within sight of the river Nile. Along the road we passed long lines of vehicles outside the gas stations.

"What's going on?" I asked our Egypt director, Farid.

"We have an acute shortage of fuel, as well as growing shortages of medicine and imported goods," he explained. "The fuel problems are also impacting our electric power plants. Many places are experiencing regular blackouts."

When we got to Minya, we needed fuel and worried that we wouldn't be able to fill up. Fortunately, the bishop's staff kindly helped us secure enough for the return journey to the capital.

These shortages, growing concerns about the competency of the president, the apparent creeping Islamization of the country, the breakdown in social services, and continuing high unemployment all helped to fuel massive protests on June 30, the one-year anniversary of Morsi's inauguration. Across the country, tens of millions came out to the streets to call for the president to step down.

The following day, on July 1, the Egyptian armed forces issued an ultimatum, giving the country's political parties forty-eight hours to meet the Egyptian people's demands. Four ministers resigned that day, leaving the government with members of the Muslim Brotherhood only.

But President Morsi publicly rejected the ultimatum and vowed to pursue his own plans for national reconciliation and a resolution of the political crisis. So on July 3, Minister of Defense Abdul Fatah al-Sisi, who ultimately became commander-in-chief of the Egyptian armed forces, removed Morsi from office and appointed Adly Mansour, the head of the Constitutional Court, as the interim president.

To many in the outside world, former President Morsi looked to be the victim in much of what was happening. While it may be true that he was elected in June 2012, it was only by the slimmest majority and only by 15 percent of Egypt's total population. Nevertheless, with a *winner-takes-all* attitude, he took this as a mandate to do what he wanted. His government was not inclusive; it was loaded with Muslim Brotherhood leaders—some with previous convictions for violence and few with any real qualifications for the posts to which they were appointed. Unlike a president in a working democracy, or even his predecessor, Morsi refused to step down in the face of massive unrest. And so, as the country's last line of defense, the army removed him—with the vast majority of Egyptians supporting its actions.

In many ways, Mohammed Morsi's year in power highlighted the complexities and frailties of a modern democracy. Even if he really was elected by a majority of the voters, was it a meaningful democratic process?

For democracy to work there are key institutions that need to be in place, such as a free and fair press, an independent judiciary, law and order in society. However, even these are insufficient unless the system also has an educated electorate and a society that recognizes everyone's right to be treated equally under the law.

Soon after their 2012 election victory, a leader in the Muslim Brotherhood said that he did not recognize democracy as a God-given model for an Islamic society. He went on to say that their party saw democracy as a "bus," which the Muslim Brotherhood was happy to use to get where they wanted to go—and now they were getting off the bus!

From the start of the anti-Morsi demonstrations in June 2013, the president's supporters had started their own sit-in in Rabaa Al-Adawiya Square, a key intersection on the city's east side. These occupations of public spaces only grew after the July 3 removal of the president and, as the days passed, became increasingly ugly, with demonstrators also blocking other major squares and intimidating local residents into providing food or access to their bathrooms.

Coptic Christians Under Pressure

For almost six weeks, demonstrators called for violence against the army, the police, the liberals, and, specifically, the Coptic Christian community. During this time, more than eighty churches were attacked, with many burned to the ground. In addition, dozens of monasteries, Christian schools, associations, bookshops, Christian-owned businesses, and homes were also looted and destroyed. It was the worst persecution of Christians in Egypt in seven hundred years.

It took a heavy toll on the persecuted. Christians we interviewed in one village shared their disappointment at how their longtime Muslim neighbors had stood by without helping while they were attacked, family members tortured or murdered, and their homes looted. They did not know how they could continue to live in that village any longer.

SAT-7 carried weekly and daily reports on the events, giving church leaders a platform to speak into the situation and to call for restraint. The new head of the Coptic Orthodox church, Pope Tawadros urged both Christians and the Muslims who were going to protect churches to keep themselves safe. "We care for people, not buildings," he stressed. "We can repair buildings but we cannot restore a person killed or injured."

Dr. Safwat El-Baiady, the president of the Protestant Community in Egypt, called for Christians to show their attackers the meaning of forgiveness and unconditional love. He also went on to share with SAT-7 viewers his concern for the impact all this violence may have on the children watching these events in the streets or on television, hoping that we would not lose a generation.

SAT-7 broadcast several worship services from burned-out churches in yet further testimony that the church is its people, not its buildings. Several beautiful music videos were also recorded in the ruins of such churches and broadcast or made available online. One was called *Heavenly Church*. It showed musicians and church members singing about the attacks, acknowledging that those who burned their church thought they were pleasing God, and responding to them with words of forgiveness and love.

For me, the most moving memory was to see the graffiti left on the wall of a burned church in Upper Egypt. On the blackened walls, the perpetrators had written, "We hate you." But underneath those words, someone from the church had responded in white paint: "But we love you and forgive you."

The Cyprus Banking Crisis

As our SAT-7 Egypt office was dealing with the events in that country, our international office in Cyprus faced its own crisis. In March, we held our annual partners' meeting, Network 2013, in Limassol, Cyprus. But the Friday before its start, all the banks in Cyprus went into a lockdown, pending the outcome of negotiations with Europe for a multibillion-euro bailout for the country and its banks, which had been badly hurt by neighboring Greece's own banking crisis. Suddenly we had no access to our accounts to pay the conference hotel or to pay salaries or other costs. For two weeks, individuals and businesses were limited to very small daily cash withdrawals and a freeze on any other banking transactions. This period ended with a "haircut" on all accounts, whereby the Central Bank confiscated all monies in excess of 100,000 euros in any one account.

Unfortunately, we had just received in our main operational account all the money we needed to pay end-of-month expenses, such as salaries and rent, as well as the Network conference costs, and we lost the equivalent of about $50,000. Though we appealed the haircut on the basis that we were a charity, the bank rejected our appeal, pointing out, as if they were proud of the fact, that they had also taken millions of euros from the account of a foundation set up to help the orphans of Cypriots killed in a tragic plane crash some eight years earlier.

We would spend the next couple of years trying to reestablish safe international banking facilities for the organization, eventually locating these in Germany.

The banking crisis in Cyprus also came at a time when our income for the work had flattened. A few months prior, at a special executive board meeting in New York City, one of our supporters suggested that we needed to "drill more holes" if we wanted to grow our income. In other words, we needed to look at diversifying our income streams.

One new initiative to come out of this conversation was the idea of starting an Arabic channel for the United States – something many Arabs living in North America had requested. Sadly, this did not attract the expected new funding or even cover its own costs.

As an organization we had always made ministry to people *in* the Middle East and North Africa *the* priority. To have continued with this new channel could have led to serious "mission creep," and so, after just a year of broadcasting, I had to pull the plug on it.

Broadcasting Hope

In the meantime, the situation in Syria was continuing to unravel.

Inspired by the Arab Spring uprisings across the Middle East in early 2011, young people in Daraa, in southern Syria, painted anti-regime graffiti on public walls. Fifteen teens were arrested and tortured, which in turn prompted local demonstrations calling for their release. More, mostly peaceful, protests spread rapidly across Syria. But as the marches gained momentum, President Bashar Assad's regime unleashed its military firepower.

The next year, an array of poorly organized opposition groups formed rebel brigades, many armed by foreign governments, seizing key cities in the north, including parts of Aleppo, Syria's largest city. And by 2013 much of the country was under the control of increasingly militant groups, some of whom funded their operations by kidnapping wealthy individuals or VIPs and demanding a ransom for their return.

In March of that year, Mar Gregorios Yohanna Ibrahim, the Syrian Orthodox archbishop of Aleppo and a member of the SAT-7 international council (formerly the international board), had attended our council meetings and Network 2013 in Cyprus, where he had shared his concerns over the rising tide of violence in the country. He was especially worried about the plight of its Christian population, much of which had already been internally displaced or were to be counted among the million or more refugees living across the border in Turkey, Lebanon, or Jordan.

A mere four weeks later, on April 22, Mar Gregorios was kidnapped, together with Metropolitan Paul Yazigi, the Greek Orthodox archbishop in Aleppo. They were on a trip north of the city, near the Turkish border, to negotiate the release of two priests who had been abducted two months earlier. The bishops' driver was killed on the spot and the bishops abducted.

Mystery surrounded their disappearance. No one received any credible ransom demand, and, despite the occasional rumors of their whereabouts and possible imminent release, they have never been seen again.

Between these tragedies and the millions of lives lost or displaced, Syria needed to feel hope. On December 25, 2013, SAT-7 broadcast a Christmas service from the Christian Unity Church in Damascus. Despite all the violence and the tragedy of what was happening in their country, the Christians in Damascus wanted to show the world that they were able to celebrate the birth of our Savior. Maissa, the program's producer and a well-known presenter on Syrian National Television, said she hoped that the service would minister to Syrians both within and outside the country. "Hatred is filling the hearts of so many," she said, "but we wanted to share with them the hope that we have because of Christmas and our trust in the Prince of Peace. We also wanted SAT-7 viewers everywhere to see this program and remember to pray for us in Syria as well as others in difficult situations."

In March 2014, Network was held, for the first time, in Turkey. It attracted a record attendance of more than 250 partners and supporters from twenty-five different countries, including some in Asia—which I saw as an indicator of the growing worldwide concern for the troubled Middle East region.

The theme of this meeting was "Broadcasting HOPE in an Era of Hopelessness." I used the keynote address on the opening day to focus on the seemingly hopeless situation in the Middle East and North Africa in the wake of the Arab Spring.

But I did not leave it there. I went on to show how our different channels, not just those broadcasting in Arabic, were bringing a message of hope. SAT-7 was supporting isolated believers; presenting testimonies of hope; modeling inclusiveness, reconciliation, and forgiveness; empowering women and children; supporting church unity; and providing counseling services for our viewers. As the region was on fire, by God's grace we continued to stand strong, offering Good News. The people of every Middle East country needed to hear it. But in particular, the Iraqis.

The Church in Iraq

The suffering of the church in Iraq began long before the Arab Spring.

The apostle Thomas is cited as the one who brought Christianity to the Assyrians of northern Iraq in the first century. The area quickly became the center of Eastern Christianity and Syriac literature. However, in the early centuries after the Arab Islamic conquest of the seventh century, Assyria was dissolved as a geopolitical entity.

From the late thirteenth century to the present time, Assyrian Christians have suffered both religious and ethnic persecution, including a number of massacres. One of the worst was when the fourteenth-century Mongol warlord, Timur, had seventy thousand Assyrian Christians beheaded in Tikrit, and another ninety thousand in Baghdad.

During the First World War, the Assyrian population of the Ottoman Empire also suffered the Assyrian genocide, which accounted for the deaths of up to three hundred thousand Assyrians in Iraq and neighboring countries. Unlike other genocides taking place at the same time, there were no central orders to deport Assyrians. The attacks against them were inconsistent and sometimes carried out at the initiative of local politicians or Kurdish tribesmen. In many cities, all Assyrian men were slain, and the women forced to flee. Exposure, disease, and starvation during the Assyrians' flight increased the death toll.

In 1987, at the time of the last Iraqi census, 1.4 million Christians lived in the country. They were tolerated under the secular regime of Saddam Hussein, though their Aramaic language was repressed, as was the giving of Syriac-Aramaic Christian names. Saddam also exploited the religious differences between Iraqi's Christian denominations, such as the Chaldean Catholics, the Syriac Orthodox, and the Assyrian Church of the East.

However, many more Christians emigrated before and during the 2003 invasion of Iraq, after which violence against Christians increased, with reports of abduction for ransom, torture, and killings. Christian clergy were especially the targets of such treatment. Some Christians were pressured to convert to Islam under threat of death or expulsion, and women were ordered to wear Islamic dress.

Some very sad calls came in to the live shows being broadcast from Lebanon, especially the popular weekly program *From Me to You*. In 2010, a few days after a terrible attack on a Baghdad church, a woman called Rawad, the host of the program. She was crying as she spoke of the tragic loss of life, including that of their priest, of women and children, and the caller's own niece. Rawad was also in tears as he listened and gently offered words of comfort. Astonishingly, the caller concluded with a prayer of forgiveness for those who had harmed her family and friends. Almost immediately another call came, this time from a Muslim. He was amazed by the woman's forgiving response and expressed his solidarity with his Christian Iraqi brothers and sisters.

For me, this was Christian television at its best. There were no slogans or clever sermons; only the powerful, authentic faith of Middle Eastern Christians living out their lives on screen. Everyone could see the love of Christ in this woman's unconditional forgiveness of people who had hurt her so badly. This was so different from the *eye for an eye* mentality that prevails in much of the region, and it was obvious that the Holy Spirit touched many viewers through her on-air testimony.

In the summer of 2011, Saeed, a SAT-7 producer from Lebanon, received permission to visit northern Iraq where he was to interview church leaders, government officials, and lay people about the current situation of the Christians in the country. His local crew comprised a Sunni Muslim researcher and facilitator and a Shia Muslim cameraman. Both, to Saeed's surprise, carried firearms!

As Saeed got to know his team, he began to feel that both were "sent by God" to help him. They accompanied him day and night for the whole of his stay and opened many doors for his visit. And when they went into the homes of displaced Christians, they cried together with Saeed as they recorded horrific stories.

One mother from a city near Baghdad told the team how her daughter, Vivian, failed to come home from school one day. Worried, the woman went to the house of Vivian's friend to see if anyone knew where she might be. They told her that as the girls were walking home from school, a black car with hooded, armed men had stopped them and taken Vivian, instructing the other girls to go straight home.

In tears, this mother continued her story in front of the camera. "We waited for a phone call to understand why she had been snatched and what the kidnappers wanted," she said. At 7:00 p.m. the call came. "What do you want? Money?" she had asked them. They'd replied, "No, we want you to suffer because her father is a traitor."

After seven days, some young men arrived at their home and asked the woman to come outside. They were aware of Vivian's situation and told the woman about a girl who had been killed and just thrown in the city square, suggesting that it might be Vivian. "They helped me hurry to the square, where we saw the body covered with a blanket," she said. "Her body was burned and her face disfigured. She had been violently raped and left to bleed to death."

This was just one story! Church bombings, assassinations, and threatening letters from extremists had become too familiar to Christians in Iraq, forcing many to find sanctuary in the Kurdish-administered region in the north of the country. And church leaders were not exempt. Two or three years earlier, sixty-five-year-old Archbishop Paulos Faraj Rahho of the Chaldean Catholic church preached a special message on forgiveness, beginning with the text, "Father, forgive them, for they do not know what they do . . ." Six days later he was kidnapped in Mosul and murdered.

When reporting back on his visit, Saeed shared how he "was amazed to find SAT-7 on the screen in every Christian home we visited! Even when we entered the home of the deputy governor of the Kurdish province of Duhok, Girguis Shlaymun, the TV was on and SAT-7 was onscreen." The deputy governor was an Assyrian Christian and told Saeed, "Everyone is watching the channel, especially in Kurdistan!" Many others shared how it was a vital lifeline, bringing them hope and encouragement.

In April 2012, SAT-7 aired its first-ever live show from Iraq. Rita cohosted the program with Jamie, Joyce, and Rawad (all musicians from the program *From Me to You*). We recorded it outdoors in the city of Erbil in front of a live audience. When looking to rent a five-camera outside broadcast vehicle, crew, and satellite uplink for the event, the team discovered that the owner of the largest television equipment rental company in the city already knew SAT-7 well. His father regularly watched SAT-7, and his daughter loved SAT-7 KIDS! We got all we needed for a fraction of the normal rental costs.

The three-hour show included moving testimonies from local Christians in the audience, worship music in both Arabic and Kurdish, live calls from viewers across the Middle East, and storytelling sessions, brilliantly illustrated by a local sand artist. Iraqi Christians were encouraged by the visit of their Lebanese brothers and sisters. And it was an event I also would not forget, not least of all because I watched it over lunch on an iPad in a Panera Bread restaurant in the United States.

This was so amazing to be able to see such an event, more than six thousand miles away, live on a handheld device. We were now living in a very different world to the one that had existed when SAT-7 was first launched sixteen years earlier.

My Own Visit to Baghdad

By the time of my visit to Baghdad in May 2014, fewer than four hundred thousand Christians remained in the country, and almost 250 churches and cathedrals had been destroyed. Christians who were too poor or unwilling to leave their ancient homeland mainly fled to Erbil.

Farid Samir, our Egypt office director, George Makeen, the SAT-7 Arabic programming director, and I landed in the country on May 30, just a week before the Islamic State in Iraq would start its takeover of Mosul. Our purpose there was to learn more about the ways in which we could better support the church in Iraq in their work and witness for Christ. To do that, we were set to meet with many different church leaders, government officials, and local media.

My first impressions of Baghdad were stunned ones. Of course, there was the intense summer heat and dust. But even more, I was shocked to see the huge number of unfinished or war-damaged apartment and office buildings, often occupied by squatters; the endless military checkpoints; the razor wire and blast walls around any building of importance; the evident poverty despite the country's oil wealth; the unreliable internet and electricity, undermined by thousands of illegal hook-ups; the daily curfews; and the unexplained gunfire at night. It felt like a vision of a world collapsing into anarchy.

Passing through the checkpoints with Pastor Joseph, our host for the visit, seemed relatively painless. The soldiers took one look at the cross hanging from his rearview mirror and at Pastor Joseph's ecclesiastical robes and just waved us through. This was a country where Christians were respected by the security forces as peaceful, nonthreatening noncombatants.

On our first day there, we hosted a luncheon for key influential people at the hotel where we were staying, the Al Marwa. A dozen people attended, including Dr. Saad Maa'n Ibrahim, the official spokesperson for the Ministry of the Interior; Moaed Al Lamai, the head of the Iraqi Journalists and Media Syndicates; and Rasha, a presenter on Iraqi National Television. Over lunch I presented SAT-7's mission, as well as data on our audiences in Iraq, which at that time astonishingly included more than two million children watching SAT-7 KIDS. I also discussed how we were seeking to make a positive contribution to Iraqi civic society, which included broadcasting Jesus' radical teachings on forgiveness, a key to breaking the endless futility of taking an eye for an eye.

The response was both interested and respectful, and we were subsequently invited to visit the minister of the interior two days later, with a police escort being provided from our hotel.

The Ministry of the Interior was mostly staffed by Shia Muslims and a few Christians. The minister went to great lengths to explain the government's position on the Christians of Iraq—how they were living in the land before the rise of Islam and how, today, Muslims were in fact "their guests."

We also met the minister's aides responsible for the security of the country's churches and for community policing. They promised help with future visits, broadcast licenses, and services, and even the use of the National Theater for any special events. We concluded our time there with a tour of the ministry's media department, where I was asked to take part in a live radio interview, sharing impressions of my visit to Baghdad and talking about SAT-7's holistic Christian approach to broadcasting.

Pastor Joseph's Alliance Church was probably the best attended church in Baghdad at that time, with nearly six hundred members and at least two hundred attending the Sunday evening service where I was speaking. The congregation included a lot of people from outside the Christian community, and the church had an active media group, with whom we later met separately to discuss possible future cooperation.

Pastor Joseph also took us to visit Rev. Maher Fouad, a local pastor and the head of the evangelical community in Iraq. Rev. Fouad and I had met almost twenty years earlier, at a conference in Korea where he remembered me sharing with his Arab pastors' breakout group the dream of launching SAT-7, a station that he and many others now watched regularly. Since most of his flock of three hundred had left Baghdad, he had been able to spend more time in developing a local Christian radio station, where we now met. Its signal covered all of Baghdad, and they had just expanded to include a repeater station in Basra.

Pastor Joseph, George, Farid, and I also spent time with other church leaders, including Archbishop Emanuel Dabaghian from the Armenian Catholic church. His enthusiasm for ministry was evident as he showed us around his beautiful cathedral. He spoke of many coming to Christ, especially in reaction to the current violence being committed in the name of Islam. He shared how most of his ethnically Armenian congregation had emigrated. Pointing to all the empty pews, he exclaimed, "Look how much room we now have for new believers to join us!"

In fact, several church leaders and one of the men we met at the ministry of the interior each mentioned to us a survey conducted in 2011 that showed that 32 percent of Iraqis had turned away from religion and had either become atheists or deists, mostly as a result of the violence being committed in the name of religion and their loss of trust in religious leaders.

We also met with Father Mina of the Coptic Orthodox church in Baghdad. They used to have 180,000 members, mostly Egyptians working in Iraq, but since the war, that number had dropped to just a couple of thousand.

Similarly, Father Joseph of the Assyrian church of the East and his son, Father Origan, shared with us how they too had seen most of their community leave for the United States or Europe. But they claimed they were not disheartened, and continued their ministry as best they could.

Canon Andrew White, known to many through his media appearances as "The Vicar of Baghdad," showed us around his church and told us of their different social ministries. These included a medical clinic and the distribution of five thousand food parcels a week to local people in severe need. The church, St. George's Anglican, was located inside Baghdad's "Green Zone," a heavily protected area of the capital where many government offices and diplomatic missions were located. Despite being positioned between a state television station and government offices, both of which had been bombed during the 2003 war, the church had only lost its stained-glass windows, escaping any structural damage.

Andrew was a longtime enthusiastic supporter of SAT-7, having even lent his phone to children at their social center who wanted to call in to live programs on SAT-7 KIDS. Our visit ended with an enjoyable meal at a high-security restaurant on the banks of the river Euphrates, which flows through the city.

Perhaps the most moving part of our visit to Iraq was to Monsignor Pios Cacha, the vicar general of the Syrian Catholic church in Baghdad. He had studied at the Catholic Seminary in Maadi, Egypt, at the same time as I had lived there in the 1970s.

We met at the Church of Our Lady of Deliverance, where there had been a devastating massacre a couple of years before. On October 31, 2010, six jihadists from the Islamic State of Iraq forced their way into the church during the Sunday evening Mass. They began systematically killing worshipers who would not convert to the Islamic faith. But even the younger children remained faithful to Jesus and were slaughtered in front of or together with their parents and Sunday school teachers.

An hour or so after the attack began, and upon hearing the ongoing slaughter taking place inside the church, Iraqi commandos stormed the building, resulting in the jihadis detonating their suicide vests. Fifty-eight worshipers, priests, police officers, and bystanders were killed, and eighty were wounded or maimed.

The explosions and firefight badly damaged the church, but the Iraqi government completely and beautifully restored it. If it had not been for the gruesome pictures in the vestibule, we would never have known that this quiet and peaceful church had been attacked in this terrible way.

However, despite the renovations, the new blast walls and razor wire placed around this and all other churches in Baghdad after this tragedy, and despite the armed, mostly Christian soldiers guarding the churches night and day, the remaining congregation had mostly left Baghdad.

We knelt and prayed in silence in what had now become less a place of regular worship and more of a shrine commemorating the witness of these twenty-first-century martyrs, who had chosen to remain faithful to their Lord rather than be spared a violent death.

With so many Christians having already left Iraq, the theology of staying or leaving often came up in conversations. The clergy who had decided to stay felt the call to be salt and light, to maintain two centuries of "presence" and witness in their country. Others, especially those church leaders who had already relocated to the West, felt that the situation was hopeless and that they should encourage the remaining Christians of Iraq to leave, to be safe, to preserve their faith and traditions, even if it be in exile. However, all those I spoke with saw the decision to stay or to leave as a personal choice, one that each family had to make for themselves.

While Farid and George continued their journey by road north to Erbil, after our five days together, I needed to travel to the UK for meetings. My Turkish Airlines flight was scheduled to leave out of Baghdad at 10:15 a.m. I left plenty of time to get to the airport, knowing there would be a lot of security checks, but I did not expect so many! We went through a dozen regular checkpoints just getting out of the city and then, a few miles before the airport, my taxi was stopped and I had to go on foot through a security check and then continue my journey with an airport-approved vehicle and driver. Arriving at the airport, I had to line up a safe distance from the terminal with other passengers in the hot morning sun, while sniffer dogs checked our luggage, bag by bag.

We were then allowed to approach the terminal, but not to enter it before we and our cases were electronically screened. Once inside the terminal, I thought things would go faster. They did not! My bags and I had to go through another full screening before I was allowed to enter the check-in area. Once checked in, I had to go through yet another full screening before I could leave the check-in area and go to my gate. And then, before boarding the flight, which I very nearly missed, I had to endure yet another bag and body scan! Someone in the airport explained to me, in a hushed voice, that these multiple checks were because the different security services did not fully trust one another.

The day after I left Baghdad, on June 4, the Islamic State of Iraq's surprise invasion of Mosul began. This marked yet another turning point in Iraq's sad, long history and was especially difficult for the region's Christians, Yazidis, and other non-Sunni Muslim groups.

A few weeks later, in early July, the Islamic State issued a decree that all Christians in the areas under its control must pay a special tax equating to almost $500 per family, or convert to Islam, or die. On July 18, the jihadists seemed to change their minds and announced that all Christians would now need to leave or be killed. Many Christians fled to the nearby Kurdish-controlled regions of Iraq.

Christian homes became the property of the Islamic State and were painted with the Arabic letter ن (nūn) for Nassarah, which is derived from "Nazarenes," or believers in Jesus of Nazareth. Most of those who fled had their more valuable possessions stolen and, heartbreakingly, some even had their children seized.

According to Patriarch Louis Sako of the Chaldean Catholic church, this became the first time in the nation's history that no Christians remained in the city of Mosul.

Winter Descends on the Rest of the Region

It was not just in the Arab World that things became more difficult. In Iran, all Farsi-speaking church meetings were stopped and believers were harassed in new ways. On December 27, 2012, Pastor Vruir and fifty other believers were arrested at a home meeting where they were celebrating Christmas. Their arrest also resulted in the main Assemblies of God church in Tehran closing. After being held for several weeks at the infamous Evin Detention Center, and with pressure from international human rights groups, Vruir and other believers were released on bail.

But at the end of the following year, on December 19, 2013, despite suffering serious health issues, the Revolutionary Court of Tehran sentenced Vruir to three-and-a-half years in prison, finding him guilty of "anti-government activities and the promotion of ideas contrary to the sanctity of the Islamic Republic of Iran."

Four years later, shortly after his release, Vruir tragically died from kidney failure, leaving behind his wife, Rima, and their three beautiful children.

Hearing these countless stories from the Arab Winter and its chilling effect on neighboring lands caused the SAT-7 team and me to realize anew the urgency of our work. We may not have been able to halt the violence in this region, but we could contribute something positive—and that was to continue providing a broadcast platform for the church in the Middle East to share the gospel, with its powerful messages of love, hope, and forgiveness—meeting people at their points of need.

Chapter 13

New Opportunities
and Challenges

A t our SAT-7 executive board meetings in November 2014, we approved a three-year strategic plan for 2015–2017 to work alongside our already established long-term goals, which included "making the gospel available to everyone in the Middle East and North Africa, especially to those who would never otherwise have the opportunity to hear it."

For this new three-year plan, we also wanted to focus on strengthening our organizational capacity, better resourcing the new team in Turkey, developing our video strategy for social media, and stepping up the quality and scheduling of on-air programming.

We deliberately held these meetings in Beirut so that our board and senior staff could also be present that week for the formal opening of the new SAT-7 Lebanon studios. On November 15, nearly four hundred guests crowded into the recently finished facilities. It was one of the wettest days of the year. The rain was so heavy that the road leading up to the studios in Mansourieh was more like a river. At one point I wondered if our minibus would begin to float and the current carry us back to Beirut!

It was also the first real rain-test for the new building—and it failed. We held the event in one of the three new studios under the patronage and in the presence of the patriarch of the Maronite church, with deputies from the Lebanese Parliament, government and military officials, and the leaders of other churches.

Just a few minutes into the opening speech, a cascade of water descended onto the temporary stage. It poured in through one of the ducts for the yet-to-be installed air-conditioning and seemed to be a kind of syphon, with a sudden downpour repeating itself every ten-to-fifteen minutes.

By the second deluge, it almost became humorous as people now knew to avoid that part of the stage! Fortunately, this repeated reminder of the storm outside did little to dampen the happy spirit of the occasion as we dedicated and commissioned for service the new building with its administrative offices, editing suites, set and equipment storage areas, and almost ten thousand square feet of studio space.

In his speech the Maronite patriarch, Bechara Boutros Al-Raii said, "Truth, love, freedom, and justice are the four principles that form the basis for peace in the family, in society, in church, and in government. SAT-7 serves all these principles—proclaiming, teaching, educating, and building culture. SAT-7 is a gift from God, from whom every good gift comes."

It was like a dream come true to see the building finished, well, *almost* finished. Because, apart from the need to fix the water problem, we would take more than another year to fully complete all the sound insulation, fix the extensive lighting grids and air-conditioning in the studios, and deal with the inevitable bugs that come with any new building. But those were all issues we gladly dealt with!

SAT-7 KIDS Goes to Iraq

The following month, Essam Nagy, the Egyptian producer and presenter of SAT-7 children's program *Why is That*, made a life-changing visit to Iraq. With some apprehension but a strong sense that God was leading him there, he and a cameraman left Cairo a week before Christmas and flew into the northern part of the country, hoping to give a voice to the displaced children who had suffered so much since the rise of the Islamic State. He was especially interested in finding the "Jesus Tent," which he had read about on the internet, a place of worship the refugees had created from bits of other tents and clothing.

They arrived in Erbil at 3:00 a.m. and took a taxi to Ainkawa, an area in the Kurdish-controlled part of Iraq to which many displaced Christians had fled. There they found makeshift encampments everywhere, with Christians occupying all and any incomplete buildings.

"Do you know the whereabouts of the Jesus Tent?" Essam asked the driver.

"No, I have not even heard of it," the driver said. "We now have so many people in the city that it is difficult to know where anything is any longer."

As Essam and his cameraman were checking into the Czech-owned, ostentatiously called Karlovy Vary or "Swan Lake" Hotel, they spotted across the road a large church, the grounds of which were crowded with blue tents for the displaced. It was the Mar Eliya Monastery. Essam walked over to peer through the wrought-iron gates, thinking that this would be a good place to begin recording with children in the morning. Then he saw it—the Jesus Tent!

"Can you believe it! Of all the places it could have been, it's here!" he called out to the taxi driver and his cameraman. Staring through the darkness, he saw the smiling face of a baby—the child Jesus, one of the pieces of a nativity scene set up outside the tent.

How appropriate! Essam thought, remembering how the young Jesus had also been a refugee, fleeing to Egypt in the days following his birth.

The following morning he met Father Douglas Al-Bazi, who oversaw the makeshift camp. From the moment they entered the gates of the church grounds with their camera and microphone, children recognized Mr. Know, as Essam is known on his weekly program. Many children ran up and took Essam by the hand and dragged him to the Jesus Tent. He was able to talk and pray with them, and he interviewed some about their journeys and lives over the previous six months. Despite the pain on some of their faces, they were bursting with energy and laughter. And many presented Essam with drawings of the Christmas story to share with the viewers of SAT-7 KIDS.

The biggest surprise was the children's awareness of what was going on around them and their forgiving attitude to those who had expelled them from their homes and lands. They even prayed for them, that God would open their hearts and give them peace. Much of this thinking obviously came from the church and their Christian parents, with whom Essam also spent time talking. While these families now lived in very difficult circumstances, they held little bitterness. Their most common concern was to get their children back into school.

On the second day, Essam and his little team went to an unfinished local shopping mall to record more stories with the refugees there. A local church had rented the unfinished construction site and erected makeshift metal partitions to afford each family some privacy and protection from the elements. Essam spotted children everywhere, boys playing soccer and girls singing. And again, as soon as they saw Essam, they rushed to greet him. Essam recorded many interviews and began to really feel the pain of the children and their parents.

Here, in this unfinished mall, they met Myriam, a polite and calm nine-year-old. She took Essam by the hand and told him that she wanted to share her story on camera. She talked about her life before they lost their home and had to flee to Ainkawa. Though she missed her comfortable home and her friends, the things she missed most were her school, where she had always been a star pupil, and her friend Sandra. Despite her admitted sense of loss, she still saw God as her loving Father and Jesus as her Savior and Friend. She also shared on tape how she forgave the Islamists, and she ended the interview by singing a beautiful hymn. Ten minutes into the interview, Essam could not contain his tears. Myriam's focus left the camera and she went to console him.

This interview, while recorded for broadcast, went viral on the internet. It was translated into dozens of languages and was even posted on the home pages of some of the Arab World's leading media outlets. Some called for schools across the region to show this message of unconditional forgiveness to all their students.

Essam revisited Myriam several times over the coming years. During his trips he found her in a temporary school in Ainkawa and reunited with her best friend Sandra. Eventually, during Easter 2019, he visited her and her family back in their home in the city of Qaraqosh, in the Nineveh plains.

After their trip to the "shopping mall," they continued on to a Yazidi displacement camp. Yazidis are a Kurdish subgroup with monotheistic religious beliefs similar to those of other Abrahamic religions and can be traced back to ancient Mesopotamia. In 2014, an estimated five hundred thousand Yazidis lived in Iraq. Most Muslims considered them to be non-Muslims, so they became the Islamic State's special focus for genocide.

As Essam and his cameraman approached the camp gate, a guard stopped them. "Do you have a permit to film?" he asked.

"No," Essam replied.

"Then you cannot enter. We are tired of people coming here and filming our misery, and then going away and nothing changing!" He paused. "Which network are you with, anyway?"

"I am with SAT-7. I host a children's program—"

"Oh, SAT-7 KIDS?" the man said, as his eyes lit up. "You can come in!"

The encampment was very poor and dirty in comparison to the situation in which the displaced Christians were living. As they entered the muddy camp, some of the children immediately recognized Mr. Know from his weekly program, which they had watched every Friday before being displaced from their homes. Soon he had a small crowd of kids around him, all wanting to be filmed!

Three young girls came forward, saying they knew a song from SAT-7 KIDS and wanted to sing it for the camera. They sang from memory the Arabic version of "Jesus Loves Me": "Jesus loves me, this I know, for the Bible tells me so . . ."

Essam's heart burst with love for these children as he listened to them sing and then recite Scripture they had learned from the programs on SAT-7 KIDS. God had led Essam to this land for a purpose, part of which Essam now knew was to show him that our work was making a difference in the lives of children—a difference that we all hope will stay with them the rest of their lives.

Blood on the Sand

Two months later, on February 12, 2015, the Islamic State of Iraq and the Levant released a five-minute video, which showed twenty-one Coptic Christian construction workers on a beach in Libya being beheaded because they refused to renounce their faith. These Christians had been kidnapped in the Libyan city of Sirte a few weeks earlier. Twenty of the men came from different villages in Egypt, and the last was thought to have been from Ghana. According to some sources, this twenty-first man was not originally a Christian, but when he saw the immense faith of the others, and when the terrorists asked him if he rejected Jesus, he reportedly said, "Their God is my God."

The president of Egypt, Abdul Fatah al-Sisi, announced a seven-day period of national mourning. The center of Sunni Islamic learning in Egypt, Al-Azhar, condemned the incident. The United Nations Security Council, French President François Hollande, and US Secretary of State John Kerry also addressed the killings. Pope Francis telephoned Coptic Pope Tawadros II to offer his condolences.

SAT-7's Arabic channel carried a series of live programs that week, addressing the murders. On the first evening after the news broke, Isis Ghattas, the mother of two of the victims, Bishoy and Samuel Estafanus, and her surviving eldest son, Bashir, called into the live show. She told SAT-7 audiences how she forgave those who had murdered her sons and explained how Bashir's and her faith had even been strengthened as they followed the Bible's instruction to "love your enemies and bless those who curse you." She went on to thank the Islamic State for recording the faithful testimony of each of her children before they were killed.

At dawn a few days later, the Egyptian and Libyan military conducted airstrikes on Islamic State facilities in Libya, though, sadly, this did not stop another massacre of about thirty Ethiopian Christians just two months later.

There are countless more stories to tell from the Arab Winter, many of them tragic and many of them still unfinished. But it is clear that the evil being perpetrated in this part of the world is causing many to stop and think. And through it all, we are seeing that the living God and His church in the Middle East are meeting people in their pain and need.

More Growth

In April 2015, after nearly twenty years of being based in the Hawaii Nicosia Tower and with a growing staff of forty, from sixteen different countries, it was time to move our international office. The final trigger was discovering that the owners of our building had plans to redevelop the whole area, meaning that we might need to relocate at rather short notice. We found two floors in a nice building in the municipality of Strovolos, some four miles out of the city center, where the rent was much less expensive per square foot.

We had been in the new space only a few weeks and were still unpacking files when we were invaded by Iranian actors! Parts of the office suddenly became the set for a new SAT-7 PARS Christian drama series called *Swamp*. They needed it to shoot the drama's office scenes, with our staff standing in as extras. Thankfully, the rest of the content for the series was shot in other locations in Cyprus.

It actually took us a full six months to settle in and get organized to the point that we could invite local VIPs in, on November 12, for a formal office-opening celebration with the mayor, and a blessing of the premises by local clergy.

During this year, SAT-7 KIDS also launched its on-air school for the growing millions of Iraqi and Syrian children whose education had been disrupted by war. The *My School* programs made available to them daily lessons in Arabic, math, and English, with other subjects to be added later. Thanks to the fact that, even in the refugee camps, hundreds of thousands still had access to satellite television, the programs quickly found many enthusiastic young viewers, encouraged by their parents.

The first series of lessons was for four-to-five-year-olds, quickly followed by another series for five-to-seven-year-olds. To our delight, the programs also attracted illiterate mothers and others who watched and learned with the children. We invited Syrian and Iraqi refugees living in Lebanon to the studios there to take part in *My School*, as well as in other programs. And our counseling staff and presenters received special training in working with traumatized children, helping to meet their emotional and spiritual needs in the studio, online, and through our programs.

Marianne, the host of the popular worship program, *Let's Sing Together*, regularly invited refugees to her live show, encouraging viewers to call in and pray for them.

Lynn, a refugee from Syria, shared, "I now understand why we came to Lebanon—to meet Marianne and to learn more about God's love through SAT-7 and the Christians in this country. This has helped me put my faith and trust in Jesus!"

More Challenges for SAT-7 in Egypt

In October 2015, with the required permission of State Security, I made another busy visit to our team in Cairo. On Saturday, October 10, after I had already checked in for my 4:00 p.m. flight back to Cyprus, I received a call from our Egypt studio director, Farid Samir.

Officers from the Ministry of Communications and Information Technology's Censorship Department had just arrived at the studios, presented a search warrant, and had called Farid to go to the studios immediately. They were apparently looking for an illegal satellite uplink and had trouble understanding that our live shows were sent to the SAT-7 broadcast center over the internet and not via satellite.

The invasion was a mix of confusion, random confiscations, and politeness. For example, the officers were careful not to interrupt the crew who were recording a program in our studios at that time and checked to make sure that they did not need any of the equipment they were in the middle of confiscating! They took several new cameras, a video switcher, laptops, editing stations, IT equipment, and hard drives containing many programs that were still in the process of being edited. The total value of the equipment was about $100,000, not including the value of all the programs on the hard drives.

I was anxious about what this all meant for the staff and SAT-7's work in Egypt, but having already gone through passport control and not having permission for a re-entry to the country, I had no choice but to take my flight and try to catch up on events as soon as I landed back in Cyprus. But I could not help feeling that the timing of the raid on the studio was planned for just after my departure.

As I heard from some of the studio staff, and later from Farid himself, in the late afternoon, the officers took Farid, along with the confiscated equipment, to the local police station. They were set to hold him there overnight, but following the intervention of Egyptian church leaders, the police agreed to release him on condition he show up at the prosecutor's office the following day.

During a two-hour hearing on October 11, the prosecutor brought charges against Farid relating to the incorrect registration of a television channel, failure to hold government and software licences for certain editing activities, and failure to comply with regulations concerning live broadcasts through the internet.

Farid and our lawyer refuted these charges. They showed that the Censorship Department's report contained factual errors and presented evidence to confirm that SAT-7's registration and licences were in good order.

Farid was then released pending further discussions between the prosecutor's office and the Censorship Department to determine whether the case should proceed to court or be dismissed. In the meantime, all the equipment continued to be held, and SAT-7 was forbidden from transmitting any new live shows from Cairo.

Two days later, I was touched to hear that our staff in Cairo had begun to collect money to help with any legal costs or fines that SAT-7 might need to pay or to help replace some of the confiscated equipment in case it was not returned. One member of staff even donated his children's school fees, while another offered his monthly mortgage payment.

I was also moved to see so many Egyptian Christians change their Facebook cover photos to the SAT-7 logo or call us to find out how they could help. Widows came to the office to offer their gold wedding rings and other women brought their jewelry, saying that they "did not need them as much as they needed us to stay on-air." A church in the impoverished Cairo district of Imbaba came to the office with a huge bag of coins they had collected, reminding us of the poor widow in the New Testament who gave what she had cheerfully and sacrificially.

The decision over whether or not the case should go to court was supposed to be made within two weeks, but as that deadline passed, the case did not seem to be moving forward. And people were now focused on the upcoming elections. Farid took the opportunity of the stalemate to make a brief visit to Cyprus to debrief us in more detail than he felt comfortable sharing over the phone, and to get some relief from the continual stress he was now living under. It was also a chance for him to see if he might be on a no-fly list at Cairo's airport.

Not only did Farid have all the pending charges hanging over him, but the police then claimed to have found someone in Luxor with the same name who was wanted for assault. They wanted to de-tain Farid and take him in a prison transport to Luxor for an identity check—even though Farid's national identity card number was quite different from that of the alleged assailant. Farid's lawyer made the four-hundred-mile journey to Luxor and got this accusation dropped on a technicality, because that case was now more than five years old.

The situation was not helped by several Egyptian newspapers publishing articles about SAT-7, linking us to other, less religiously sensitive channels broadcasting from outside the region. The honor-ary president of the Protestant churches in Egypt and chair of the

SAT-7 Egypt board, Rev. Dr. Safwat El-Baiady, took a bold lead in publicly refuting the press allegations. Christian journalists and the president-elect of the Protestant churches, Rev. Dr. Andrea Zaki, supported his actions.

In early November Egypt's President Abdul Fatah al-Sisi made a state visit to London. One of our supporters in the House of Lords, Baroness Elizabeth Berridge, co-chair of the All Party Parliamentary Group on International Freedom of Religion or Belief, took the opportunity to raise the issue of the seizure of SAT-7's equipment. The president's response was gracious and he promised the baroness to look into the matter, assuring her that SAT-7 would get back its equipment. I then worked with Baroness Berridge to prepare a briefing for the Egyptian ambassador in London, outlining the events to date, listing the equipment confiscated, and giving an overview of SAT-7's international council and operations worldwide.

Two weeks later, Rev. Dr. Safwat El-Baiady received a phone call to confirm that the SAT-7 equipment would be returned. We were relieved and anticipated receiving everything back. There followed a number of positive meetings with the district attorney for South Cairo. In addition, the national press interviewed Rev. Dr. Andrea Zaki about the ongoing situation. We also spent several weeks tidying up our paperwork with the Censorship Department and verifying that our internet services were all properly licensed.

But as Christmas approached, we still had no equipment nor any permission to resume live broadcasts over the important holiday season. Unable to do much in Cairo, some of the team traveled to Iraq and helped with a memorable three-day Christmas "Prayer for Peace" rally, which SAT-7 broadcast live from the National Theater in Baghdad. More than one thousand people packed into the theater each night to worship and pray for their war-torn country. We posted short clips and songs from the event on Facebook, attracting more than a million additional views across the region.

We also broadcast a Christmas special from the battered Christian quarter of Homs in Syria, showing how the community there was trying to get back on its feet after being under siege for the previous two years. A third program—which shared the hope and joy of the season, despite the heavy atmosphere hanging over the region and our office in Egypt in particular—was an exclusive Christmas concert recorded in our studios in Beirut with the renowned Lebanese singer Majida El Roumi.

Eventually, on January 28, 2016, without any warning, all the confiscated equipment and hard drives were returned in perfect order to the Cairo studios. The staff were jubilant! I was in Malta for a conference when Farid sent me a text message with the news. Tears of joy came to my eyes.

And the good news continued when, on February 17, Farid received official confirmation that the case against him had been closed and all charges dropped.

No one understands why the Censorship Department came after us. Some speculated that we were shut down to show a balanced approach by the government, who had recently, ahead of new parliamentary elections, closed a number of channels belonging to Egypt's Muslim Brotherhood. Others thought that some of our programs had included content that the security service found unacceptable. Others thought that it was our attempt to import new television production equipment that triggered the action, because of new restrictions on such equipment. Regardless, we are grateful to God for the final outcome!

Celebrating God's Provision and Moving Forward

In April, we hosted Network 2016 in Nicosia, attracting 350 guests to come together and celebrate twenty years of ministry. Over the past two decades, God had enabled the organization to grow from one two-hour broadcast a week to now broadcasting 840 hours each week, across five channels in three languages; from four staff to more than two hundred, now based in eleven different locations. Interactions with our viewers had grown from hundreds a year to hundreds of thousands.

The conference was also a good time to showcase just some of our new and creative programming: *Stories with the Sheikh,* retelling the book of Genesis in the style of a traditional Arab storyteller; *Marriage Madness,* a sitcom dealing with the realities of everyday relationships; *Dancing with Refugees,* a documentary in which a SAT-7 crew spent time with displaced Syrian families in the mountains of Lebanon; *Copts Got Talent,* a talent show from Egypt; *With Jesus,* special episodes recorded when an Egyptian worship team visited orphans in war-ravaged South Sudan; *DokDok's Family,* a children's drama about a teenage inventor, aimed at showing how we can all use our talents to help others; *Little Painter,* a Farsi program teaching children about Jesus through art; *Smile Magazine,* for Persian teens; *The Preachers of Anatolia,* a Turkish program addressing common misconceptions about the Christian faith; and *New Life,* a new devotional program in Kurdish.

Twenty years before, I could never have imagined the seemingly endless creative energy of my Christian brothers and sisters from so many different backgrounds and church traditions. I marveled and thanked God for how He had provided for this ministry in terms of people, funding, security, as well as the ways He helped us overcome so many obstacles. I thanked Him for using us all, including our partners and supporters, to touch the lives of millions. And I thanked Him for the ways He showed Himself faithful to us every step of the way.

I had definitely needed faith with each step of SAT-7's growth! As our staff and budgets continued to grow, so had our financial needs. But over my previous two decades in the Middle East, before the launch of SAT-7, I had seen God provide in special ways, starting with little things—such as receiving the $100 a month we needed to live on when we first joined OM. Later I had to trust God for larger project funds. With the launch of the monthly magazine, the needed funding grew to nearly $7,000 a month. And when SAT-7 started, we needed to see $130,000 a month of support come in . . . and this kept on growing as broadcast hours expanded and new channels were added.

We continued to have faith and we saw over and over the goodness of God in the words *Jehovah-Jireh*, the Lord will provide!

I had found that living a life of faith, daring to believe, puts us in positions where we can watch God work. And as we see Him work, that builds our faith even stronger.

Our faith was strong!

A few weeks later, on May 30, the night before the exact anniversary of the first broadcast twenty years earlier, more than six hundred Egyptian Christians came together for a four-hour celebration, carried live on SAT-7. The guests included Egyptian government and church leaders from all the main denominations, many of whom delivered speeches between music from different choirs and a musical operetta written especially for the evening. In my own speech I recalled the early days and its many challenges. And I honored the many, especially those from North Africa, who had been brave enough to go on-screen when the consequences of doing so were still unclear.

But it was Isis Ghattas Dawood, the mother of two of the twenty-one Coptic Christians murdered by the so-called Islamic State on a Libyan beach the year before, who left the biggest impression that evening. She again shared how her loss had made their family stronger in their faith as they sought to obey the biblical injunction "to love our enemies and bless those who curse us." For the audience present and the millions watching live, Isis voiced her forgiveness and shared how she prayed for her sons' killers. She spoke of how her two boys, Bishoy and Samuel, "had chosen martyrdom rather than renounce their faith." She ended by saying, "If my children weren't scared to die for their faith, why should I be?"

The audience at the event immediately rose to their feet in a standing ovation.

In July 2016, the marketing company IPSOS conducted audience research for us in ten different Arab countries. The results showed that the audience for SAT-7's Arabic channels had grown by more than 40 percent over the preceding five years, to a total of nearly 22 million. The data surprisingly showed that audiences in Saudi and

Algeria were especially encouraging, with more than 2 million self-confessed viewers in each. And on the SAT-7 KIDS channel, just the program *My School* had a regular audience of 1.3 million children.

At our international management team and executive board meetings that November, we made some important decisions, rationalizing our Arabic channels. We decided to stop the relatively expensive SAT-7 PLUS channel on the HotBird satellite, recognizing that the SAT-7 ARABIC and SAT-7 KIDS channels broadcasting from the Nilesat orbital position had been on air without incident for six years, and that the SAT-7 PLUS channel was now watched mostly by Arabic speakers in Europe. Important as these viewers were, they were not our primary audience. And in any case, they had better options than those in the Middle East to watch the channels online.

Also, by November, the brutal war in Syria was now in its fifth year, with no signs of abating. Around half the now 12 million displaced Syrians inside and outside the country were children. Another 6 million people had been displaced from their homes in Iraq and Yemen by conflict. In total, almost ten thousand schools in these countries had been damaged, destroyed, or occupied by the displaced or by militia groups. At our board meeting, in light of the popularity of the *My School* programs, we decided to launch these on a separate channel alongside other educational programming for these millions of children now without any formal schooling.

This new channel, to be called SAT-7 ACADEMY, would give more air-time for broadcasting programs to the different age groups we were trying to simultaneously cater to, as well as allow us to repeat programming for people in different time zones. We planned to launch the channel in September the following year, with many new programs made in partnership with local NGOs, under the leadership of Juliana Sfeir and George Makeen.

Juliana was Lebanese and appointed as the SAT-7 ACADEMY channel manager. She was a long-term producer with SAT-7 who specialized in social impact programs dealing with women's and human rights, as well as having been the lead producer for the *Theological Education for Arab Christians at Home (TEACH)* programs.

George, originally from Egypt but now based in Cyprus, was SAT-7's programming director for all Arabic channels and had worked with the organization since the 1990s.

Both passionately believed that education was key to releasing potential in people and to help them think critically, keeping them from becoming yet more victims of the radical political and religious propaganda that was now so rampant in the region.

The executive board made one other important decision that November: they appointed Rita El-Mounayer as SAT-7's deputy CEO. I was quickly approaching my seventieth birthday—and as much as I loved SAT-7 and my work there, it was only right that I plan to step down before I passed my "best before" date. So I had long before suggested to the board that it was time to begin looking for my replacement.

Initially, the executive board had wanted to open the search for a new CEO to applicants from outside the organization, but the SAT-7 international council stepped in and indicated that they felt the appointment of a new CEO to succeed the founder was especially challenging and far more likely to fail if the next CEO were not appointed from within the ranks of SAT-7's existing leadership.

We identified Rita as the most likely candidate, especially as, a year before, she been given responsibility to manage all the channels, including the Turkish and Persian-language ones, and had done a great job in bringing them closer to each other under the banner of "ONE SAT-7." Now as deputy CEO, she could learn the ropes from me before she stepped into my role.

The following year, in March 2017, Albert Fawzi formally took over as the new executive director of SAT-7 Egypt, following Farid Samir and his young family's departure to Europe. And in anticipation of the SAT-7 ACADEMY launch, as well as the need to rationalize programming on SAT-7 KIDS, Andrea Elmounayer became the channel manager for KIDS. Andrea was another long-term member of SAT-7's staff and had been a creative producer of children's programming since the early days. She was also involved in the launch of the new, tablet-friendly website for SAT-7 KIDS.

During this year we also formed a SAT-7 Hong Kong committee, comprising volunteers from different Chinese churches to help with fundraising both there and in mainland China. The Chinese in Hong Kong and Singapore quickly made the historic comparison between China and the Middle East when it came to the use of Christian media. In the 1950s, Christian short-wave radio had been used to send the gospel into China, and these broadcasts continued faithfully for many years without there being any tangible signs of success. Broadcasters like FEBC received fewer than a dozen letters a year from the country. And yet, years later, it became clear that these broadcasts had been catalytic in a massive turning to Christ, increasing the size of the church in China from just 4 million to somewhere between 40 million (the current Chinese government number) and 100 million.

Kuan Kim Seng, dean of St. Andrew's Cathedral in Singapore, expressed it this way at one of our Network meetings in Turkey: "Millions of children regularly watch SAT-7 KIDS, and in ten years' time, they will become adults, having heard about Christ. Imagine what God can do in their lives. We should pray for the children of the Middle East, that they will change their societies!" The Hong Kong committee shared this vision, and they were trusting God for great things in the decades to come.

On August 17, 2017, the test broadcasts for SAT-7 ACADEMY began, with a full schedule launching on September 1. The response was positive, especially from those working with children in the refugee communities. They found the colorful and entertaining programs a great supplement to their own on-the-ground educational efforts. That year, the theme for the annual SAT-7 Week of Prayer was "Equipping the Next Generation," with a special emphasis on the region's children. And the SAT-7 KIDS channel celebrated its tenth year on-air.

If 2017 had been full of changes, 2018 more than matched it! In April, Reinaldo Santos was appointed as the executive director for the recently registered SAT-7 Brazil support-raising office. Additionally, two members of the senior management team announced plans to move on. These included our chief financial officer (CFO),

Iren Frändå, and our chief operations officer (COO), Andrew Hart. Though each had their own good reasons for leaving, their departures left a hole in our leadership team as we were also working toward a CEO transition.

Andrew accepted an appointment as CEO of another media ministry, PAK7, for the 230 million people of Pakistan. PAK7 was a new initiative we had been invited to "adopt" but we had clearly defined our ministry to include Arabic, Turkish, and Persian-speakers in the Middle East and North Africa, and this did not include Pakistan. However, this did not stop us from sharing with the PAK7 team—as we had with other Christian channel start-ups in Central Asia, Indonesia, Ethiopia, and other parts of the world—our experience, policy documents, contacts, programming, and other things to get them started. But in this case, we were also sharing a member of our management team!

In addition, by August 2018, we found ourselves in another difficult financial position. And in God's faithfulness, He again provided. Just when we needed them, funds showed up. Unaware of our situation, a faithful supporter in the UK sold his company and donated all the proceeds to SAT-7. Jehovah-Jireh!

That summer, we commissioned a new round of research studies to try and assess both the impact of turning off the SAT-7 PLUS channel and starting SAT-7 ACADEMY. And in light of so many new online opportunities, we were also interested to see if satellite television was still the most strategic way for us to invest in the region.

The results of the study showed that 2018 marked the twenty-second year of continued increases in the number of people with satellite television in the Middle East-North Africa. "Why?" some asked. For me it was obvious: because satellite is still the only uncensorable visual media in the region; it's inexpensive compared to streaming, especially when people pay by the megabit; it is easy for nonreaders to navigate; and it is available everywhere. So, satellite television was still clearly a strategic opportunity and would remain so for some years to come.

We did, however, discover that the audiences for satellite television now included fewer viewers from the new generation, which consumed most of its news and entertainment online. More than three million SAT-7 videos were now being watched each month on YouTube, with almost the same number again on Facebook. It was therefore important for us to move forward on both fronts. Consequently, we recommitted to making available more and more customized and original content online, especially for the SAT-7 ACADEMY programs, knowing that this would enable kids to work at their own speed and repeat individual programs as many times as and when they needed.

The research also showed that most of the millions who watched SAT-7 ACADEMY were also watching the SAT-7 ARABIC and KIDS channels. The fact that the new channel was not attracting much of a different or unique audience led us to conclude that the *My School* programming might as well stay on and enrich the SAT-7 KIDS channel, and that we should make the needed repeats available through a strengthened SAT-7 ACADEMY online-learning platform, where all programs could be available on-demand. This decision was made easier by the fact that we were already having trouble scheduling the *My School* programming on a single channel covering the five time zones across the Arab World and for all the different age groups!

So it was with mixed feeling that the SAT-7 ACADEMY satellite channel ended on October 31, and instead it became a "brand" for educational programming on the other channels as well as an online platform.

Other new online initiatives included the production of *Mamaland,* a special online parenting series of short videos for women. Our regular audience interactions had indicated that this subject was important to millions, and so the programs were well researched and addressed in an attractive way the key concerns parents had. As people progressed through the online video lessons, they also received opportunities to view other material of a more overtly spiritual nature, such as "How to Pray with Your Children." Thousands signed up for the online course, and we learned a lot about how we might use such an approach in the days ahead.

At the end of the year, we faced another cash-flow crisis, though I was heartened by the fact that the production teams did not want to stop any of the special Christmas programs, and many volunteered their time as well as helped create homemade Christmas decorations for program sets.

As 2019 began, no one was aware of the great pandemic that would paralyze much of the world in the following year. Instead, we were focused on our own changes that lay ahead.

In March, at our international council meeting, we appointed His Eminence Archbishop Angaelos of the Coptic Orthodox Diocese of London as the new chair. He replaced Rev. Dr. Habib Badr, who was stepping down after nearly two decades in that role, one where his wisdom and insights had helped me personally as we navigated all the changes in the region and the growth of the ministry.

And at the end of that month, I stepped down as CEO, handing over the role to Rita El-Mounayer. She had come a long way since the early days when she scripted, produced, and presented SAT-7's first children's program. As I shared at the handover ceremony at Network 2019, "Rita has always been a quick learner. She is keen to study, read widely, and develop herself. This, along with her passion for ministry, intelligence, hard work, and great interpersonal skills, have all helped position her for this exciting and challenging next step. I really believe that she is going to be exceptional in the role of CEO."

I continued to be available to Rita for the next year, as and when she felt she needed my input. Apart from this, I moved into the new, nonexecutive role of SAT-7 Founder and President. This included my continued presence on several SAT-7 ministry boards and the SAT-7 international council, especially helping with any residual legal affairs.

I knew the change would take some getting used to, but the one feeling I had not expected to deal with was that of guilt! Each morning as I woke up, I had to remind myself that it was okay for me not to feel guilty for not being responsible for the worldwide ministry of

SAT-7, its people, and its current challenges. But, of course, I could feel responsible to pray for the ministry and its new leadership, which I joyously do.

SAT-7's Continuing Work

When I first came to the Middle East nearly fifty years ago, even the idea of walking around with a cell phone was unimaginable, and no one would have believed it if they were told about a future with satellite television, smart phones, or social media.

And even when SAT-7 was in its research and development phase in the early 1990s, only a few hundred websites existed in the world. Very few people had a personal email account. There was no Skype, Zoom, WhatsApp, Signal, or other inexpensive ways to communicate globally. And a single analogue satellite television channel cost an unbelievable $2 million a year to lease. People were still using VHS tape machines to record and play their favorite videos. There were no online Bibles or other Christian resources, and the idea of an Arabic-language Christian television channel going live from its studios in Cairo was unthinkable.

But as we have, year by year, embraced the use of new technologies, God has blessed our humble efforts and the ministry of SAT-7. A study the now-late James Engle (creator of the "Engle scale") did in Algeria in 2000, just four years after our first broadcast, showed that half of all the people in new churches at that time had come to faith through or had been greatly helped by watching the SAT-7 broadcasts—men, women, children, and teens, literate and illiterate, urban and rural.

Years later, as we move forward, what does the future hold and how will SAT-7 rise to meet it? If 2020 taught us anything, it was that we never really know what the future holds or how our lives might suddenly change as a result of a pandemic, war, or some other global catastrophe.

As communicators there are a lot of new technologies that we expect will change the way we work in the short and long terms.

These include parallel developments in Artificial Intelligence (AI); quantum computing; neurotechnology; the power of new 5G networks to connect people and "things"; immersive virtual-reality (VR) experiences for training, tourism, and entertainment; to name a few.

With so many changes, we face real legal and ethical considerations. Will new internet controls censor us—especially in parts of the world where there is already little or no free press? And as more and more people get their news and information from one or more of thousands of different and often unverified sources, will this further fragment and polarize societies?

While there is much uncertainty about the future, and no one knows what will be the next "big thing" on the internet, as communicators we do know it is still true that *content is king*, and good content will always find audiences. This content may not look like the visual media of today, but we know that we will need to increasingly offer short-form video for hand-held viewing. We know that great visual quality is important for the bigger screen, and we will need to stay abreast of all new trends in social media if we want to be effective in providing seekers with secure and easy-to-access content and live counselors. And in the Middle East and North Africa, I pray we will also see a better collaboration between Christian media ministries, and even stronger relationships formed between SAT-7 and on-the-ground churches or informal Christian fellowships.

May God continue to give us wisdom, vision, and creativity as we navigate a very different future with all its exciting opportunities and challenges.

Chapter 14

The Surprising Middle East

The Middle East and North Africa (MENA) have always been a poorly understood place, by both the general public in the West as well as by Middle Easterners themselves. There are many reasons for this, including the continuous stream of bad news from the region (the only news that can make its way through the plethora of local news in most countries) and the lack of transparency and severe censorship within the region itself.

Another reason the Middle East and North Africa is poorly understood is that it is complex and cannot be understood with broad generalizations. Each of the region's two-dozen countries are as different to each other as the countries of Europe.

But there are many things most of these countries do have in common: almost two-thirds of the population are under the age of thirty; there are relatively low levels of functional literacy; unemployment is rampant among the young and especially young women; women's rights are still trampled on, with an average 30 percent of women having experienced physical violence by an intimate partner, and honor killings still widely accepted; there is little freedom of the press, with journalists often being harassed or detained; new social media has given young people a new opportunity to speak out against political and religious leaders; Christians and other minorities currently face the worst persecution in a thousand years; and at the same time, many in the general population are turning away from religion.

To these issues we can add the ongoing pan-regional tensions and the unfinished conflicts in Syria, Iraq, Yemen, Libya, and in the Palestinian territories, which by the start of the 2020s had already left almost 2 million dead or injured, more than 15 million displaced, and another 50 million shattered by grief and loss.

There are multiple national and international agendas at play, with proxy wars taking place between those from a Shia Muslim tradition and those from a Sunni Muslim background; between those who are for inclusion and coexistence and those who are wanting a theocracy; and so on.

But I especially want to look at the rising loss of trust in all forms of authority, including religious authority, that has emerged in recent regional studies such as the 2018–2019 BBC/Arab Barometer study of the Arab World, the 2018 KONDA survey in Turkey,[1] and the already mentioned 2020 research carried out by the Group for Analyzing and Measuring Attitudes in Iran.

All of these studies, and many national surveys—conducted in Saudi, Iraq, and other Arab countries—point to a turning away from traditional religious belief. Some people just reject all religious belief, while some declare themselves deists, retaining a belief in a God but rejecting the religion they were brought up with. Others go all the way and declare themselves atheists, something that would have been impossible to conceive of a generation ago. Atheism is apostasy, it brings shame on the person and his or her family and is punishable by death in some countries.

Why are we seeing this turning away from religion? From the discussions I have had in different countries over the past few years several factors have surfaced.

First, religious extremism. Many have been appalled by Muslims killing other Muslims in the name of their common God. The

---

1. See Hurtas, "Turks Losing Trust in Religion."

rise of the so-called Islamic State in 2014 only served to widen such attitudes.

Others have been turned from religion by the hypocrisy and the corruption they have seen in religious leaders, especially in theocracies like Iran.

Ihsan Eliacik is a Turkish theologian whose work set the stage for an Islamic group called the Anti-Capitalist Muslims. In a 2019 interview with Al-Monitor, he stated the surprising fact that Muslim societies that have religiously conservative governments tend to be put off from Islam. "According to recent research of mine, similar outcomes are currently seen in three countries in the Islamic world—Saudi Arabia, Iran, and Turkey," he said. "They are all ruled by religious governments, but in all three countries atheism and deism are spreading, while religiosity is declining [and] suspicion toward religion is growing. Because of those governments, people begin to think that Islam is in fact a lie and they have been deceived."3

This disappointment and loss of trust in religious leaders and religion was exacerbated by the disappointment many people had at the way the 2011 Arab uprisings turned out. At the time, people believed that these would lead to new freedoms, new employment opportunities, and being able to live with dignity. But all they got was chaos and destruction. And disappointment led to a loss of hope, even among the region's Christian populations, motivating many more to make the hard decision to emigrate.

But for most Christians and Muslims in the region, emigration has never been a legal or practical option, something that has only added to their loss of hope, noticeably pushing up despair and suicide rates, especially among the young.

It is in this context that there has never been a more important time for Christians to broadcast, on-air and online, messages of hope in our region. But I do not mean just academic, theological messages of hope. I mean a whole gospel, to minister to the whole person, authentically touching all areas of human need: the spiritual, the emotional, the psychological, the socioeconomic, and the educational.

But it is not just taking a holistic approach. It is also seeing God's Holy Spirit at work in the lives of our viewers, sometimes in a very special way through visions and dreams. The story of Aziz is typical of such interventions. He is a young Iraqi who had been a militant, fighting with a violent Islamic group in Syria. He telephoned SAT-7 to explain that he had been hiding in a destroyed church during a battle when he had a life-changing vision. He saw the broken pews restored and Christians filling the building, worshiping God.

A man in white, radiating light, walked over to him and touched his shoulder.

The militant recognized Him as Jesus Christ from the *Jesus* film he had watched on SAT-7's Arabic service. And it was to a SAT-7 counseling line that Aziz turned after he left the ruined church a changed man.

"The living Jesus Himself came to me," he said. "He called me and I told Him, 'I want to follow you.'"

Shortly after his first call, Aziz went into hiding but he has continued to call SAT-7 periodically since. He can speak only briefly and has to call from different phones to protect his security.

On one occasion he said, "I'm still here. Don't forget me. I want to follow Jesus."

Media continues to give the Christians of the Middle East and North Africa the opportunity to come out of their churches and homes and to be the "salt of the earth," a "city on a hill," a "lamp on a lampstand." Over the past quarter-century, the Christians of the region have shared their lives through media with millions who may never have spoken with a Christian before. They have shared their sorrows, their joys, and the faith and hope that is theirs. As individuals and a community, they have shown the unconditional forgiveness of God through their own public acts of forgiveness, sometimes in the wake of terrible acts of violence against them.

God is using this witness to bring many to Himself and, in the fullness of time, I believe that the rest of the global church will be surprised, even stand in awe, when all that is happening today, in secret, becomes clear to everyone.

And what a privilege that SAT-7 has been part of God's work.

If there's one thing I have learned from my time living among our Christian brothers and sisters in the Middle East and North Africa it is that most of them please God every day through their bold faith in Him, in daring to believe. And they have also helped show me that *not* daring to believe is far more dangerous.

Acknowledgments

While this book has named many of the staff, board or council members of SAT-7 and its associated ministries, many have not been mentioned, either for their own sakes or because of a lack of space. But their contributions—as paid staff, volunteers, or workers on loan from other ministries—have all richly contributed to the story of SAT-7 and its impact on the lives of millions in the Middle East and North Africa. Their nonmention in this book will only add to their reward as good and faithful servants when their pilgrimage on earth is over.

I would, however, especially like to thank my editor, as well as Andrew Hart, Julia Jolley and others who have helped me check and improve the manuscript.

And, lastly, I would like to especially thank my personal supporters, some of whom have faithfully encouraged and prayed for me and my family in our life of faith for five decades.

Bibliography

Farnham, Bruce. *My Big Father: The Story of Kenan Araz.* Waynesboro, GA: OM Literature, 1985.

Hurtas, Sibel. "Turks Losing Trust in Religion under AKP." *Al-Monitor*, January 9, 2019. https://www.al-monitor.com/pulse/fa/originals/2019/01/turkey-becoming-less-religious-under-akp.amp.html?skipWem=1.

Maleki, Ammar, and Pooyan Tamimi Arab. "Iranian's Attitudes toward Religion: A 2020 Survey Report." https://gamaan.org/wp-content/uploads/2020/09/GAMAAN-Iran-Religion-Survey-2020-English.pdf.

CPSIA information can be obtained
at www.ICGtesting.com
Printed in the USA
BVHW070505270621
609767BV00005B/9